2/17

Trafficked Children and Youth in the United States

D1417487

The Rutgers Series in Childhood Studies

The Rutgers Series in Childhood Studies is dedicated to increasing our understanding of children and childhoods, past and present, throughout the world. Children's voices and experiences are central. Authors come from a variety of fields, including anthropology, criminal justice, history, literature, psychology, religion, and sociology. The books in this series are intended for students, scholars, practitioners, and those who formulate policies that affect children's everyday lives and futures.

Edited by Myra Bluebond-Langner, Board of Governors, Professor of Anthropology, Rutgers University, and True Colours Chair in Palliative Care for Children and Young People, University College London, Institute of Child Health.

ADVISORY BOARD
Perri Klass, New York University
Jill Korbin, Case Western Reserve University
Bambi Schieffelin, New York University
Enid Schildkraut, American Museum of Natural History and
Museum for African Art

Trafficked Children and Youth in the United States

Reimagining Survivors

ELŻBIETA M. GOŹDZIAK

Rutgers University Press

New Brunswick, New Jersey, and London

Library of Congress Cataloging-in-Publication Data

Goździak, Elżbieta M., 1954- author.
    Trafficked children and youth in the United States : reimagining survivors / Elżbieta M.
Goździak.
        pages cm.—(The Rutgers series in childhood studies)
    Includes bibliographical references and index.
    ISBN 978–0-8135–6970–3 (hardcover : alk. paper)—ISBN 978–0-8135–6969–7 (pbk. : alk.
paper)—ISBN 978–0-8135–6971–0 (e-book (web pdf) : alk. paper)—ISBN 978–0-8135–7569–8
(e-book (epub) : alk. paper)
    1. Child trafficking—United States. 2. Child prostitution—United States. 3. Child prostitutes—
Rehabilitation—United States. I. Title

    HQ144.G779 2016
        306.74'5—dc23
        2015028622

A British Cataloging-in-Publication record for this book is available from the British Library.

Visit our website: http://rutgerspress.rutgers.edu

Manufactured in the United States of America

Contents

Acknowledgments

Authors, like Oscar winners, are often advised to keep their acknowledgments short. However, where a book project based on several years of field research is concerned, very many people contributed to the endeavor. I would like to express my gratitude to all of them.

First, many warm thanks to my research team members: Micah N. Bump, Julianne Duncan, Margaret MacDonnell, and Mindy Loiselle. Without them the original study that gave birth to this book would have never been possible.

My deepest gratitude goes to the U.S. Conference of Catholic Bishops and the Lutheran Immigration and Refugee Services for facilitating access to the survivors of child trafficking and their caseworkers and indulging my never-ending questions. Sr. Mary Ellen Dougherty, Juliane Duncan, and Nathalie Lummert of USCCB were particularly instrumental in getting me into the field of child trafficking. At LIRS, Annie Wilson and Chak Ng were also indispensable to paving my way into the assistance programs for trafficked minors.

Two friends and colleagues, Marisa O. Ensor of the University of Tennessee and Anahi Viladrich of the City University of New York read an earlier version of the manuscript and provided invaluable recommendations to strengthen this book. I am very grateful for their frank assessments.

I am particularly indebted to Marlie Wasserman, my editor at Rutgers University Press, and her team for their enthusiastic support of this project. I would also like to thank the anonymous reviewers who critically evaluated my book proposal and provided invaluable advice to improve the text.

This research would have not been possible without the financial support of the National Institute of Justice. NIJ financed the original study that spearheaded this research and has continued to support several of my forays into human trafficking research. Along the way I worked with outstanding project officers at NIJ: Jennifer Handley, Karen Bechar, Maureen McGough, and John Picarelli. I would like to thank them all for their enthusiastic support of my research agenda on human trafficking.

Heartfelt thank you to the Rockefeller Foundation for supporting my residency at the Bellagio Center in Italy where the book prospectus took shape.

Many thanks to my research assistants—Sara Graveline, Whitney Skippings, and Minna Song—who masterfully copyedited and formatted this book. Special thank you goes to Michael Sliwinski who helped me wordsmith this text and corrected the nonnative English speaker's quirky ways of expressing herself.

The real heroes of this effort are the survivors of child trafficking! Thank you from the bottom of my heart!

**Trafficked Children and
Youth in the United States**

Prologue

Afong Means Strength

It was a crisp fall afternoon in 2013. I was waiting in front of the Silver Diner in suburban Maryland to meet Evelyn.[1] Several years older than when I first interviewed her, Evelyn has not lost her exuberance. Pushing her ten-month-old son in a stroller to the restaurant where we planned to have a late lunch, Evelyn smiled and waved as soon as she spotted me. With one hand holding onto the baby's carriage, she used her other arm to envelop me in a warm hug.

Evelyn is a survivor of domestic servitude. For two years she lived in her trafficker's house in Greenbelt, Maryland, completely isolated from outside contact. She was not permitted to speak with her family, go to school, or even answer the door. In 1995, Evelyn's mother and uncle sold her to Theresa Mubang, an acquaintance of Evelyn's maternal uncle, to settle an old land dispute in Cameroon. Mubang brought Evelyn to the United States when she was barely ten years old. Mubang, a naturalized U.S. citizen, traveled on an American passport, but Evelyn used fraudulent documents to cross international borders. Evelyn thought she was coming to the United States to fulfill her childhood dream of attending an American school, but the reality was different from the life she imagined watching *The Cosby Show* and *The Fresh Prince of Bel Air*. Instead of the idyllic life of hopping on a school bus every morning, learning English, and making new friends, Evelyn was forced to care for Mubang's young children around the clock and perform never-ending household chores. When she was allowed to rest, she slept on the floor. If her cleaning was not up to Mubang's standards, Evelyn was beaten with an extension cord or locked up in a basement without food. Mubang's son urinated on Evelyn regularly to humiliate her. When she tired of beating Evelyn, her captor scratched the girl. If ever there was a poster child for a trafficked minor, Evelyn is it.

Evelyn's body testifies to the physical violence she endured: she has scars and burns to remind her of the ordeal. A decade after she escaped, it is still difficult for Evelyn to recount not just the scars on her body but also the verbal abuse Mubang wielded as skillfully as the rod she used to discipline her. However, the insults, the cruelty, and the violence did not squash Evelyn's spirit. Throughout her ordeal Evelyn refused to give up. She persisted, day by day, with a defiantly hopeful outlook and a head held high.

When the opportunity arose, Evelyn escaped. She found help, first from a distant relative and then from Lutheran Immigration and Refugee Services. In 2003, when Evelyn was nearing her thirteenth birthday, the U.S. government officially recognized Evelyn as a trafficked child. She was now eligible for federally funded assistance to victims of child trafficking—help was on its way. Evelyn is grateful to Lutheran Immigration and Refugee Services, to her foster "auntie," and especially to her pro bono attorney, Melanie Orhant. With Orhant's expert legal assistance, Evelyn received a special visa for victims of trafficking (T-Visa) that allowed her to stay in the United States, be placed in foster care, and attend school. Throughout this lengthy process, Evelyn observed Orhant, who at the time was a managing attorney for the Break the Chain Campaign, helping other victims rebuild their lives in America. Melanie's passion and dedication inspired Evelyn. During our first interview in 2006, Evelyn told me she wanted to be like Melanie: to advocate on behalf of trafficked victims, participate in antitrafficking activities, and lead support groups for survivors. Truth be told, I was a bit skeptical about her ability to accomplish her goals. Evelyn has proven me wrong; she has achieved her dream of becoming a self-described "activist against modern-day slavery." Evelyn speaks at events for the Break the Chains Campaign and collaborates with Survivors of Slavery, a nonprofit organization, which "supports survivors of modern slavery who want to lend their voice to the 21st century abolitionist movement."[2] Recently, Evelyn went on a retreat with a group of young women who had been trafficked for sexual exploitation. She said that she drew strength from the retreat and hoped that sharing her story was helpful to the other women.

Evelyn's strength manifests itself in many different ways. An excellent student in Cameroon with a strong yearning to learn new things, Evelyn was told over and over again that she was "dumb," "dirty," and "unworthy," and that she would never amount to much. Though she struggled in high school in America, these insults did not prevent Evelyn from pursuing her dream of attending college. While her spoken English was passable, she was illiterate in written English. Reading, writing, and solving math problems posed insurmountable challenges at times. Discouraged, she dropped out, but not for long. She enrolled in a GED program and after getting her diploma went on to earn an associate degree in social work from a local community college. With a new boost of confidence, she enrolled in an online BA program in homeland security at the University of Maryland. She will graduate in 2015.

Strong and determined to succeed, Evelyn continues to show incredible resiliency in the face of adversity. Unfortunately, her life is not free of struggles. A few years ago a stranger on the street raped her at gunpoint. She thought that she would not be able to trust a man ever again. Yet a few years later she found a loving partner in Malcolm, the father of her son. Their son Molima, "My Heart," as his father calls him, is the center of Evelyn and Malcolm's lives. Evelyn and Malcolm are engaged to be married. They are hopeful for a good family life.

A few dark clouds still overshadow Evelyn's happiness. For a long time, she could not understand why her mother sold her to a stranger. How could a mother give up her own flesh and blood? The inability to understand her mother's actions weighed so heavily on Evelyn that she fell into depression. She thought that the only way she could shake off the feeling of despair would be to confront her mother. With the help of an older brother living in Europe, Evelyn saved money for an airline ticket and in 2012 went to Cameroon. Evelyn shared with me excerpts from the journal she kept while visiting her family in Cameroon.

She left her homeland a little girl of ten, taken across the ocean by a stranger, but she returned on her own terms, a young woman of twenty-seven. Although bitter about her mother's involvement in her trafficking, Evelyn was startled by her own joy and excitement at seeing her mom. Tears ran down both of their cheeks as they hugged for the first time in almost two decades. Evelyn's mother would not let go of her daughter even when Evelyn's siblings came to embrace her. Surrounded by family members, mother and daughter held each other for over an hour.

A few days after visiting her mom and then her dad, Evelyn finally met her maternal uncle, a man she used to call father. Burdened by the thought of being treated as chattel, Evelyn confronted her uncle. Looking him in the eye, Evelyn wanted to know what role he had played in her trafficking. At first he said he merely arranged for Mubang to take Evelyn with her to the States, but later admitted that money changed hands. Fearing that other people in her hometown might treat their children like disposable goods, Evelyn spent a few days organizing meetings and speaking to parents, children, and civil society groups about child trafficking and its effects on young victims. Ever the activist, she hopes that these discussions raised awareness about trafficking in children.

Today, Evelyn is not free of economic difficulties. Recently, she lost her job as a security guard. "It was one of those 'he said, she said' stories; my word against my coworker's word," she told me. The company let her go.

Unfortunately, Evelyn did not qualify for unemployment benefits. As a result her fiancé is now the sole breadwinner. An artist from Cameroon, Malcolm has to supplement rare artistic commissions with a job as a manual laborer. They try to economize as best as they can, but some days they go to bed hungry. Evelyn is ill-prepared to understand the intricacies of networking and job-hunting in America. She wishes that the programs providing assistance to survivors of trafficking focused less on mental health counseling and more on employment services.

As we finish up our lunch, Evelyn says she has faith that things will improve. I do not doubt that Evelyn will persevere. Afong is Evelyn's middle name, given to her by her grandmother, and *afong* means strength in the language of Evelyn's childhood.

Introduction

Researching and Writing about Child Trafficking

I use Evelyn's story to introduce the central theme of this book: the coexistence of agency and vulnerability, and the interplay of trauma and resiliency in survivors of child trafficking. Evelyn's story is representative of the resiliency and perseverance of countless survivors of child trafficking; yet it is also unique in terms of her own approach to healing and rebuilding her life post-trafficking. It represents the vulnerabilities and calamities that do not always disappear once victims escape their trafficking ordeal. The focus on resiliency and survivorship, rather than trauma and victimhood, signifies a departure from the prevailing public discourse about trafficked children and youth that deploys gut-wrenching narratives about girls kept as sexual slaves and sold into domestic servitude. Journalists and service providers alike portray them as hapless victims forced into the trafficking situation and hardly ever as actors with a great deal of volition, often willingly participating in the decision to migrate. With an emphasis on agency, this book gives these young people a voice and allows them to ascribe their own meaning to their trafficking experiences. Ultimately, this book provides a fresh take on the social world about matters that concern them the most as they rebuild their lives in America: securing good jobs, being able to send remittances home, learning English, developing friendships, and finding love.

In this book I also juxtapose programmatic responses—based on the principle of the "best interest of the child"—with the young survivors' perceptions of their experiences and service needs. I explore the tensions between the adolescents' narratives of their trafficking and the actions and discourses of foster care and child welfare programs. The former are grounded in culturally diverse conceptualizations of childhoods, and the latter are based on Western, middle-class ideals of childhood, which yield programmatic responses toward trafficked minors. My aim is to contribute to the unfolding discourse on human trafficking that takes a more agentic and harm-reductionist approach found in the works of Laura Agustín,[1] Denise Brennan,[2] Elizabeth Bernstein,[3] Julia O'Connell Davidson,[4] Pardis Mahdavi,[5] Svati Shah,[6] and Carole Vance.[7] I engage theoretical questions about children and childhoods, agency and vulnerability, and trauma and resilience. Practically, I aspire to reconcile the gap between the young survivors' perceptions of their need to recover from violence and exploitation (based on indigenous coping strategies, resiliency, and notions of agency and survivorship) and the current institutional response (based on notions of vulnerability, victimhood, and dependency on adults).

Researching Child Trafficking

I have written about this research before, providing the anatomy of the research grant that spearheaded this study and discussing the trials and tribulations this project entailed.[8] Nonetheless, I do want to stress that methodologically and pragmatically, research with survivors of child trafficking to the United States is complicated. In the United States, in order to conduct human trafficking research that highlights the perspectives of trafficked persons themselves, researchers have to work closely with service providers. Trafficked minors are considered an extremely vulnerable population and service providers are charged with protecting them from further exploitation as well as from the possible adverse effects of recounting their experiences in the course of research interviews. While some assert that since the passage of the UN Convention on the Rights of the Child in 1989, "listening to the voices of the children has become a powerful and pervasive mantra for activists and policy makers worldwide,"[9] not all social service providers see research as a way to empower survivors of child trafficking. Caseworkers are often skeptical that participation in research will provide young people with an opportunity to bring about justice. They often argue that seeking justice is the role of pro bono attorneys, not trafficked youth. Ironically, many service providers do not see the value of listening to adolescents to inform program design. They think professionals know better what is in the best interests of the trafficked children and adolescents. Anthropologists often lament how difficult it is to convince practitioners about the value of research and gain their permission to recruit survivors of trafficking to participate in empirical studies.[10]

When I first started researching child trafficking over a decade ago, I began by "studying up":[11] looking at existing decision makers, policies, and programs set up to prevent child trafficking, protect trafficked children, and prosecute perpetrators. Access to trafficked children and adolescents, guarded by their protectors almost as closely as by their traffickers, was impossible and research funds scarce; most of the money appropriated by the U.S. Congress for anti-trafficking activities was spent on direct services to victims or information campaigns.[12] Later on, as I gained the trust of service providers, I was slowly able to meet a few survivors of child trafficking and begin "studying down," examining the perspectives of survivors of child trafficking, analyzing the meaning they ascribe to their trafficking experiences, and identifying the service needs and strategies they employ to rebuild their lives in America, and "sideways," comparing the experiences of various survivors and assistance programs.[13] In 2006, I received a grant from the National Institute for Justice and started interviewing survivors of child trafficking and their helpers in earnest. My team and I traveled to many cities and towns around the country to meet trafficked minors, their foster parents, and caseworkers. These encounters varied in duration and intensity, but rarely allowed for prolonged participant observation of a singular program or individual survivor. There are no communities of trafficked children and youth;[14] many of the study participants lived with foster families and were scattered around the country, often miles away from the locality where they were first found.

Similarly to other anthropological studies of mobility and mobile populations, in this study the research encounter took the form of *unsited (or mobile) field.*[15] Although I spent several years gathering information about some 140 adolescents and young adults—most of them girls—trafficked for sexual and labor exploitation before they turned eighteen years of age, few of these interviews stemmed from "accidental encounters" or "chance events."[16] I mostly relied on the scheduled "interview moment." I have also relied on close collaboration with service providers who cared for the survivors of child trafficking. They facilitated access to the girls and boys, determined whether the adolescents were in an appropriate frame of mind to grant the research team an interview, waited on hand to counsel the youth should recounting of the trafficking ordeal trigger a traumatic response, and occasionally arranged interpreters.

This collaboration has been met with some criticisms from fellow researchers that precisely because of the close connections between the researchers and the practitioners, the study would be less "objective" and the involvement of the child advocates and service providers in the study would be self-serving. Given the alternative—no access to survivors or program staff—I had few qualms about pursuing this study as a joint project between university-based social scientists and service providers. The practitioners that joined my team—an anthropologist turned child welfare specialist, a social worker, and a therapist specializing in counseling abused and neglected children—were firm believers in the value of practice-based action research, and welcomed this rare opportunity to collaborate with me, a cultural anthropologist and migration scholar, and my colleague, a Latin American specialist. The team worked closely together to ensure interdisciplinary perspective and methodological rigor. All team members were trained in ethnographic interviewing techniques and research ethics.

The fact that, to date, no books based on empirical research with foreign-born survivors of child trafficking to the United States have been published was an additional incentive to undertake this project. The vast majority of existing publications on child trafficking—in the United States and globally— focus on "women and children." The surveys of literature on human trafficking I conducted over the years[17] indicate that child victims are often subsumed under the women and children heading without allowing for analysis that differentiates the needs of this diverse demographic. Thirty percent of the publications I reviewed do not differentiate between male and female children. It is noteworthy that women and children are lumped together in antitrafficking legislation and the dominant antitrafficking paradigm when in all other instances, including labor laws, great care is being taken to separate child labor from adult labor.[18] Many writers use the word "children" but focus on underage girls or even young women over eighteen years old; research on trafficked boys is essentially nonexistent, as is research on men trafficked both for sexual and labor exploitation.[19]

In the early 2000s, when the study that gave birth to this book commenced, services for trafficked children were in their infancy. Practitioners were very keen on exchanging experiences to enhance their ability to provide the best possible care. However, many were not aware that the existing assistance programs were created in an empirical vacuum. It was a rare opportunity for an anthropologist and a scholar of international migration to be able to share research findings from the very beginning of the project.

The project began with an online survey of programs assisting survivors of child trafficking. The survey aimed at assessing the scope and scale of assistance offered to survivors, the challenges programs encountered as they prepared to serve trafficked children and adolescents, and, of course, the programs' willingness to participate in the qualitative part of the study. In the end, fifteen programs in ten states—Arizona, California, Florida, Maryland, Massachusetts, Michigan, New York, Pennsylvania, Texas, Virginia, Washington, and the District of Columbia—were researched. The bulk of the fieldwork was conducted between 2006 and 2007, paired with follow-up visits with survivors and service providers in 2013 and early 2014, as well as many encounters with programs and policymakers in the interim. My colleagues from the U.S. Conference of Catholic Bishops and the Lutheran Immigration and Refugee Services introduced me to many of the program staff. The program staff in turn facilitated contacts with their current or former clients, survivors of child trafficking.

While unable to spend more than two or three days at each program and just a couple of hours with each survivor, I nevertheless characterize this study as ethnographic.[20] I traveled to "the field" to see the programs in action, participated in or organized working meetings with a variety of case workers, attorneys, and law enforcement representatives working with survivors of child trafficking, conducted focus group discussions and individual in-depth interviews with program staff, and interviewed many of the survivors in their place of residence, at their worksite, or at the programs where they were being served. This on-site research is very different from the approach used by attorneys, law enforcement, and to some extent social workers and psychologists as well as other "experts" who are mainly interested in facts. They often forget to consider the context that frames the survivors' experiences or analyze the situation from the youths' point of view. Claiming "the best interest of the child" as the compass of their actions, they nonetheless end up fitting the information obtained from the survivors into predetermined legal or child welfare frameworks.

In contrast, my aim was to listen to the trafficked girls and boys in order to present their points of view. My primary objective was to convey how the survivors conceptualized their trafficking experiences and their traffickers, what they perceived as their most urgent needs, and how these perceptions differed from the conceptualizations and the approaches of the service providers. I wanted to tell *their* stories. The ethnographic details come from their narratives, not my analysis of court documents and case files. Case files and court documents, where included, are meant to inform and add to the narratives of service providers and child advocates whose voices I also wanted to capture. Case file reviews provided an excellent opportunity to see how the stories elicited by social workers differed from the narratives the youngsters shared with the research team. By and large the narratives found in case files were presented to fit the trauma paradigm that underpinned the rehabilitation programs, while the stories the girls and boys shared with us contested many of the assumptions made by law enforcement and program staff about what happened to the girls and boys and what course of action was in their best interest.

This study stems from the conviction that anthropological research can make a significant contribution to the antitrafficking field. Of particular import are insiders' narratives that can greatly inform the antitrafficking field "where ideology passes as knowledge."[21] While the young people in this study had been interviewed by a variety of people, including law enforcement, immigration officials, pro bono attorneys, and service providers, these stories were elicited to accomplish particular goals—to inform prosecutorial proceedings, obtain immigration relief, or establish eligibility for services—that are not always commensurate with the young people's desire to narrate their experiences. In a small way, this project attempts to contest the image of "the forcibly trafficked child" whose childhood had been lost and needed to be reclaimed. It contrasts the stereotypical portrait of a trafficked child with the diversity of experiences and voices that ought to be heard to facilitate long-term socioeconomic self-sufficiency and psychosocial well-being of survivors of child trafficking in order to facilitate integration into the American society.

A Few Words on Terminology

I have made intentional decisions regarding the words and phrases I use in this book. Public discourses use the word "children" to refer to trafficked minors whether they are four or seventeen years old. The law also designates individuals under the age of eighteen as "children." In this book I deliberately use words like "children," "adolescents," and "youth" or even "young people" to differentiate between age groups, to recognize the principle of the "evolving capacities" of people eighteen years of age and younger, and to discuss the different levels of agency they have. I call the young people I write about "minors" when I mean to stress that they are underage and that in the eyes of the law they have not attained the age of majority. I also use "girls" and "boys" to indicate gender. Many publications use the phrase "trafficked children" as if the youngsters they write about were devoid of sex and age.

When I want to stress the girls' and boys' strength and resiliency, I opt for the word "survivor." It is not a perfect term—some of the girls and boys are still dealing with the aftermath of the suffering they endured—but it is better than the alternative: victim. I do realize the legal necessity to use the term "victim" in some circumstances; after all, to be eligible for services and immigration relief, these young people—or their pro bono attorneys—had to prove that they were victims of the crime of human trafficking. Money set aside by the federal government for victims of crimes pays for the assistance they receive. However, in the context of this research the narratives I elicited speak to the ability of the children and adolescents to survive, sometimes against all odds. Furthermore, therapeutically speaking, assigning them the identity of victims is counterproductive. I explore all of these issues in-depth later in the book. Here, I want to signal that the terminological choices I made throughout were not purely stylistic, but rather quite purposeful.

Finally, I do use the term "child trafficking" although very few of the girls and boys I studied were small children when they were trafficked. There were two children under three years of age, and the youngest girls were ten years old, but the majority of the cases were older adolescents. My choice is again deliberate. Regardless of the age at the time they escaped or were rescued from their traffickers, all of the survivors were referred to programs specifically designed to serve victims of *child* (my emphasis) trafficking, aimed at assisting these young people in reclaiming their "lost childhoods." Legal provisions and service eligibility determination were also tied to the phenomenon termed child trafficking.

The Young Survivors

And now without further ado, permit me to introduce several of the young girls and boys featured in this book. I have decided to draw attention to these particular girls and boys because they show the array of minors officially recognized by the federal government as trafficked children. Some readers might question whether all of the young people I am about to introduce fit the average person's understanding of who is a trafficked child and who isn't. I too asked myself whether I would qualify all of them as trafficked victims or perhaps smuggled minors who ended up in severe exploitation. The fact remains: the federal government deemed all of the protagonists of this book to be victims of child trafficking and accorded them appropriate legal status. I do not claim that they are representative of the population of trafficked children and adolescents since the size of the sample is limited and caution needs to be taken not to generalize on the basis of 140 youngsters, even though at the time when this research began this group constituted the universe of the foreign-born minors in federally supported assistance programs for victims of child trafficking. Despite the small sample size, diverse patterns—type of trafficking, length of time in the trafficking situation, and especially conceptualizations of and reaction to the trafficking ordeal as well as attitudes to the provided services—have begun to emerge.

None of the girls and boys were kidnapped or physically forced to accompany their traffickers to the United States. Many did not consider the people who brought them to the United States to be traffickers. In many instances parents, or smugglers paid by their family members, brought the girls to the United States. Without exception, all of the girls and boys in this study believed they were coming to the United States to find employment and in some cases educational opportunities. None sought out work in the sex industry and yet some ended in sexual exploitation. Others worked in bars and restaurants but law enforcement labeled their experiences "sex trafficking" even though the girls denied that they were sexually exploited. Several of the younger girls—ten or twelve year old—ended up in domestic servitude. A group of Peruvian boys—the only males in this study—worked in construction. They were paid meager wages and lived in squalid conditions.

The girls and boys spent varying length of time in the trafficking situation. Some were kept in domestic servitude for several years, while others escaped their situation relatively quickly. Some ran away from their traffickers, others were extricated by law enforcement. The sample also included girls whose trafficking exploitation was preempted. They were neither sexually exploited nor forced to toil in a sweatshop or domestic servitude. The fact that they traveled with strangers to the United States from far-flung corners of the world coupled with their young age was sufficient to declare them victims of child trafficking when they were apprehended at the border or in an airport.

The short vignettes below are presented to introduce the readers to the girls and boys. They are not meant to showcase archetypes of survivors of child trafficking, but rather aim to emphasize the diversity of experiences. They are also not meant to provide a comprehensive narrative of each youngster's trafficking ordeal; rather they are to facilitate the readers' first encounter with the youth. In subsequent chapters, the stories are fleshed out and additional girls are introduced to illustrate different themes explored in this book, but for now let's just meet some of them for the first time.

Fatima

During a trip to Morocco, Fatima's uncle and aunt suggested she go with them to the United States. They promised to send her to school in exchange for taking care of their infant son. Fatima's parents thought it was an excellent idea and readily agreed to the proposed plan. Fatima liked the scheme as well because she loved school and knew it was hard for girls to get a good education in Morocco. She liked babies and was happy to exchange babysitting for a chance to finish high school and maybe even go to college. Fatima's parents traveled to the United States with her and stayed in her uncle's house for several months. Fatima's mother did all the housework, cooked for the whole family, and cared for her brother-in-law's baby boy. After her departure, twelve-year-old Fatima was expected to take on household chores and babysitting as well as help out in a coffee shop her uncle owned. Uncle Youssef threatened to report Fatima to the authorities if she did not perform her duties well. The threat was effective: Fatima's tourist visa had expired and she feared deportation.

Fatima is one of the girls trafficked when they were relatively young— preteens—into domestic servitude. Fatima comes from Africa where child circulation is a cultural norm and relatives living in cities take in young girls (and sometimes boys) to provide them with educational opportunities in exchange for babysitting and housekeeping services.[22] Unfortunately, in the case of Fatima the relatives turned out to be unscrupulous and abused her. Fatima exemplifies the girls who have been very resilient and ultimately persevered against all odds. Others were more vulnerable and had a harder time coping with the aftermath of trafficking.

Belen

Belen is the third of four children born to a middle-class family in a large city in Mexico. Her father was a local politician. Although Belen was very close to her dad, she believed that her mother did not love her. Other family members shared Belen's reservations; her grandfather thought his son married beneath him. He accused Belen's mother of being a gold digger. When Belen was ten years old, her father committed suicide in front of her. Within a few months the family fell apart: Belen's mother left and the children had to fend for themselves. Belen's uncles and aunts took two of the older siblings in, but Belen and her younger brother were left in the family home. Some of her father's relatives tried to take possession of the house and turn Belen and her brother out, but Belen fought back and on her fourteenth birthday, the court ruled in her favor and she became the legal owner of the house. She provided for herself and her brother by getting food from her friends. At some point she also got a job in a factory where her sister's boyfriend worked. Unfortunately, her brother got into drugs and, as she said, "I lost control of him." At seventeen she decided to go to the United States. She tried to come legally, but was refused a tourist visa. She contacted an uncle in Pennsylvania and asked him for help. Belen's uncle arranged for a *coyote* to smuggle her across the U.S.-Mexican border, but as will be seen later things did not turn out too well for Belen.

Analisa

Analisa was born in 1986 in Honduras, in a small town outside of the capital city of Tegucigalpa. She comes from a large family with ten siblings. Her parents separated when she was an infant; it is unclear whether they had a legal or common law marriage. Her father remarried and moved to a different town. Her mother fell ill and was unable to care for Analisa. Baby Analisa was sent to live in a coastal town with her maternal grandmother, where she spent the next twelve years. In 1998, Analisa's grandmother fell ill and sent her to live with her biological father and his wife. Analisa had not seen her father since infancy and reported feeling like a stranger in his household. Her stepmother was not happy to have to care for Analisa. When Carmen, her adult daughter from a previous marriage, came to visit from the United States and offered to take Analisa back with her, Analisa's stepmother readily agreed. Analisa was uncertain what her father thought about this plan. Analisa reported wanting to take advantage of the opportunities Carmen presented. However, instead of going to school, Analisa ended up working as part of a cleaning crew Carmen managed.

Belen and Analisa exemplify youngsters who faced unexpected problems—parental illness or family breakdowns resulting from death or divorce—that forced them to seek employment in the United States. In some cases the idea to migrate came from the girls, while in other situations a family member or a friend planted the idea. Early in the study, I heard social workers hypothesizing that their families marginalized the trafficked girls and boys or that those were pathological families who forced their children into the trafficking situation. By and large, these hypotheses proved to be wrong. Larger forces of poverty and lack of child welfare safety nets to fall back on were the culprits; extended families or stepfamilies—especially those already abroad—were the only support systems when the going got tough.

Catalina

Catalina, trafficked from Mexico to California, was seventeen years old when she entered the program for trafficked minors. She was placed in a group home for pregnant and parenting teens. Catalina had a toddler son, Manuel, whom she loved but was ill prepared to care for, according to the program manager. Little was known about her trafficking ordeal and she was not willing to talk about her experiences with her caseworker. Everybody surmised that Catalina must have had some horrendous experiences because she appeared constantly on edge and her emotions were described as "volatile." When she was angry she often took her anger out on Manuel. Six separate incidents of child abuse were recorded in her case file and Child Protective Service was called to give Catalina a stern lesson about child abuse and proper parenting.

Flora and Isa

In 2002, Flora and Isa's mother arranged for her fifteen-year-old twin daughters to be brought to Fort Worth, Texas, to escape the poverty of the hurricane-ravaged city of Choluteca in their native Honduras. They were smuggled across international borders with a group of thirty young women lured to Fort Worth with promises of good jobs as waitresses or housekeepers. When Flora and Isa arrived in Fort Worth, their mom was there to greet them with open arms. The rest of the young women were ordered by the smugglers to change into skimpy outfits and forced to work off smuggling fees of up to $8,500 per person at a bar.

At first, the twins did not work and stayed in their mother's apartment, but as boredom set in they convinced their mom to ask their uncle if they could work in the bar their mother managed for him. He agreed, and the two joined several other young women in selling marked-up beer tickets for $10 a glass. At the end of the night, each girl kept $4 of each sale and the owners kept the rest. On a tip from a concerned resident, immigration officials raided the bar and Flora and her twin, along with several other girls, were taken from the bar and referred to a foster care program.

Magdalena

Magdalena, from a small pueblo in Mexico, is one of eleven children. She has seven brothers and three sisters. Just like her mother, Magdalena never went to school; she is illiterate in Spanish and continues to have difficulty learning English. She described herself as being close to her mother and her grandmother, but distanced from her father. When she turned thirteen, she left home to work in a restaurant in a nearby town. That's what girls in the village did: went to town to look for work and catch a husband. Within a few months she met Jorge, a man in his twenties who wooed her and said he wanted to marry her. Magdalena liked him and believed he would marry her. Jorge sent her to the United States to stay with his sisters in New Jersey and promised to join her there. It turned out that Jorge's sisters operated a brothel. Jorge was skilled at manipulation and continued to call Magdalena after the sexual abuse began, saying: "This is just temporary until I come to be with you." Jorge also sent Magdalena pictures of a house he was supposedly building for her family with the money she was making as a sex worker.

Julia

When I first met her in 2006, Julia, originally from El Salvador, had just turned eighteen. The FBI picked up Julia a year earlier in the course of an investigation of a ring of alleged sex traffickers bringing girls and young women to work in cantinas in Florida. The rescue operation took place a day after Julia arrived in the United States. Julia thought she was coming to Florida to work as a nanny, but it soon became apparent that her smugglers had other ideas. The first inkling that something was amiss came when one of the men she traveled with started making unwanted sexual advances. The older women in the group protected her, but Julia's guard went up. When the group arrived in Florida, Julia was brought to an apartment where several other girls and women lived. She quickly learnt that she would have to work in a bar wearing provocative clothes to attract Latino immigrant men to buy expensive drinks. She felt duped and violated. She feared that the worst was yet to come. Although frightened by the FBI squad descending on the apartment in the middle of the night, Julia said later she realized that she was spared a more dreadful ordeal.

Lin

Lin, a Chinese girl who grew up in a village on the border with North Korea, is the youngest of three children. She lost her father to a dramatic car crash at a young age. Lin has happy memories from the time before the accident. She remembers singing with him in the mornings and going on long walks in the afternoons, skipping through orchards. A couple of years after his death, Lin's aunt immigrated to the United States. She sent money to support Lin for the next few years. Lin lived in a school dorm, took classes in the morning, and worked as a cashier in the afternoon. After a while, Lin decided that she wanted to join her aunt in the United States. She and her two cousins approached Park, a Korean female snakehead (smuggler) to help them travel to the United States. Lin talked to other people who had used Park as a smuggler and confirmed her good reputation. Lin's trip to the United States took five weeks, according to her estimation. It started in her native village. From there, she and her two cousins were taken to Beijing, where the group left for Guinea in Africa. From Africa the girls were taken to Brazil and then to another country whose name she does not remember. The last stop before reaching the United States was Mexico. In Mexico, Lin and her cousins lived with a Korean family for a few days. There they met Mr. Li, their driver, who repeatedly tried to rape the girls. They attempted to cross the Mexican-U.S. border in Texas. The girls were told that it would take about an hour by truck, but it took much longer—four hours, by Lin's calculation. The trip was grueling; she remembered how cold the truck was, like a refrigerator. She also recalled a rather confusing series of events involving changing cars and drivers. From the truck bed, the details were murky; Mr. Li apparently left the car for a while, but eventually returned. As they approached the border, Mr. Li got into a serious car accident, and died. The girls were taken out of the wreckage and into custody. "Two policemen appeared and started asking us a lot of questions," recalled Lin. As the girls narrated their story, the Border Patrol determined that they were victims of trafficking.

Peruvian Boys

In 2002, acting on a tip from a concerned neighbor, federal agents raided three houses on Long Island in New York and uncovered fifty-six Peruvians, including thirteen unaccompanied boys ranging in ages from five to seventeen years old, living in cramped and squalid conditions. The Peruvians included both unaccompanied children and families, with some children accompanied by their mothers and fathers. A husband and wife team had brought them and other families to New York from Lima on fraudulent visas to work in the construction industry. Prosecutors said the couple charged would-be immigrants up to $13,000 each. When the migrants arrived on Long Island, the jobs did materialize, but they were not as lucrative as promised. The work was tiring, often involving sixteen-hour days with no lunch breaks. Court documents suggest that the traffickers forced the families to hand over their passports and almost all their earnings, leaving them with $50 a week to buy food. They threatened that they would call *la migra* if anyone complained. The traffickers also said they would hurt the migrants' families in Peru if they tried to escape. At the time of my research, these were the only boys identified as victims of trafficking. Since then, the number of boys in the United States has grown considerably and in recent years has surpassed the number of girls. Most of the identified boys have been trafficked for labor.

As these vignettes show, the girls and boys I studied were born outside the United States and were trafficked to this country across international borders. I want to stress that this book does not focus on US-born commercially sexually exploited children who only recently have become part of the child trafficking discourse and praxis under the label of domestic minor sex trafficking. I am a scholar of international migration and my sole focus is on mobility across international borders.

The Chapters Ahead

This book follows the framework of "capture," "rescue," and "restore" within which policymakers and service providers place both the discourse and the assistance provided to trafficked minors. I begin, in part I, with discussion of moral panics that overshadow the discourse of child trafficking, the imagined scale of the phenomenon, and the motivations of the "new abolitionists"—the advocates and service providers working with young survivors of human trafficking. In the following three parts I contest the myths and unpack the realities of captivity, rescue, and rehabilitation of survivors of child trafficking. The closing chapter is an evaluation of the efficacy of the system of care for trafficked children and its impact on the long-term well-being of the young survivors. It also includes a prognosis for the antitrafficking field. In the epilogue I narrate my return visits to some of the survivors—now young adults, some with children of their own—to check on their progress in adjusting to life after trafficking and integrating into American society. I also recount recent conversations with social workers that worked with the trafficked children and adolescents featured in this book to find out what adjustments, if any, they have made in their social work practice with trafficked children.

Part I

Moral Panics

Moral panics about child trafficking precede the current preoccupation with the trafficking of minors by more than a century. In 1885, William T. Stead, editor of London's *Pall Mall Gazette*, set off a series of "maiden tribute" exposés with the story of Lily, portrayed as being sold by her mother to a brothel owner for a sovereign. He sought to open the eyes of the public to the grim realities of the "white slave trade" in young English girls trafficked to brothels on the Continent.[1] The reprints of Lily's story sold in the thousands. The articles were then published in book form and sold on both sides of the Atlantic to the great acclaim of abolitionists fighting to outlaw prostitution.

Stanley Cohen, author of *Folk Devils and Moral Panics*, summed up the impact: "Societies appear to be subject, every now and then, to periods of moral panic. The moral barricades are manned by editors, bishops, politicians and other right-thinking people. Sometimes the panic passes over and is forgotten, except in folklore or in collective memory; at other times it has more serious and long standing repercussions and might produce such changes as those in legal and social policy or even in the way society conceives of itself."[2]

In 2002, Lukas Moodysson, a Swedish director, produced *Lilja 4-ever*, a brutal story of the downward spiral of Lilja, a trafficked girl from the former Soviet Union. Abandoned by her mother, who migrated to the United States, Lilja ends up in Sweden where she is forced to perform sexual acts for a large number of clients. The film was embraced by many humanitarian organizations and was used in numerous information campaigns against human trafficking in Eastern

Europe. In Moldova, the International Organization for Migration bought distribution rights and organized screenings for some sixty thousand people, mainly teenage girls, young women, and a smattering of government officials.[3]

These stories are just two examples of how a crusading journalist and a zealous moviemaker, acting a century apart, incited temperance activists, purity reformers, rescue workers, and the general public to believe in widespread sex slavery and made discourse about forced prostitution a permanent fixture of journalism and the mass media.[4] Despite the differences in time and place, these exposés generated similar responses in terms of creating legislation, pushing for reforms, and fostering heated discussion around sex trafficking. Moreover, by focusing on coerced prostitution, media campaigns against trafficking and crusades for child protection obscured the everyday exploitation of adolescents (and adults) in forced labor and domestic servitude.[5]

Less about the poverty that has prompted many youngsters to cross international borders in search of jobs, contemporary panics about international trafficking in children and adolescents give raise to heartbreaking images of "tidal waves" of underage sex slaves and indentured servants. Stripped of caution, stretched to their most alarming possible meaning, and tossed into public debates, these images are treated by the rescue industry—antitrafficking advocates, service providers, and policymakers—as reliable sources of proof of the magnitude of trafficking of girls under the age of eighteen.

Furious about these "tidal waves" of trafficked victims, U.S. politicians vowed to crack down on so-called modern-day slavery. Congress passed the Trafficking Victims Protection Act in 2000 and triggered a worldwide war on human trafficking that reached its peak during the years of the Bush administration. Despite political will, new legal tools, and a substantial commitment of resources, a mere eight thousand-plus victims, including some eight hundred-plus children, have been identified since 2000,[6] a far cry from the estimates of fifteen thousand foreign-born minors being trafficked into the United States annually.[7]

The chapters in this section set the stage for understanding both the historical antecedents and contemporary manifestations and discourses about child trafficking, its scale, and societal and institutional responses. Together, they debunk the prevailing myths about the victims (they are mainly adolescents, not small children), characteristics of child trafficking (it's not all about sexual exploitation), scale (no "tidal waves" have been found), and empirical evidence (policies and services are created in an empirical vacuum). They show how images of the "typical" trafficked minor—a young, naïve, pretty girl lured, deceived, and sexually exploited—feed the dominant conceptualizations of child trafficking and how social practices involved in constructing and legitimizing these images are used to design "evidence-based" assistance programs for survivors of child trafficking.

1

"Tidal Waves"
of Trafficking

It was a warm and sunny morning in early May 2003 in Miami, Florida, but the temperature in the conference room oscillated between frosty and feverish. We were discussing child trafficking, a topic that can at once send chills up one's spine—"How could we have ever allowed this to happen in the twenty-first century?"—and excite advocates who want to "erase this scourge here and now!" The U.S. Conference of Catholic Bishops (USCCB) and Georgetown University's Institute for the Study of International Migration had organized the first in a series of three regional meetings aimed at improving identification of minors trafficked to the United States across international borders. Around the table were Immigration and Customs Enforcement agents, local law enforcement officers, federal prosecutors, researchers, and representatives of civil society organizations working with unaccompanied refugee children, commercially sexually exploited children, runaway youth, street kids, and foreign-born adolescents trafficked to various U.S. cities. The discussants were outraged that a mere twenty-four trafficked girls have been identified between July 2001, when the U.S. Department of Justice issued regulations implementing Section 107(c) of the Trafficking Victims Protection Act (TVPA),[1] and May 2003, when we gathered in Florida. Twenty-four adolescent girls out of the estimated thousands of foreign-born minors trafficked every year to the United States.[2] The conference participants were eager to identify individuals and organizations—service providers, child advocates, law enforcement,

Good Samaritans—and networks—antitrafficking task forces, juvenile justice systems—that were most likely to come into contact with trafficked minors. At minimum, they argued, border guards, immigration officials between ports of entry, staff at detention centers, local law enforcement, and health and social service providers must be more vigilant. "Identification improvements must be made in these areas," they said, and vowed to do their best to enhance their identification strategies.

Fast forward to April 2004. I was sitting in another conference room, this time in Houston, Texas. A similar cast of characters was assembled to take part in the second conference on identification of victims of child trafficking. Again, conference participants debated procedures, mechanisms, and coordination efforts necessary to increase the identification of victims of child trafficking. Other topics were quickly added to the already long list of items for discussion. Participants were eager to debate the need for increased training on all aspects of the trafficking of minors; dissemination of information to raise awareness about the phenomenon, appropriateness, and availability of services for victims of child trafficking; evaluation of programs for minor victims; and strategies to ensure immediate care of all children and adolescents in trafficking-like situations.[3] The list was growing exponentially, while little had changed in terms of the number of identified victims of child trafficking. Since the meeting in Miami a year earlier, twenty-one additional girls had been found. By the time we met for the third and last time, in the spring of 2005, in Portland, Oregon, the total number of survivors of child trafficking hovered around fifty—a drop in the proverbial bucket.

The conference participants never questioned the existence of large numbers of foreign-born minors trafficked to the United States, nor doubted that with intensified efforts and increased resources they would be able to rescue more victims. In fact, some of the civil society actors present started planning capacity assessments. They assumed that very soon they would need to serve large numbers of child and adolescent victims. I wondered whether I should have suggested that such assessments might be premature or posited that perhaps so few victims of child trafficking have been identified because there are not as many victims as anticipated. After all, we were finding, on average, one girl a month. I decided against talking about these issues publicly. During a coffee break, I approached several participants with my doubts. Without exception, my interlocutors gasped: "How could you entertain such a radical idea?"

Eight years later, as I am writing this book in the fall of 2014 and summer of 2015, the number of foreign-born minors trafficked across international borders has increased, but not by much. At the last count, between 2001 and 2014 a total of 841 victims have been identified and given letters of eligibility for federally funded services, a far cry from the estimated "thousands" of children supposedly trafficked to the United States every year for purposes of sexual and labor exploitation.[4] To resolve this discrepancy, it is necessary to first understand the established view of child trafficking and its impact on institutional responses.

What Is Child Trafficking?

Simply stated, child trafficking involves the recruitment, transport, harboring, or receipt of children or adolescents (under the age of eighteen) into a situation involving severe exploitation: forced labor, debt bondage, commercial sexual exploitation, pornography, or the unlawful removal of organs. Legally speaking, trafficking of adults always requires force, deception, and coercion, but when a third party moves or uses children in prostitution, pornography, or for the removal of organs, force or coercion do not need to be present to deem these acts child trafficking.[5]

In the eyes of both international and U.S. law, minors under the age of eighteen do not have the same legal capacity as adults to engage in certain forms of work. The vulnerability of children, related to the biological, physiological, cognitive, behavioral, and social changes "taking place during the growth and maturation process, distinguishes children from adults . . . and thus also their trafficking situation."[6] This is a problematic definition of "children," as it lumps all individuals under eighteen years of age together and ignores the principle of "the evolving capacities of the child."[7] This principle is a new concept in international law. It recognizes that as children acquire enhanced competencies, there is a diminishing need for protection and a greater capacity to take responsibility for decisions affecting their lives. The Convention on the Rights of the Child allows for the recognition that children in different environments and cultures, and faced with diverse life experiences, will acquire competencies at different ages. However, despite this recognition, the principle is not always applied to migrating children. Children and adolescents who migrate, be it legally or illegally, but end up in exploitative circumstances are always trafficked, according to U.S. and international law. "If children have been recruited and transported for the purpose of exploitation, they have been 'trafficked' no matter if they consented to move."[8] Sometimes minors who have not been exploited yet—like Lin and Julia—are also considered victims of trafficking.

It is not my intention to add to the chorus of scholars who have debated the merits and limitations of the trafficking definition or recount their arguments.[9] I am not solely interested in what the law says as much as how it is interpreted on the ground—how the definition of "child trafficking" is operationalized and how a victim of child trafficking is determined. Legal experts have pointed out that, in the case of trafficked adults, law enforcement determines who is a victim and is therefore eligible for immigration relief and associated services. Legal scholars emphasize that law enforcement often bases this decision on who would make a good witness for the prosecution.[10] Since minors do not need to cooperate with law enforcement in order to be eligible for federally supported services, this argument falls flat. And yet there is still someone who decides who is a victim and who is not. Some children get in, others are screened out.

When I started presenting preliminary findings from this study, many researchers often asked how I determined whom to include in the sample—what criteria I used to deem a particular youngster a victim. "My job was easy," I would answer. I studied what was at that time the totality of the children and adolescents trafficked across international borders. My sample constituted the universe of the minors whom the federal government accorded a status of a victim of child trafficking and deemed eligible for services for trafficked children. I chose not to use my own sampling criteria, but rather unpack the adolescents' contestations of the labels the government affixed.

The Scope of the Phenomenon

In the late 1990s, the high-profile Cadena-Sosa[11] and Paoletti-Lemus[12] cases had American law enforcement on high alert for other human trafficking situations involving immigrants. Anthony DeStefano, in a 2008 study of U.S. policy on trafficking, notes that "[f]rom the Northern Mariana Islands to Chicago, Bethesda, Maryland, New York, and other cities, investigators were discovering cases of migrants who had been forced or tricked into jobs that usually involved prostitution, although officials were finding instances of garment sweatshop labor as well."[13] These alarming news reports raised fundamental questions: What is the scope of human trafficking in the United States and around the world? How many of the trafficked victims are children and adolescents?

A study by Richard Estes and the late Neil Weiner on the commercial sexual exploitation of children is often cited as the authoritative source on the number of minors trafficked into the United States.[14] Indeed, in the early 2000s Estes and Weiner, citing field interviews with stakeholders, estimated that approximately 15,000 children were trafficked to the United States annually. They projected that at least half of these youngsters, about 8,500, fall prey to commercial sexual exploitation as part of their trafficking experience. Mia Spangenberg, who studied child trafficking in New York City for ECPAT-USA, put forth the same statistic in her report without questioning its reliability.[15] These two reports were the only studies of foreign-born children trafficked to the United States when I began my research.

These estimates were predicated on the early figures cited in the now-infamous April 2000 report *International Trafficking in Women to the United*

States: A Contemporary Manifestation of Slavery and Organized Crime by Amy O'Neill Richard.[16] An analyst at the State Department's Bureau of Intelligence and Research at the time, Richard indicated that the trafficking problem in the United States varies in size given differing definitions of what constitutes trafficking and that research was based on limited case studies. These caveats, however, did not stop her from quoting wide-ranging estimates that put the number of trafficked women and children (lumped together) at 700,000 to two million worldwide and at 45,000 to 50,000 people trafficked annually to the United States.[17] The demand for numbers, any numbers, meant that, in the words of a United Nations report on trafficking, "Organizations feel compelled to supply them, lending false precisions and spurious authority to many reports."[18] Thus began the number game.

Richard's report cited Central Intelligence Agency figures that were later disputed. A front-page article in the *Washington Post* criticized the U.S. government's alarming statements about "tidal waves" of trafficked persons entering the country for being based on methodologically flawed estimates.[19] The same criticism about worldwide estimates promulgated by the U.S. Department of State has been expressed in different fora by the United Nations Educational, Scientific and Cultural Organization (UNESCO), the U.S. Department of Justice,[20] and the Government Accountability Office. The Government Accountability Office concluded that statistics provided by the State Department's Office to Monitor and Combat Trafficking in Persons office were problematic because of "methodological weaknesses, gaps in data, and numerical discrepancies."[21] According to Jay S. Albanese, a criminologist at Virginia Commonwealth University, "There's tons of estimates on human trafficking. They're all crap. . . . It's all guesswork, speculation. . . . The numbers are inherently unreliable. The estimates of trafficking, both in the U.S. and worldwide, are not based on actual counts, and the basis for the estimates is not reproducible, so they fluctuate in unexpected ways and cannot be relied on to assess the extent of trafficking."[22]

Following these criticisms, the State Department in their annual Trafficking in Persons (TIP) report downgraded the number to 17,500 victims trafficked annually into the United States.[23] This new number did not provide breakdowns by age or gender, but the public discourse has continued to focus on women and children. In the past couple of years the TIP reports ceased to provide estimates of human trafficking altogether. Instead, the country narratives now focus on the number of victims provided assistance in any given year and the number of prosecutions of traffickers.[24] I am sure this strategy has been deployed to deflect discussions of the scale of trafficking, a topic that continues to embarrass the State Department and other federal bureaus that simply cannot come up with a reliable methodology to properly count victims of trafficking. On the other hand, this new emphasis on assisted victims shows how small the numbers of identified victims continue to be despite increased resources for governments and civil society groups to find trafficked persons.

More recently, an unpublished but widely circulated report prepared by Senator Tom Coburn's office, aptly titled *Blind Faith: How Congress Is Failing Trafficking Victims*, again took issue with flawed estimates of the scope of human trafficking and the exorbitant resources spent on antitrafficking initiatives.[25] Academics invariably begin their discussions by emphasizing that the number of trafficked persons worldwide—including children—is indeed difficult to measure and have subsequently called for improved methodologies to describe the unobserved.[26] The U.S. federal government sponsored several studies to improve identification strategies, but so far they have not yielded any significant increase in identified cases.[27] Most of the studies repeat the same old adage about trafficking being a hidden crime. The Coburn report mentioned above concluded, "Human trafficking statistics are inaccurate and inflate the number of victims because they often include persons who are merely *at risk* of being trafficked or who are considered economically disadvantaged rather than actual trafficking victims."[28] Moreover, variables used to assess risk factors are often limited to poverty levels and the status of women in particular countries. These are often opinions, not facts grounded in empirical data. Poverty, the social standing of women, and migration are not good proxies for measuring trafficking risks. Not every poor woman is equally prone to seek smugglers or fall prey to force, fraud, and coercion.

Even when the cited figures are presented as less then reliable, they are always portrayed as the "tip of the iceberg"—never the iceberg itself. In 2005, Kevin Bales, for example, estimated that twenty-seven million people labored as slaves in the early 2000s.[29] During the same time period, the UN Entity for Gender Equality and the Empowerment of Women indicated that 500,000 to two million people fell victim annually to trafficking. A 2002 International Labor Organization report on child labor estimated that 1.2 million children are trafficked annually into forced and bonded labor or are forced to become child soldiers.[30] Ten years later, in 2012, the International Labour Organization reports estimated that 20.9 million people are victims of forced labor globally and are trapped in jobs into which they were coerced or deceived and which they cannot leave. Minors aged seventeen years and below represent 26 percent of the total (or 5.5 million victims).[31] The agency never provided any explanation for the alleged increase in forced labor.

Some argue that the clandestine nature of trafficking is the reason why it is difficult—if not impossible—to estimate the scale of the phenomenon. In response to this claim, some call attention to other difficult-to-count populations—the homeless, unauthorized migrants, sex workers—and suggest methodologies that have allowed both researchers and policymakers to count the uncountable. Courtland Robinson of Johns Hopkins University, for example, conducted a study to measure risks associated with trafficking and labor violations among Burmese migrant workers in Thailand. He used an adaptive sampling method, respondent-driven sampling, to estimate the prevalence of labor violations in the migrant worker population.[32] Guri Tyldum and Anette Brunovskis report using several different data collection techniques in a study of human trafficking and transnational sex work in Oslo, including quantitative and qualitative methodologies, rapid assessment (i.e., capture-recapture estimation of women in street prostitution), telephone surveys of female sex workers operating through individual advertisements, and respondent-driven sampling.[33] The authors make an important observation about the necessity to decide not only how to count but also who to count: persons at risk for trafficking, current victims (still hidden both from law enforcement and the general public), or survivors (those who have escaped the trafficking situation on their own or have been found, usually by the police). These methodologies hold promise for more accurate estimates.

The discrepancy between the estimates and the actual number of victims is staggering. In 2013, the U.S. State Department indicated that there were 44,758 victims identified globally; of those, 10,603 were victims of trafficking for labor exploitation. During the same year there were only 1,199 labor-related prosecutions, and 470 labor-related convictions, while the remaining were sexual exploitation cases.[34] In 2011 the International Organization for Migration, a major service provider that assists trafficked individuals, globally provided assistance to trafficked persons on 5,498 occasions. The actual number of trafficked persons was smaller, because some clients received assistance more than once. At present the International Organization for Migration is not able to provide the exact number of beneficiaries they served. They do indicate, however, that 62 percent of these cases included adults (aged eighteen and over), 36 percent included minors, and 2 percent were unknown. Sixty-two percent of these cases involved females. More than half of the cases involved trafficking for forced labor (53%). About a quarter (27%) of the clients served suffered sexual exploitation. Other categories of clients included women who experienced forced marriage or were victims of organ trafficking (7%), people forced into begging (5%), and individuals trafficked both for sexual exploitation and forced labor (5%). In 2011, individuals were mostly trafficked across borders (64%), but also internally (31%), and sometimes both across borders and internally (1%).[35]

Since the passage of the TVPA in 2000 through the end of FY 2014, 4,477 trafficked adults and 841 children have been certified eligible for federally funded services in the United States. Lower-than-expected numbers of identified victims and prosecuted cases are attributed to several factors: the often-repeated claims, discussed above, regarding the clandestine nature of the trafficking phenomenon; inadequate enforcement of the provisions of the TVPA and limited resources for antitrafficking efforts;[36] insufficient coordination among governmental agencies;[37] law enforcement agencies with limited experience in dealing with the crime, which makes identification of human trafficking challenging;[38] or the fact that the estimates far exceed the reality and gravity of the situation which, in the absence of reliable data, take on mythical proportions.[39]

Researchers who have compared the discourse about "modern-day slavery" with historical accounts of "white slavery" or forced prostitution of white, mainly Irish, women support the latter supposition: "a number of contemporary historians question the actual extent of the 'white slave trade.' Their research suggests that the actual number of cases of 'white slavery' . . . was very low."[40] This does not mean that historians negate the existence of white slavery, but historical research proves that its incidence was greatly exaggerated and that perhaps the same can be said about contemporary human trafficking.[41]

Some experts suggest that the government should broaden its strategies to include an enhanced screening of children and adolescents at U.S. borders, particularly unaccompanied minors. Each year, immigration officials apprehend a large number of minors at U.S. borders. Some return voluntarily, others are returned because of bilateral understandings. Under the provisions of the Trafficking Victims Protection Reauthorization Act of 2008 all unaccompanied minors should be screened and their protection needs identified despite the existence of any formal or informal agreements about immigration of minors between the United States and the country of origin.[42] Legal provisions notwithstanding, most apprehended Mexican underage migrants are speedily returned to Mexico. Of the 11,577 Mexican minors apprehended at the border in the first seven months of FY 2014, only 494 were placed in Office of Refugee Resettlement custody; the rest were sent back to Mexico. The Congressional Research Service estimates that some 43,000 children, including 35,000 children from the neighboring countries of Mexico and Canada, are immediately returned each year.[43]

Little is known about the children who return to their countries of origin. Recent years have also seen an increase—projected to reach 60,000 or more in FY 2014[44]—of unaccompanied children entering the United States from Mexico, El Salvador, Honduras, and Guatemala. A report *Children on the Run*, issued by the UN High Commissioner for Refugees, cites violence in their homes and exploitation as the main reasons for children leaving their home countries in such unprecedented numbers. In Mexico, children reported that the criminal industry of smuggling people into the United States aggressively recruits minors, often to be drug mules but sometimes simply with promises of better opportunities. Children and adolescents also reported abuse by caretakers, sexual violence, deprivation, regularly witnessing atrocities in society, and hope for reunification with their families as reasons for coming to the United States.[45] Experts stress that there is a good possibility that both the population of children and adolescents who returned to their homelands as well as the minors in federal custody include trafficked individuals. Except for the UN High Commissioner for Refugees study, there is, however, not much research on these youngsters, especially the ones who were returned home. It is therefore impossible to say how many of these children might have been trafficked.

A significant number of victims of child trafficking had been referred to the federal government but were determined ineligible for federally funded services; in other words, they were not deemed to be victims of child trafficking. Between 2004 and 2007, USCCB and LIRS referred 151 cases of child trafficking to the federal government, accounting for an estimated 800 to 2,300 individual victims. Only twenty-three minors (14 of the 151 cases, accounting for 3 percent of the individual victims) received federal benefits. The remaining children did not receive benefits. Based on the information USCCB and LIRS had at the time of the referrals, both agencies considered all of the referred children to be victims of child trafficking according to the law.[46] It is worth realizing that even if all of these referrals were recognized as trafficking cases, the numbers do not come even close to the estimates of trafficked minors.

The reasons why so many girls and boys did not receive benefits are numerous and demonstrate that despite a legal definition of the phenomenon, child trafficking is operationalized unevenly and perhaps even capriciously. In some cases federal law enforcement agents or U.S. attorneys were simply not sympathetic to the young people's plight. In other cases the legal system deemed them victims of smuggling rather than trafficking despite the fact that according to the law minors do not have volition and cannot consent to being smuggled. In at least one case, underage victims of arranged marriages were considered to have been kidnapped rather than trafficked. This distinction makes little legal sense since kidnapping involves force and coercion, as does trafficking of minors. In still other cases, the children were reluctant to disclose detailed information about their experiences, which led to insufficient evidence of the crime of trafficking. In yet another case, a convicted sex offender brought a group of choirboys to the United States from Zambia, promising to pay them for their singing. Since he did not pay, they went back to Zambia before the case could be thoroughly investigated. In several instances, the minors' original story changed and federal law enforcement chose not to endorse benefits. Lack of sufficient evidence to support the endorsement of trafficking benefits led to the children being placed in removal proceedings and receiving deportation orders. There is little systematic data on these children. Field coordinators and case managers at the USCCB and LIRS kept notes,[47] but there should be a central database of these children and at least a minimal follow-up to ensure their protection.

By late 2005, human rights and child advocates started expanding the category of victims of child trafficking. Victims of child trafficking were no longer limited to foreign-born minors trafficked across international borders. "Advocates argued that there was a class of domestic trafficking victims: U.S. citizens and residents who traveled inside national borders as forced laborers—invariably young people and children used for sex."[48] As a result of these advocacy efforts, the TVPA was amended in 2008 to include domestic trafficking victims: U.S. citizens and lawful permanent residents. This cohort is comprised mainly of persons who used to be called commercially sexually exploited children. More recently, this phenomenon is referred to as domestic minor sex trafficking and defined as "the commercial sexual abuse of children through buying, selling, or trading their sexual services."[49]

The 2008 amendment to the TVPA suddenly opened a new opportunity to indicate the enormity of human trafficking in the United States and boost the number of trafficked children and adolescents to astronomical proportions. The U.S. Department of Justice says that as many as 300,000 young Americans are victimized by some form of human trafficking each year. Various advocates, including the "Real Men Don't Buy Girls" ad campaign, picked up the Department of Justice statement and began to claim that between 100,000 and 300,000 children are "enslaved and sold for sex in the United States."[50] What the advocates are forgetting is that the projected numbers of domestic minor sex trafficking and commercial sexual exploitation of children are as muddled as the numbers put forth a decade ago about foreign-born victims of human trafficking. Using respondent-driven sampling, Richard Curtis and his colleagues attempted to estimate the prevalence rates of commercially sexually exploited children in New York City.[51] Despite a rigorous methodology, the researchers encountered only a handful of victims, again underscoring the gap between estimates of trafficking and the number of officially identified cases.

It is not my intention to suggest that domestically exploited teen sex workers do not deserve attention and help, but I do wonder why the system set up to protect and assist commercially sexually exploited children was insufficient and why they had to be subsumed under the trafficking label. They are U.S. citizens and do not need immigration relief or special eligibility for services. The logical conclusion is that they are important to the numbers game. This numbers game is played just as much in other countries.[52]

In November 2007, Denis MacShane, the former British Foreign Office minister who described London as "Europe's capital for under-aged trafficked sex slaves," announced that according to Home Office estimates, 25,000 sex slaves currently work in the massage parlors and brothels of Britain.[53] Politicians and religious groups still repeat the media story that 40,000 prostitutes were trafficked into Germany for the 2006 World Cup—long after leaked police documents revealed there was no truth at all in the tale.[54] A report by the Foundation against Trafficking in Women asserts, "One problem in attempting to glean anything meaningful from trafficking statistics is that it is rarely clear exactly what is being measured. . . . [T]he term 'trafficking' is anything but unambiguous, and can refer to a number of different situations."[55] Trafficking is often confused with smuggling or irregular migration.[56] "[W]hen statistics are available, they usually refer to the number of migrant or domestic sex workers, rather than cases of trafficking."[57]

At present, no U.S. or international agency is compiling accurate and comprehensive statistics. The National Human Trafficking Resource Center, promoted as the only national center to receive calls from foreign-born victims of trafficking, has proven to be ineffective and does not yield much reliable data.[58] The Human Trafficking Reporting System of the Department of Justice is the only system that collects data from the investigations conducted by state and local law enforcement agencies. However, per their own admission, "the data integrity is not of a satisfactory standard to permit valuable conclusions to be drawn from it."[59]

Why would agencies rely on faulty data to contribute to the legend of "tidal waves" of trafficking in persons? And why do these accounts persist? Perhaps because in the human trafficking field, empirical proof is set aside while ideology takes center stage.

Ideology versus Evidence

"In no area of the social sciences has ideology contaminated knowledge more pervasively than in writings on the sex industry," asserts Ronald Weitzer.[60] The dominant antitrafficking discourse "is not evidence-based but grounded in the construction of a particular mythology of trafficking," concurs Jyoti Sanghera.[61] These claims certainly extend to trafficking for sexual exploitation, where canons of scientific inquiry are often suspended and research serves a particular political and moral agenda.[62] Activists involved in antiprostitution campaigns have conducted much of the U.S. research on human trafficking for sexual exploitation.[63] These activists adopt an extreme (i.e., absolutist, doctrinaire, and unscientific) version of radical feminist theory, which does not distinguish between trafficking for forced prostitution and voluntary migration (legal or undocumented) for sex work and claims that all sex workers are victims of trafficking. As Weitzer points out, few of the radical feminist claims about sex trafficking are amenable to verification.[64] These morally—and politically—driven debates result in claims that "sex trafficking reached epidemic levels worldwide, victimizing 'hundreds of thousands' or 'millions' of people every year,"[65] and "its incidence has . . . *skyrocketed* in recent years" (emphasis in original)[66] These claims are impossible to substantiate given the lack of baseline data. The use of inflated figures is a common characteristic of moral crusades.[67]

The discourse on trafficked children parallels in many ways the discourse on trafficked women and assumes that "migrants can be neatly divided into moral categories such as adult (strong, active, agent) or child (weak, passive, victim), and smuggled (complicit in a crime against the state) or trafficked (victim of a crime against the person)."[68] Research shows the inadequacies of these binaries.[69] In her research in Ghana, Tempane Natinga demonstrates that children who remain in their place of birth, working for their own families, can be exploited, but migrant children who move for work may have positive experiences that provide them the opportunity to develop skills and earn an income that they can spend on necessities. However, Western antitrafficking advocates often see them as "child laborers" and "victims of trafficking," rather than as working children.[70]

Although the academic and policy literature on international migration of minors is growing, the prevailing focus on trafficking risks is misleading. Children and adolescents are "either imagined in the shadow of parents, that is, their parents are considered the primary migrants using their adult networks, or girls and boys are seen as vulnerable interlopers into adult environments."[71] Critical discussions about child trafficking require a more nuanced examination of children and adolescents' experiences of cross-border and internal migration. Empirical research from many parts of the developing world on the reasons why children and adolescents migrate, especially for work, dispels the sweeping conceptualization of underage labor migrants as passive victims of trafficking.[72] However, given the absence of empirical studies of the contacts and networks used by young labor migrants, "the risk exists that all children's migration, particularly when others are involved and when it concerns work, will be framed as trafficking."[73]

Moral crusades propagated by activists and, to a certain extent, by service providers whose funding depends on maintaining the gravity of the trafficking problem "typically rely on horror stories and 'atrocity tales' about victims in which the most shocking exemplars of victimization are described and typified."[74] In reality, limited numbers of victims have been identified and even fewer have been studied to be able to make such gross generalizations. Policymakers, advocates, and service providers must not rely on such dramatized accounts and should adjust their efforts to account for the reality of lower-than-purported trafficking statistics.

Looking Forward

Research fulfills a number of roles, one of which is to offer an independent and critical assessment of current policy and practice. The list of issues that need to be investigated in future research projects is long, but the most important is a critical engagement with the production of "knowledge" that fuels public debate about human trafficking. Where does this knowledge come from, and how is it used? The United States prides itself in leading the antitrafficking movement and providing policy and programmatic guidance to other governments. The data and the knowledge the government uses must therefore be valid, reliable, and based on empirical research.

In order to acquire the broadest possible picture of the trafficking phenomenon, several different data collection methods, including quantitative and qualitative methods, need to be tested. Estimation methods that have been gaining currency in studies of hidden populations, including rapid assessment, capture-recapture methodology, and respondent-driven sampling, should be tested in research on human trafficking. These methods demonstrated success in studying the difficult-to-count populations—the homeless, street children, and women in street prostitution—and hold promise for more reliable quantitative research on trafficked persons.[75] Collaboration with scholars who have had a long history of conducting research on sex work could be very fruitful in testing the applicability of data collection methods developed and utilized within the sex industry research arena to studies of trafficking in persons. Similar collaboration ought to occur with researchers studying illegal migration. There has yet to be a discussion of the applicability of methods utilized by Jeffrey Passel or George Borjas to estimate the number of undocumented immigrants in the United States to arrive at similar estimates of the number of children (and adults) trafficked into the United States.[76]

Rigorous ethnographic and sociological studies based on in-depth interviews with survivors of child trafficking would provide baseline data and paint a more accurate portrait of trafficked children and youth. Too often victims of child trafficking remain one-dimensional figures whose stories are condensed and simplified, which is counterproductive to the development of culturally appropriate services. In order to develop appropriate assistance and treatment programs for survivors, increased attention needs to be paid to the expertise and practical knowledge of nongovernmental organizations and their experience in working with different groups of trafficking survivors: girls and boys trafficked for labor and sexual exploitation; unaccompanied children and youth; and young people trafficked as part of a family unit.

Given the fact that services to trafficked persons are still developing, monitoring and evaluation studies should be an integral part of every assistance program, public and private. Well-designed monitoring and evaluation studies, particularly external evaluations, can identify effective policies and "best practice" approaches as well as assess the success of different programs. Particularly important are longitudinal studies of the effects of rehabilitation programs on the ability of survivors to integrate into the new society or reintegrate into their native one. The United States has spent a considerable amount of resources supporting assistance programs to victims of human trafficking, but no follow-up studies have been conducted on any of the survivors—children or adults—once they graduate from these programs. Have survivors of trafficking for sexual exploitation been accepted by their families and local communities? Are survivors of trafficking for labor exploitation at risk for revictimization? How are the children who had been trafficked with the approval of their families doing? These are just some of the questions that require answers to inform sound policy and practice.

In the end, the problem of assessing whether we are dealing with "tidal waves" of child trafficking or smaller cohorts of victims is a symptom of the need for empirically grounded knowledge of child trafficking. Sound empirical research will yield substantive improvements in policy making and service provision. Policymakers and program staff will gain a better understanding of the processes involved in trafficking of minors and in-depth knowledge of their characteristics and service needs. Most important, this knowledge will build upon the survivors' own accounts and conceptualizations of their experiences and not theoretical deductions. At the moment, however, the unsubstantiated estimates of the scale of child trafficking continue to feed the moral panic promulgated by the new abolitionists, the subject of the next chapter.

2

The Old and New Abolitionists

Tales of the exorbitant scale of human trafficking gave rise to the development of national and international antitrafficking policies and robust systems of care for trafficked persons, including victims of child trafficking. In her provocative book *Sex at the Margins,* Laura Agustín named the complex system of antitrafficking projects and the ever-expanding number of antitrafficking advocates "the rescue industry."[1] She argues, along with other authors, that to fight "modern-day slavery," faith-based organizations—the main actors in the antitrafficking field—operate on a rescue-based model.[2] The model involves pursuing "'rescue' operations in which they generally work with law enforcement to 'bust' local brothels suspected of keeping underage girls as prostitutes. The model is to extract or rescue individuals and put them into shelters for 'rehabilitation' and, presumably, their safety."[3]

The rescue industry focuses almost exclusively on women and children trafficked for sexual exploitation as well as sex workers whom the rescuers perceive to have been trafficked, whether they have chosen or been forced into sex work. Exploited men and boys—in the sex industry or in other forms of labor—do not draw much attention from the rescuers, nor do women and girls in forced and exploitative labor or domestic servitude. It is often said that advocates prioritize sex trafficking victims because they match law enforcement's image of the ideal victim—weak, vulnerable, blameless, defenseless women and children worthy of compassion.[4] The critics of the rescue industry focus primarily on evangelical Christians and secular feminists.[5] The network of antitrafficking advocates and service providers is, however, much broader. It includes those who stand on ideological barricades pushing for new protocols and laws, those that hold prominent positions in the federal government, and the social workers that assist trafficked minors (and adults) without much fanfare.

In this chapter I introduce policymakers, child advocates, social workers, and foster parents involved in "rescuing and restoring" trafficked children and adolescents. I also discuss the types of publicly supported services that are available for trafficked minors. Together, these elements provide a comprehensive background for understanding how foreign-born trafficked children and youth under the age of eighteen are protected from victimization and assisted in integrating into the wider American society. I begin by tracing the history of the abolitionist movement and present the contemporary, federally funded system of care for minors trafficked across international borders to the United States for labor and sexual exploitation. Understanding the prurient interests of the anti-white-slavery campaigners in prostitution and their simultaneous disregard for other forms of labor exploitation illuminates our understanding of the contemporary rescue industry, its preoccupation with sex trafficking, and its focus on women and girls.[6]

Old Phenomenon, New Importance

The origins of the contemporary trafficking debate date back to the end of the nineteenth century when feminists such as Josephine Butler brought involuntary prostitution into the international discourse under the term "White Slave Trade," a term derived from the French "Traite des Blanches," which was related to "Traite des Noirs," a term used in the beginning of the nineteenth century to describe the black slave trade.[7] "White Slavery" referred to the abduction and transport of white women for prostitution. "For long years past the slaughter of the innocents has been going on," Josephine Butler wrote to her sister in 1898 about international child prostitution. "We knew it not, or only had a partial knowledge of it. Now we know, and before God we are responsible for that terrible knowledge." In a manner similar to today's antitrafficking campaigns, the issue was covered widely in the media, a number of organizations were set up to combat it, and national and international legislation was adopted to stop the trade.[8] The nineteenth-century movement against "white slavery" grew out of the abolitionist movement against prostitution, which campaigned in England and other western European countries as well as in the United States against the legalization of prostitution.[9]

The first international agreement against "white slavery" was drafted in 1902 in Paris and signed two years later by sixteen states.[10] The International

Agreement for the Suppression of the White Slave Trade did not equate "white slavery" with prostitution. Initially, the agreement addressed the fraudulent or abusive recruitment of women for prostitution in another country, although later, in 1910, its scope was broadened to include the trafficking of women and girls within national borders.[11] In 1921, during a meeting held under the auspices of the League of Nations (later to become the United Nations), the trafficking of boys was also incorporated into the agreement. In 1933 a new convention was signed in Geneva. The International Convention for the Suppression of the Traffic in Women condemned all recruitment for prostitution in another country. The abolitionist standards of the 1933 convention were reiterated in the 1949 UN Convention for the Suppression of Traffic in Persons and the Exploitation of the Prostitution of Others, which stated, "Prostitution and the accompanying evil of the traffic in persons for the purpose of prostitution are incompatible with the dignity and worth of a human person and endanger the welfare of the individual, the family, and the community of a person."

In the international arena, a renewed interest in human trafficking was influenced by developments regarding migration flows, the feminist movement, the AIDS pandemic, child prostitution, and child sex tourism in the 1980s.[12] In the 1990s trafficking in human beings, particularly women and children, reappeared on the agenda of the UN General Assembly, the Commission for Human Rights, the World Conference on Human Rights in Vienna in 1993, and the World Conference on Women in Beijing in 1995. By 1996, seventy countries had ratified the 1949 Convention.[13]

In November 2000, the UN General Assembly adopted the UN Protocol to Prevent, Suppress, and Punish Trafficking in Persons, Especially Women and Children, also known as the Palermo Protocol.[14] The Palermo Protocol was a result of two years of negotiations at the UN Center for International Crime Prevention in Vienna. The Protocol was the target of heavy lobbying efforts by religious and feminist organizations, on the one hand, and human rights advocates, on the other hand. These two groups of activists represented two opposing views of prostitution. The Human Rights Caucus saw prostitution as legitimate labor, while the Coalition Against Trafficking in Women, representing religious and feminist activists, saw all prostitution as a violation of women's human rights.[15] The Coalition Against Trafficking in Women argued that trafficking should include all forms of recruitment and transportation for prostitution, regardless of whether force or deception took place,[16] while the Human Rights Caucus, which supported the view of consensual prostitution as work, argued that force or deception was a necessary ingredient in the definition of human trafficking. The Caucus also maintained that the term "human trafficking" should include trafficking of women, men, and children for different types of labor, including forced sweatshop labor, agriculture, and prostitution.[17] The two groups also presented differing views on the notion of consent. The Coalition Against Trafficking in Women argued that prostitution is never voluntary, because women's consent to sex work is meaningless since they do not realize the exploitation they will experience. The Human Rights Caucus, on the other hand, stated, "No one consents to abduction or forced labor, but an adult woman is able to consent to engage in an illicit activity (such as prostitution). If no one is forcing her to engage in such activity, then trafficking does not exist."[18]

In the end the signatories of the Protocol rejected the definition championed by the feminist and religious groups represented by the Coalition Against Trafficking in Women and defined human trafficking as "[t]he recruitment, transportation, transfer, harboring or receipt of persons, by means of the threat or use of force or other forms of coercion, of abduction, of fraud, of deception, of abuse of power or of a position of vulnerability or of the giving or receiving of payments or benefits to achieve the consent of a person having control over another person, for the purpose of exploitation."[19] In less legalese language, the definition of human trafficking emphasized that force, fraud, or coercion must be present for a particular labor or sexual exploitation to be recognized as human trafficking. As will be seen later, this definition was modified in relation to children and youth under eighteen years of age. With the Protocol in place, many international organizations, such as the International Labor Organization, the United Nations Children's Fund, the International Organization for Migration, and the European Union, have engaged in vigorous antitrafficking campaigns.

Focus on Women and Girls

"Human trafficking is the only area of transnational crime in which women are significantly represented—as victims, perpetrators, and as activists seeking to combat this crime," writes Louise Shelly.[20] It is difficult to assess the accuracy of this statement since the statistics regarding the scope of human trafficking are not very reliable. However, it is important to point out that policymakers, advocates, and researchers do focus on trafficking of women and girls to the detriment of paying attention to the trafficking of men and boys. Originally, the protocol addressing trafficking was to be entitled "Trafficking in Women and Children," omitting men entirely. Only later was the phrase "especially women and children" included. The Smuggling Protocol, on the other hand, "has no such coda and no specific emphasis on gender. Smuggled migrants are assumed to be men seeking work elsewhere without proper documentation, while trafficked persons are assumed to be duped victims, usually women."[21] This gendered distinction is rooted in stereotypes of women and girls as victims and men and boys as less vulnerable to exploitation. This ideology not only presents a distorted view of women, but also harms men. Trafficked men are invisible. Exploitation of men and boys is not readily recognized and thus is much more difficult to address.

The focus on women and girls is also related to the fact that the trafficking discourse centers on trafficking for sexual exploitation to the detriment of other types of trafficking.[22] Women and girls are considered to be particularly vulnerable to trafficking because in many parts of the world they have low social status, limited access to education, few rights to property, and scarce opportunities to participate in the political process.[23] While low socioeconomic status might indeed be a risk factor for trafficking, highly educated women are not immune to being trafficked. In fact, empirical studies confirm that the trafficking of women and girls from Eastern Europe and the former Soviet Union—in many instances highly educated individuals—is not as rare as the argument linking the lack of educational opportunities with trafficking would have us believe.[24] Poverty as a root cause of trafficking also needs to be further explored. Not all poor women or girls resort to migration to improve their economic situation. In the early 2000s, when the antitrafficking field was holding Eastern European women trafficked for sexual exploitation under a magnifying glass, there were few reports about trafficked Bulgarians despite the fact that Bulgarian women were as poor as Ukrainian or Polish women. In September 2002, at a conference in Brussels, a staff member from the U.S. embassy in Sofia asked me what I thought of the fact that we heard nothing about trafficking of Bulgarians. I did not have an answer but thought that the Bulgarian case was proof that poverty was not a sole indicator of risk for trafficking.

The gendered (as well as raced, classed, and sexualized) discourse on human trafficking stems from the current disconnect "between the broad legal definition that embraces any worker who experienced force, fraud, or coercion and the narrow latitude of activist and policy discussion that focuses on sex work."[25] It does not result from exceptional vulnerability of women and girls, real or perceived. The centrality of women in the trafficking discourse "maintains the gendered divide around which earlier definitions of trafficking settled and thus reinforces the general, dominant image of trafficking as pertinent only to women's and girls' lives." The concept of gender inequality continues to guide research, "with situations of poor women and girls becoming the main concern of those involved with antitrafficking work."[26]

Finally, the gendered dimension of human trafficking relates to broader issues of women and migration. Despite the continued feminization of migration—half of the world's migrants are women[27]—there remains a "bias that women and girls need constant male or state protection from harm, and therefore must not be allowed to exercise their right to movement or right to earn a living in a manner they choose."[28] "Some countries (e.g., Bangladesh, Myanmar, and Nepal) have even prohibited women from migration because of the fear that they will end up in trouble."[29] This bias often conflates migration with trafficking and contributes to the notion that women are the main victims of trafficking. Critics have argued that antitrafficking measures have been used not necessarily to protect women from exploitation, but to police, punish, and racialize female migrants.[30]

TVPA and the Four Ps: Prevention, Protection, Prosecution, and Partnerships

In the United States, trafficking became a focus of activities in the late 1990s when two separate bills were proposed in Congress. Senator Paul Wellstone (D-MN), sponsored a bill that included provisions to prosecute forced labor in all its forms, emphasizing that involuntary servitude was not exclusive to the sex industry but was also liable to occur in agriculture, garment, food, and many other industries. Republican congressman Chris Smith, aided by Laura Lederer, then of the Protection Project, and Gary Haugen of the International Justice Mission, drafted an alternate bill and launched a forceful campaign against Wellstone's proposed legislation. Congressman Smith's bill claimed that Senator Wellstone's "focus on a range of labor issues would distract from combating sex slavery."[31]

In the end, Congress passed the Victims of Trafficking and Violence Protection Act and President Bill Clinton signed it into law on October 28, 2000. Known as TVPA, the Act was the product of a tenuous alliance between evangelical Christians and secular feminist antitrafficking crusaders.[32] Feminist organizations—such as Equity Now and the Protection Project—joined forces in the name of saving the world's women and children. The already-mentioned Laura Lederer, editor of the classic feminist antipornography anthology *Take Back the Night*, a former State Department appointee, and current president of Global Centurion, an NGO devoted to fighting modern slavery by focusing on demand, was the major link between feminist and evangelical organizations. She famously defended this alliance, saying that faith-based organizations had introduced "a fresh perspective and biblical mandate to the women's movement. Women's groups don't understand that the partnership on this issue has strengthened them, because they would not be getting attention internationally otherwise."[33]

Although the TVPA of 2000 included both sex and labor trafficking in the definition of human trafficking, the U.S. focus on sex trafficking paralleled international antitrafficking efforts. Combating sexual slavery became a key priority in the Bush administration. The Department of Justice under John Ashcroft spent an average of $100 million annually to fight trafficking domestically and internationally, "a sum that overshadows any other individual nation's contributions to similar efforts."[34]

The TVPA initially got lost in the transfer of power from the Clinton to the Bush administration, much to the abolitionists' chagrin. Gretchen Soderlund reports that in 2002 the groups behind the TVPA mobilized their constituencies to put pressure on the Bush administration to enforce the provisions of TVPA. Michael Horowitz, former senior fellow at the Hudson Institute and a senior adviser to the Religious Action Center of Reform Judaism, played a key role in the coalition that got the TVPA signed into law. Horowitz wrote to a fellow advocate that it was time to mobilize the administration to get serious about the fight against human trafficking. He worried that if left to their own devices, sex workers' rights advocates would be teaching "seven-year old girls how to get their customers to use condoms and to use techniques that make sexual penetration less painful."[35] In his opinion, the administration had to start supporting antitrafficking programs aimed at eradicating all forms of prostitution. Horowitz continues to criticize the U.S. government for not enforcing the TVPA in the international arena. "It [the TIP report] is not taken seriously by foreign governments," he said. He also added that the U.S. government response to human trafficking has become "a series of press conferences with no bite" and described the State Department as "a white noise operation."[36]

The law was aimed at accomplishing what originally came to be known at the "Three Ps": prevention, protection, and prosecution. The fourth P—partnerships—came in much later. Prevention "relates to activities such as public education and job creation intended to keep potential victims out of the clutches of traffickers and away from exploitation," developing "viable economic alternatives to their desperate migration for work" and thus getting to the root causes of human trafficking.[37] Protection describes a diverse array of assistance programs—housing, financial assistance, medical care, and mental health counseling—available to victims of severe forms of trafficking who meet certain eligibility criteria.[38] Prosecution holds traffickers accountable under criminal law and levies appropriate penalties. Partnership means collaboration between different agencies and actors.

Policymakers and antitrafficking advocates regard the TVPA of 2000 and the Trafficking Victims Protection Reauthorization Act of 2003 as the main tools to combat trafficking in persons both worldwide and domestically.[39] The passage of the TVPA launched an entirely new federal bureaucracy to deal with human trafficking. The U.S. Department of State created its Office to Monitor and Combat Trafficking in Persons (J/TIP). Other departments—the Department of Health and Human Services, Department of Justice, United States Agency for International Development, Department of Labor, Department of Homeland Security, Department of Education, and Department of Defense—followed and created their own programs to fight human trafficking. In the already cited report, "Blind Faith," Senator Coburn called the growing federal antitrafficking apparatus "wasteful, mismanaged, and duplicative." He has taken issue with the amount of money authorized to combat human trafficking, emphasizing that the dollars spent on antitrafficking initiatives have grown exponentially—from $31.8 million in 2001 to $185.5 in 2010—with agencies having difficulty keeping track of their funds.[40]

Of all the federal officials leading the antitrafficking crusade, John Miller, the first director of the U.S. State Department's Office to Monitor and Combat Trafficking in Persons (the TIP Office), was probably the best-known and most written-about figure. "Our job under this statute is to end trafficking," Miller stated in 2003. "If America fails to take the lead in rescuing the victims, there's no other nation that will." According to E. Benjamin Skinner, author of *A Crime So Monstrous: Face-to-Face with Modern-day Slavery*, Miller loved the media: "He viewed it as an essential weapon of the new abolitionist movement, and he tended to speak without a filter."[41] Indeed, he did not mince words and had a flair for using sensationalistic phrases to discuss human trafficking. Miller was one of the first people to call human trafficking "modern day slavery." In a conversation in my office, he bemoaned the fact that Colin Powell, the former secretary of state, would not use the word "slavery" to describe trafficking in persons. Colin Powell thought the term "slavery" was too politically charged and emotionally loaded. "The best I was able to do," Miller said, "was to persuade him to use slavery-like conditions."[42] Miller was highly attuned to the political importance of linguistic frames. He argued that the term "sex worker," which is preferred by some civil society actors and feminist academics, served "to justify modern-day slavery, [and] dignify the perpetrators and the industries who enslaved."[43]

Before taking over the TIP Office, Miller, a former member of the House of Representatives from Washington State and a fervent antitrafficking advocate, chaired the Seattle-based Discovery Institute, a nonpartisan organization focusing, among other things, on the theory of creationism known as intelligent design. He brought the same conservative attitudes to the antitrafficking enterprise. The Trafficking Victims Protection Reauthorization Act of 2003 elevated Miller's status, raising his rank to ambassador-at-large.[44]

John Miller believed that prostitution "fuels" the increase in sex trafficking. In 2005 a group of human rights activists, lawyers, and researchers challenged Miller's opinion by stating that his views were not supported by valid research and empirical data and that the government's focus on prostitution rather than all forms of labor trafficking was skewing the country's actions. Miller did not listen to the scholars and human rights activists. He squarely focused the administration policy on the link between prostitution and trafficking: "Sex work causes sex trafficking; thus, eliminating one would eliminate the other," he said. As DeStefano emphasizes, "This policy approach was a dramatic shift from the U.N. Protocol's position, which did not condemn prostitution. Rather it condemned the coercion or deceit used to inveigle and compel a person to do a job, which may or may not be prostitution."[45]

Miller was also a great supporter of the TIP Reports his office produced. These annual reports rank countries according to a number of indicators listed in Section 108 of the TVPA. Among the criteria are vigorous prosecution of traffickers, extradition of suspects where appropriate, protection of victims, awareness-raising campaigns, cooperation with international efforts aimed at stopping human trafficking, and prosecution of public officials who participate or facilitate trafficking in persons. Many of these reports were met with some controversy. The 2003 report was the first one to involve sanctions, while the 2004 report introduced a watch list—a probationary status of sorts. Many legal scholars and social scientists voiced skepticism about the value of this "naming and shaming mechanism," but Miller defended the reports. At a press briefing on June 4, 2004, he said that the country reports were pressing governments to do something about human trafficking: "For example, 24 countries this past year have new, comprehensive antitrafficking laws. There have been almost 8,000 prosecutions of traffickers worldwide and almost 3,000 convictions."[46] His successor, Mark P. Lagon, also spoke favorably about the TIP reports despite the fact that the reports continued to be based on anecdotal information and are not grounded in systematic research. In 2008, at a large meeting with stakeholders where he was announcing anticipated financial support for antitrafficking activities, I asked Ambassador Lagon whether his office planned to support research on trafficking or evaluate the efficacy of the programs the J/TIP office funded. Not surprisingly, the answer was "No. We might fund an evaluability assessment but do not have any plans to support basic research." Luis CdeBaca, the subsequent director of the TIP office, stood by the information published in the reports as well. Under his leadership, several evaluation efforts had been undertaken, but the results are not publicly available.[47] It is yet to be seen what impact the current acting director of the J/TIP office, Kari Johnstone, will have on the antitrafficking field. She has headed the office since CdeBaca's departure in November 2014.

In 2009, Secretary of State Hilary Rodham Clinton added the fourth P—Partnerships—to the original 3Ps outlined in the TVPA, asserting: "The criminal network that enslaves millions of people crosses borders and spans continents. So our response must do the same. So we're committed to building new partnerships with governments and NGOs around the world, because the repercussions of trafficking affect us all."[48] Almost every federal department wanted to be part of the network.[49] New antitrafficking campaigns began to be launched, often disregarding previous initiatives and duplicating efforts. The Blue Campaign launched by the Department of Homeland Security in 2010 is an example of one of the latest additions to federal antitrafficking efforts.

While the J/TIP office in the State Department has dealt almost exclusively with antitrafficking overseas—through grants supporting awareness campaigns, training programs, technical assistance aimed at establishing national antitrafficking laws, and direct services to trafficked persons, mainly women—it nevertheless set a tone for activities at home aimed at trafficking into the United States. Although most people—minors and adults—were trafficked to the United States for labor exploitation,[50] the State Department's focus on sex trafficking has affected the ways trafficked persons are conceptualized. I write more about this in chapter 8 where I discuss how law enforcement and service providers imagined that the trafficked girls were sexually exploited whether there was proof of sexual exploitation or not.

System of Care for Trafficked Minors

While many federal departments are involved in the antitrafficking activities both overseas and domestically, for the purpose of this discussion—focused on foreign-born children and youth trafficked to the United States—the most important actor is the Anti-Trafficking in Persons Program, until very recently housed in the Office of Refugee Resettlement (ORR) and currently merged with the program serving domestic victims of trafficking in the Department of Health and Human Services and its network of implementing partners. Both the State Department and the Department of Justice are often in the limelight, drawing the public's attention to human trafficking through awareness-raising campaigns led by celebrities or mounting prosecutions against notorious traffickers accused of horrendous crimes. The Anti-Trafficking in Persons Program, on the other hand, is a much less visible player, going about its business without much fanfare, dispensing grants for direct services to victims of human trafficking and working with local communities to raise awareness about human trafficking.

At first blush it might seem odd that an office established to administer the U.S. refugee resettlement program has been given a mandate to care for trafficked minors (and adults). Then again, given ORR's history of resettling unaccompanied refugee children since the fall of Saigon and the associated expertise in funding and administering programs aimed at providing linguistically and culturally appropriate services to diverse refugee populations, this connection proves suitable. Incidentally, the antitrafficking program had been added to ORR's portfolio in the post-9/11 climate when the U.S. refugee resettlement program was all but dormant.[51] Faced with the possibility of downsizing the refugee program, ORR and its implementing partners enthusiastically embraced these new challenges. However, because the number of resettled refugees has increased in recent years without substantial increases in ORR's budget, the antitrafficking program is beginning to be perceived as a drain on the agency's resources and in competition with the refugee program. The recent influx of undocumented and often unaccompanied children and adolescents from Central America and Mexico is further stretching ORR's resources, human and financial.[52]

Available Services: Social, Educational, and Health Care

Trafficked minors are eligible for a number of different services and benefits under the Trafficking Victims Protection Act. Since trafficked children and youth are often present in the United States without parents or legal guardians, ORR classifies them as unaccompanied refugee minors (URMs) and places them in the URM programs, administered by two faith-based organizations with a long history of serving unaccompanied refugee children, the U.S. Conference of Catholic Bishops and the Lutheran Immigration and Refugee Services and their local affiliates.

The URM programs operate in fifteen states and twenty cities. They are run in accordance with U.S. child welfare guidelines, and are licensed in the state in which they operate. Minors are provided shelter in a foster family, small group homes, or independent living arrangements, depending on the youth's developmental needs. These families and homes must be licensed by their state or county child welfare provider and receive ongoing training in child welfare matters. Foster care placements are based on the individual needs of a particular minor. Challenging as it might be, the URM programs strive to place the children and youth in families with similar cultural, linguistic, and religious backgrounds. The young people's special health, educational, and emotional needs as well as personality and temperaments are also supposedly taken into consideration when placing them in care. The programs have found that some children do well in family settings, while others, especially older youth, are unable to adjust to the rigors of family life and do better in small group care.

Children and youth who enter the URM programs are eligible for a wide range of benefits, including the Children's Health Insurance Program and the Temporary Assistance to Needy Families program. Youth between ages sixteen and twenty-four can receive work permits and may be eligible for Job Corps, a program run by the U.S. Department of Labor. They can also receive intensive case management services, educational services, legal representation, medical care, and mental health counseling.

Once in care, the minors are provided with indirect financial support for food, clothing, and other basic necessities. The URM program or the foster family makes arrangements to take the child/youth to initial medical and dental evaluations and for ongoing medical care. The URM program also provides intensive case management, which includes health counseling and access to pro bono attorneys to assist them in obtaining legal immigration status.

Minors in the URM program are enrolled in public schools and the URM case manager assists in connecting the child with English as a Second Language tutoring or special educational services as needed. After the initial placement period, the minor is supposed to be provided with independent living skills training, job skills training, and career/college counseling. Minors must enter the program before their eighteenth birthday and may stay in the program until they are twenty or twenty-one, depending upon a particular state's emancipation guidelines.

Although programs are supposed to evaluate family reunification possibilities for children in their care, and many do, the prevailing opinion is that unaccompanied trafficked minors do not have appropriate family members in the United States or overseas with whom they could be reunified. In one case I examined, Gulianna requested reunification with a family member in Guatemala but her request was denied by the juvenile court judge overseeing her care due to concerns about her safety were she to return to a relative of the family members who trafficked her. Gulianna's case was not unique. In most instances where family members, even more distant relatives such us aunts and uncles, were involved in the trafficking of the girls—either as smugglers or employers—the girls' wishes to go back home were ignored and formal requests denied. Law enforcement regarded the relatives as criminals. In cases where the traffickers were not related to the trafficked minors, but came from the same village or neighborhood, law enforcement and family court judges thought that going home would put the girls and their families in danger. Sensationalistic media accounts of criminals preying on family members of trafficked victims overshadowed any rationale the trafficked minors put forth in advocating for return home. Social workers also advised the youth to stay in the United States, mainly because they did not trust the government had appropriate resources to assess the safety and appropriateness of such returns.

Make no mistake, the majority of the youth wanted to stay in the United States not because they feared retaliation, but because they saw many more opportunities to earn a living in the United States. Fatima spent several years in domestic servitude in her uncle and aunt's house. He parents advised her to stay in the foster care program and remain in the United States. Her father argued that while she would have the support of her immediate family—parents and siblings—if she returned to Morocco, everyone else would shun her and she would have no prospects for a good marriage or a decent job.

In some cases, minors have chosen to emancipate from the program after turning eighteen and have joined family members in the United States. In the opinion of some child advocates, these family members may not have been appropriate to be the sole caregiver for a younger child under the age of fourteen, but may provide valuable support for an emancipated young adult.

This raises frank questions as to why a couple of years would make a difference. If the home was not appropriate for a sixteen year old, then one must question its suitability for an eighteen year old. The very cautious manner in which the URM programs evaluate whether it is suitable to release a trafficked child or adolescent to their family member residing in the United States stands in sharp contrast to the number of Central American undocumented and unaccompanied children released to families or communities in the United States. According to Mark Greenberg, acting assistant secretary of Health and Human Services' Administration for Children and Families, 95 percent of these young people get released to their families and communities.[53] It begs the question: Why is it safer and more appropriate for some minors to be reunited with families than for others?

Immigration Relief: T-Visas

Unlike antitrafficking legislation elsewhere in the world, the TVPA includes immigration relief for trafficked victims. In many other countries, the psychosocial services offered to trafficked minors and adults might be as generous as, or even more munificent than, those stipulated by the TVPA, but nowhere else do victims have access to permanent immigration relief and a path to citizenship. The United Kingdom, for example, has been very proactive in the recognition of trafficking as a serious crime, but has not adopted legal mechanisms to ensure the protection of trafficked victims, either on a short- or long-term basis. There is no specific relief from deportation that would allow trafficked victims to remain temporarily or permanently in the country if return is not viable. Instead, trafficked persons must apply for asylum, which if granted allows them to remain in the United Kingdom permanently, or humanitarian protection or discretionary leave, which are provided for defined periods of time.[54] In Italy, the much-lauded Article 18 of Legislative Decree No. 286/98 provides for a residency permit for a trafficked victim, albeit only for one year.[55] In contrast to these limited provisions, minors (and adults) trafficked to the United States can apply to remain in the country under the T-Visa program. The T-Visa provides immigration protection to minors (and adults) who experienced severe forms of trafficking and allows them to become lawful permanent residents and eventually U.S. citizens.

Eligibility for services and access to the trafficking-related visas are two separate processes that may or may not intersect. Trafficked minors are not required to have a T-Visa to gain access to assistance. All that is required is "determination of eligibility" from ORR. In fact, many social workers consider timely access to services to be more important for avoiding revictimization than the T-Visa, especially for young children. However, some of the

members) with services offered by local interfaith groups, including the Salvation Army, Catholic Charities, and Jewish Family Services, as well as secular nonprofits. The USCCB program came to a sudden halt when the Department of Health and Human Services announced that "strong preference" would be given to groups that would refer all victims to family-planning services offering the full range of legally permissible gynecological and obstetric care, including abortion in some cases.[62] The pro-life policies of the Bush era penalized the agency when a well-meaning caseworker helped a teen mother in need. The pro-choice politics of the Obama administration penalized the organization for adhering to the pro-life teachings of the Catholic Church.

Programmatic Challenges

For all their merit, the URM programs do face some challenges. One of them is finding suitable foster homes, with safe and culturally and linguistically appropriate foster parents with sufficient education and social capital to facilitate the social and economic integration of trafficked children and adolescents into the wider American society. Another is to find culturally appropriate indigenous approaches to heal traumatic experiences.

Analisa, whom we have already met, hails from Honduras. She was placed with a Spanish-speaking family from Puerto Rico. While speaking a common language certainly aided Analisa's adjustment to her post-trafficking life, the family was ill-prepared to assist her with school work, to counsel her regarding career options, and to help her with learning English. The foster parents were school dropouts with very limited English language capability. The foster father was an evangelical minister and was supported by his congregation. Neither he nor his wife was prepared to help Analisa find a suitable job.

Despite strict regulations governing foster care homes, they allowed their unmarried son to move into the family home. Analisa and Julio developed a romantic relationship that resulted in pregnancy. Analisa became a young mother—she was several months shy of her eighteenth birthday when she discovered she was with child—and had to face another challenge in her integration to the new life in the United States. Julio and Analisa love their daughter and are raising her together, but the unplanned pregnancy has curtailed Analisa's ability to attain economic self-sufficiency. At minimum, she has to provide for another human being. Childcare responsibilities limit Analisa's ability to work outside the home. If the romance did not end well, the sexual relationship between Analisa and Julio could have been perceived as statutory rape and the results would have been grim for all concerned: the foster parents risked losing their license and the agency that cared for Analisa could have been in trouble as well. Indeed, the agency was quite worried how I would interpret the relationship between Analisa and Julio. The social worker that accompanied me to the interview with Analisa wanted to make sure I understood that the relationship between Analisa and Julio was consensual. Indeed, I noted that Julio was very devoted to both Analisa and his baby. Culturally speaking, I was also aware that it was not unusual for a seventeen-year-old Honduran female to be married and have children.

Foster parents who do not share language or cultural background with the trafficked child present different dynamics and challenges. Middle-class educated foster parents have the financial means, education, and social capital needed to assist a trafficked minor in rebuilding her life, but language and cultural barriers often stand in the way of successful relationship between them and the foster child. Aurelia, a sixteen-year-old girl from Mexico trafficked to Arizona to work in a bar, was, at first, enchanted with the material wealth her foster family had: a comfortable house with a spacious backyard and a nice car. Aurelia enjoyed having a separate bedroom and her own bathroom. However, her foster parents' different cultural background proved to be a real obstacle. "It wasn't so much that they didn't speak much Spanish," she said, "but you wouldn't believe what she [the foster mother] wanted me to wear. I looked like an old lady: no sparkle, no make-up." Aurelia also did not like having a curfew, being nagged by her foster mother about schoolwork, but most of all feeling isolated in the white suburb where her foster parents lived, without access to other Latino youth.

Several older girls—usually seventeen years old or older—were placed in supervised semi-independent or independent living arrangements. In many states, survivors of child trafficking were eligible to remain in the program past their eighteenth birthday; length of eligibility differed by state, but in many localities the benefits extended up to age twenty or twenty-one. While some disliked having "too many rules" and "not enough freedom," many did really well in these programs. They enjoyed learning to live independently "the American way": learning to manage time and money, making decisions, even the smallest ones, about what to cook or what to wear. Those girls who were initially placed in a foster family and then moved to a group home invariably preferred the group home.

In addition to finding appropriate foster families, the URM programs have grappled with other challenges. Some of these challenges were much more pronounced in the early 2000s when the programs serving trafficked children were in their infancy; others persist even today, fourteen years after the TVPA legislation was enacted. In order for trafficked children to have access to the services provided under the TVPA, they must obtain the determination of eligibility letter from ORR. In previous years issuing such a letter required cooperation between ORR and the Department of Justice. The processes involved were lengthy and often left the trafficked minor in limbo for quite a long time. Currently, any individual—service provider, child advocate, and attorney—can request a letter of eligibility from ORR on behalf of a child when credible information indicates the minor may be a victim of trafficking. Trafficked minors can also receive interim assistance as they await the letter of eligibility. Thus, the hurdle that plagued the system for several years seems to be a thing of the past.

However, while establishing eligibility for services currently seems to be much more straightforward than in years past, service providers have very limited resources to continue providing services to victims of child trafficking after they are no longer eligible for the URM programs. Evelyn, whom we met in the prologue, is a perfect example of a young woman who could use career counseling and job placement services several years after she left the URM program. As graduation from college approaches, career counseling seems especially important to Evelyn. She is not sure what kinds of jobs she is qualified for with a bachelor's degree in homeland security or how to find a job that would lead to upward mobility. She needs stable employment with prospects for growth now that she has a son. Recently, by pure coincidence, I was able to connect Evelyn with a job readiness and employment services program operated by USCCB. The program includes résumé writing and other skill-building activities. We are both hopeful that the program will be helpful to Evelyn. However, survivors cannot rely on happenstance. There is a need for long-term follow-up services or at minimum a centralized clearinghouse with information survivors can access whenever they need to learn about a new facet of American life.

The intent of the antitrafficking movement is to prevent trafficking, protect victims, and prosecute perpetrators. Many prevention efforts have been mounted, but a number of children and youth have nonetheless been "captured." We must therefore "rescue" and "restore" them. The next three parts of this book unpack the myths and realities of captivity, rescue, and rehabilitation of survivors of child trafficking.

Part II

"Captured"

In the movie *Taken*, Liam Neeson plays a retired government agent whose daughter Amanda, on vacation in Paris, is captured by two mobsters running a slavery-prostitution ring. What follows—predictably—is a frantic father on a transatlantic quest to rescue his daughter. In reality, trafficked children are rarely kidnapped. Parents of "trafficked" children don't have to search for them because they know exactly where they had taken their children or whom they paid to smuggle their children across international borders. Trafficking scenarios do not follow Hollywood scripts. Trafficked children do not live privileged lives full of expensive gifts and trips to France. The children and adolescents in my study, without exception, came from poor families struggling to make ends meet. The youngsters were expected to contribute to the family's livelihood. Yet the opportunities to engage in wage employment in rural Mexico, Guatemala, Morocco, Cameroon, and China were few and far between. The nearby towns and cities also provided limited options. The United States seemed like a much better idea.

Families consulted *coyotes* or snakeheads to facilitate border crossings. Mothers and sometimes grandmothers took the risky journey with the girls to provide them with a better education or to place them in jobs in faraway America. Assessing the options available in their native villages, many families thought America was the mythical "El Dorado" where they would be able to find lucrative jobs, send money home to support a disabled father or ailing grandparent, or to provide for their own babies. They had no way of knowing that their dreams would turn into a harsh reality: not only would the big bucks fail to materialize, they faced exploitative working conditions, long hours in smoky bars selling overpriced drinks to boozy clients, endless days of scrubbing floors and looking after their employers' children, and being subjected to sexual exploitation.

The biggest shock would come when Immigration and Customs Enforcement agents raided the cantina or the fast food restaurant where they worked. Many would watch as their mothers, whom they often toiled alongside, were taken away in handcuffs by the Feds and charged with child trafficking. U.S. law enforcement's conceptualizations of who is a trafficker and what constitutes acceptable working conditions for adolescents stand in sharp contrast with the cultural and familial notions of helpers facilitating better lives abroad.

The chapters in this section present a portrait of traffickers—parents, grandparents, neighbors, and boyfriends—involved in the trafficking of the girls and boys I studied (chapter 3) and introduce a group of trafficked youngsters, extremely poor tweens and teens, with few opportunities to improve their fate other than to be smuggled across international borders in search of paid employment (chapter 4). These chapters are not meant to deny the involvement of criminal networks in the trafficking of children and adolescents, but rather to underscore the fact that family involvement in child trafficking should not be underestimated. Stories about the diverse experiences of trafficked youth and varying levels of labor and sexual exploitation show that not every young girl trafficked to the United States is chained to a bed in a brothel. Many clean hotels and motels, others serve drinks in seedy bars, and still others work as nannies. They are neither manipulated by larger-than-life gangsters nor forced to provide sexual services to countless men every night. All are, however, exploited. Overworked and underpaid, they see no possibility of accomplishing their goal: to improve their and their family's livelihood. Some are in debt bondage. For them the prospects for financial independence are even more unattainable. No matter how much they suffer, however, they do not want their moms or uncles behind bars.

3

Snakeheads, Coyotes,
and . . . Mothers

Traffickers are "restless merchants of modern slavery," operate "alien stash houses," and deal and barter slaves with little retribution across vast international networks—these are just some of the descriptions overheard during training for Transportation Security Administration agents, baggage handlers, and restaurant workers at a large international airport. Journalists portray traffickers as "thick-necked, beady-eyed thugs, members of organized crime gangs like the Albanian or Russian mob, the Italian mafia, the Japanese yakuza, Chinese triads or the Hell's Angels."[1] Activists elevate traffickers to an evil, powerful, calculating, and all-knowing entity.[2] International organizations and academic writers indicate that the traffickers' highly organized criminal networks span the world and are able to adjust to ever-changing environments and demands.[3]

Numerous authors focus on the alleged connections between sophisticated, organized crime networks and human trafficking despite the fact that there is scant empirical data to support this view.[4] Researchers make this connection based on a variety of disparate facts: people of different nationalities are often part of the same group of trafficked victims, trips over a long distance require a well-oiled organization, substantial amounts of money are involved, itineraries are able to change quickly, legal services are available on a moment's notice, and traffickers are able to speedily react to counteroffensives mounted by law enforcement agencies.[5] Europol, the European Union's law enforcement agency, has developed these arguments,[6] but many others share these opinions.[7] The U.S. Department of State reiterates these assertions, describing how traffickers enjoy virtually no risk of prosecution by using surreptitious modes of transportation and communication. Such criminals frequently avoid punishment by operating in places where there is little rule of law, a lack of antitrafficking legislation, poor enforcement of such laws, and widespread corruption.[8] Some researchers believe there is a close connection between organized crime and trafficking for sexual exploitation due to the close involvement of criminal organizations at various levels of the expansive sex industry.[9]

On the other end of the spectrum are scholars who "have questioned the assumptions behind the organization and transnationality in the trafficking-as-organized crime thesis," writes Maggie Lee,[10] citing Hobbs and Dunningham, Huysmans, Finckenauer, Loader, Levi, and Woodiwiss and Hobbs.[11] Lee explains further that the preoccupation with "external, alien actors, cultures, and organizations"—such as the Russian Mafia, Colombian cartels, Jamaican Yardies, and Chinese triads—are "part of the long-standing intellectual tradition of a criminology of the other, of the threatening outcast, the fearsome stranger, the excluded and the embittered."[12] A review of the literature on child trafficking indicates that few authors mention the involvement of family members in the trafficking of minors. When family is discussed, the discourse focuses mainly on how parents in foreign countries have been tricked by traffickers promising education, employment, and financial prosperity.[13] The fact that parents often accompany their sons and daughters on the migration journey is frequently glossed over or omitted.

The point here is not to side with one view or the other. In fact, limited empirical data makes it difficult to support either view. The involvement of families in child trafficking is worth exploring both to enhance prevention strategies and to design appropriate services for survivors of child trafficking. Awareness-raising campaigns could provide a more realistic view of the behaviors involved in cultural practices of child circulation or child fostering—for example, *restavek* children in Haiti who are sent by their parents to work as domestic servants, often indentured, or children growing up in nonnatal families in various parts of the world—to ascertain whether or not these practices lead to precarious migration journeys and put children and youth at risk for trafficking. The antitrafficking field needs to understand better the intimate nature of migration,[14] including the involvement of family and kin in smuggling and trafficking. Law enforcement representatives and service providers need to understand that vilifying family members who helped their children cross international borders clandestinely might further traumatize the young survivors. Of course, those who severely abused and exploited trafficked children and youth ought to be punished, but not at the expense of the well-being of the youngsters.

This chapter paints a portrait of "the other traffickers"—parents, grandparents, neighbors, and boyfriends—who were involved in facilitating the journey of the children and adolescents featured in this book to the United States. Although without exception their journey started as a smuggling operation, it ended—at least in the eyes of the law, if not in the eyes of the youth—in exploitation or abuse. Law enforcement considered working children to be exploited and abused, often without considering the conditions under which the youngsters worked. Therefore, the girls and boys were deemed to be victims of trafficking and their relatives were tried in courts of law on charges of child trafficking. "The Pied Piper who leads the children away with their parents' blessing is the key to this modern slavery," the journalist James Astill states. "Often one of the child's own relatives, he is commissioned to take full advantage of the extended family, and of the poor man's assumption that anywhere is better than here."[15]

The U.S. antitrafficking law treats minors under the age of eighteen as having no volition and therefore as being unable to consent to being smuggled. The law does not embrace the principle of the "evolving capacities" of the child introduced in the Convention on the Rights of the Child. This principle recognizes that as children acquire enhanced competencies there is a diminishing need for protection and a greater capacity to take responsibility for decisions affecting their lives. The Convention allows for the recognition that minors in different environments and cultures, and faced with diverse life experiences, will acquire competencies at different ages. Under the TVPA of 2000, minors—even those on the verge of adulthood, and who may no longer identify as children—are always trafficked, never smuggled, and those who help them are always traffickers, never just parents, uncles, or family friends trying to give them a better life.

The Importance of Kinship Networks in Facilitating the Journey to the United States

It is tempting to see human trafficking as a phenomenon dominated and controlled by organized crime, but in reality the picture is much more complex.[16] Smaller operations based on kinship or friendship ties may, of course, be part of larger criminal networks. In my research, however, I have not uncovered any direct evidence of such connections. Moreover, the trafficked girls did not speak of criminal networks—Flora and Isa were astounded and saddened when law enforcement dragged their mother away in handcuffs—but rather focused on the close relationships between themselves and those who helped them cross the U.S. border and find employment. "This is my mother," cried Isa, "where are you taking her?" Despite this reality, policymakers, child advocates, and service providers maintained a studied blindness toward the complicated role family and kin play in facilitating and financing the migration journeys of children and adolescents to the United States.

Researchers have paid somewhat more attention to these issues. In many studies of migration networks, kinship ties "are thought to be among the most intimate, interdependent and controllable of ties."[17] Drawing on historical examples of family and kinship systems, anthropologists have written about trafficking for sexual exploitation as a phenomenon embodying a cultural practice related to the sexual exchange of girls and women.[18] Lynellyn Long, for example, argues that contemporary sex trafficking transforms "traditional bride wealth and marriage exchanges by treating women's sexuality and bodies as commodities to be bought and sold (and exchanged again) in various Western capitals and Internet spaces."[19] Anuja Agrawal, a sociologist, questions the idea that "a large mass of women [in the Bedia community in India] can enter the sex trade while their families remain innocent bystanders."[20] Her research takes issue with the prevailing notion that dysfunctional and pathological family background is the culprit behind girls' and young women's entry into the sex trade. Instead, she shows the intimate relationship between the Bedia practice of prostitution and their familial economy. Agrawal argues that sex work is for many Bedia women a way out of poverty. She shows that the conditions under which these girls and young woman work differ significantly. Those who work in very exploitative conditions in urban brothels are barely able to benefit from this source of income, since typically the brothel owner usurps their earnings. On the other hand, those who work in brothels on the condition that they share their earnings with the brothel owner are somewhat better off. Those who are able to strike out on their own without needing to pay huge debts or share the bulk of their income can prosper. According to Agrawal, most Bedia women work under the latter two conditions and most prefer to share their income only with immediate family. Sex work is an economic strategy for the whole family in this society, not an abuse of girls and women by their kin.

These examples showcase situations that are not palatable to many, especially if the sex workers are very young. But what role do families and kin play in situations where children and adolescents seek opportunities outside the sex industry? In my research, the vast majority of families aimed at providing their children and adolescents with either educational opportunities or access to better livelihoods by helping them find jobs in restaurants, bars, cantinas, or construction. In a few instances, the parents were already in the United States and wanted to reunite with their daughters. In all of these circumstances, family and kin were essential and played a myriad of roles: financier of the migration process, smuggler across international borders, transporter within the United States, or employer, but not criminal. Both Evelyn and Fatima remarked that African families expected kin to help raise children, provide for them, and give them opportunities whenever help was needed. Fatima said that her mother always housed and fed children of relatives. "You know," she said, "they helped out in my mom's restaurant in exchange for food and a place to sleep. We were not rich, but they were poorer, so we had to help."

Anthropological research in many parts of the world has documented this informal, kinship-based fostering of children of different ages. Jessaca Leinaweaver has reviewed anthropological findings about circumstances under which children are more likely to benefit from kinship-based fostering and when it exposes them to risks. Her analysis of cross-cultural data indicates that informal kinship-based fostering is not necessarily harmful and in some instances can be beneficial, especially when it provides children with access to education or apprenticeships. Of course, the fact that in some cases this cultural practice bears certain risks is of no small concern, but at the same time should not be dismissed from consideration for children and adolescents who need help. Leinaweaver suggests that "practitioners and policy makers should support, rather than condemn or even criminalize, the informal movements of children."[21] I agree. Practitioners should at a minimum make an effort to understand the internal and international mobility of children and adolescents before they conclude that such migrations always spell child abuse and exploitation.

Many different people—parents and grandparents, aunts and uncles, cousins, in-laws, family friends, acquaintances, and strangers—were involved in "trafficking" the girls and boys I studied. In some cases more than one person was implicated in the trafficking of a particular youth. Different people played different roles in the trafficking journey, including planting the idea of migrating to the United States for work or education, providing financial resources to cover the costs of the smuggling operation, serving as *coyotes* or snakeheads who assisted the youth in crossing international borders, transporting them from the border to their destination, arranging employment, and directly exploiting and physically, sexually, and emotionally abusing the youth. In the following pages, let us look at some of these individuals.

Mom and Pop Operations

Family involvement in smuggling the children and adolescents to the United States was pervasive in my study. Close family members—parents, grandparents, aunts, and uncles—facilitated the journey of the majority of the girls. Parental involvement was most common among Honduran cases, but close family members also trafficked girls from other Latin American countries, including Guatemala, El Salvador, the Dominican Republic, Argentina, and

Mexico. Families were also involved in trafficking youth from China, Ghana, Morocco, and Cameroon. Only three girls indicated that their parents played no role in their trafficking. By the time she was planning her migration from Mexico to the United States, Belen's dad was dead and her mom had left her and her siblings. There was no parent to consult. Xue from China insisted that she contacted the smuggler directly without her mother's knowledge; case files confirmed these assertions. Anna from El Salvador also did not inform anyone about her plans to go to Texas.

Several parents or grandparents made arrangements for the children and youth to be smuggled into the United States to work or to go to school. At minimum, the young people were embarking on the migration journey with their blessing, and in most cases with their financial assistance as well. In a couple of cases originating in China parents handed their daughters over to snakeheads to smuggle the girls to the United States. Four girls, in four separate cases, were "trafficked" by their mothers or grandmothers from Honduras to New Jersey and Texas to work in cantinas or bars. Law enforcement alleged that, in some instances, this "work" included prostitution. However, there is no solid evidence to support this claim, and several girls were adamant that they did not have to provide sexual services; all that was required of them was to dance and flirt with bar patrons to entice them to buy expensive drinks.

Catalina first heard about the "opportunity" to go the United States from her grandparents. Her mother arranged a meeting with a *coyote* and her father paid him $10,000. Poor as the family was, Catalina's father decided to mortgage the family farm to raise the cash. Apparently, Catalina's grandfather later changed his mind and advised her not to travel to el Norte, but she decided to go regardless. In case files this kind of family involvement was often described as "colluding with the traffickers," although, according to the girls and boys, parents genuinely believed that they were improving their children's prospects for the future and were unaware that the smuggling would turn into severe exploitation and trafficking.

Despite the fact that some parents were more directly implicated in their trafficking and exploitation, many girls were ambivalent about thinking of them as traffickers who should be prosecuted and pay for their crimes. The story of Flora and Isa is a case in point. Flora was very guarded when talking about her family, because her mother and three other members of her immediate family were convicted of luring some thirty young women, including the fifteen-year-old Flora and her twin sister, Isa, from Honduras to Texas to work in a cantina the family owned. Neither Flora nor Isa thought they were trafficked. Neither one of them vilified their mother. Flora felt that her mother had done nothing wrong and did not understand why she was arrested and incarcerated. In order to further exonerate her mom and grandma, Flora reported that she was not being made to prostitute: "I was simply working as a waitress and dancing for men when they requested it," she said. She did, however, give a full description of the bar to the Immigration and Customs Enforcement agents, who used this information to convict six of the nine relatives involved with the establishment. In an interview with my research team, Flora said she did not want to tell on her aunts and uncles, but felt intimidated by the agents and thought she had no choice but to "tell them something." The court case notes reported that Flora was in danger of retaliation from some of the relatives involved in the family trafficking business who remained at large in Honduras. The notes also indicated that Isa would have to testify in the future as well.

Melinda expressed similar feelings about her mother and grandmother's involvement in the trafficking of several girls and young women from Honduras to New Jersey. Melinda had difficulty accepting the fact that her mother, an evangelical pastor, and her *abuela* (grandmother) had engaged in illegal activity and was devastated to learn that, as a result of her testimony, U.S. law enforcement officers worked with Honduran authorities to incarcerate both women in Honduras. Many of Melinda's post-trafficking struggles revolved around the understanding that there were some things that were not in her power—such as her mother's and grandmother's jail sentences—but would affect her for the rest of her life. "Moving towards acceptance of this has been a major advancement for Melinda," said her social worker. I often wondered if Melissa would have been less traumatized if her mother had only been deported, and not incarcerated. Many of the youth were very familiar with deportations. Several had relatives who were deported not once but twice. Incarceration, on the other hand, they believed was something that awaited murderers and thieves.

Her sister-in-law recruited Carla in Honduras, organized her smuggling into the United States, arranged her employment in the States, and provided false identity documents. According to court documents, a second sister-in-law "harbored Carla at her residence for several months, while her brother-in-law transported Carla to and from her places of employment."[22] Carla disagreed with this characterization of her living arrangements and said she was never forced to live in a particular place, but felt she could not leave the area until her smuggling debt of $7,500 was paid.

When parents or other family members were involved in facilitating the young people's journey to the United States, the youngsters thought the family was helping them to cross the border or providing financial support to pay a smuggler. Even when family members were arrested and charged with smuggling or trafficking underage minors, the youth did not vilify them. Some girls were quite upset when law enforcement or service providers referred to their family members as traffickers; even those girls who felt wronged by their loved ones had difficulty conceptualizing their actions as criminal and certainly did not want to see their relatives behind bars.

Although none of the girls in this cohort were kidnapped or smuggled to the United States against their will—they were adamant in asserting that they were able to exercise their agency and participate in the decision-making process to migrate to the United States—and some were not sexually abused or otherwise exploited, their status as minors combined with the fact that they were not attending school but working rendered them victims of trafficking in the eyes of law enforcement and the courts. The family involvement in the migration/smuggling/trafficking continuum conceptualized by the police and social service providers as criminal activities had not contributed to the girls' willingness to participate in "rehabilitation programs." All the cases discussed here indicate that the process of labeling and conceptualizing close family members as criminals might be useful for prosecution, but quite detrimental at times to the youth's long-term reintegration into the wider society. I will return to this issue in chapter 8 when I explore the rehabilitation strategies aimed at assisting the girls recover from the trauma of trafficking.

Friends, Acquaintances, Boyfriends, and "Strangers"

Let me now turn to friends, acquaintances, boyfriends, and "strangers" in order to ascertain whether more distant relationships—not based on kinship—with these actors affected the youth's conceptualization of their involvement in the trafficking process. Both Victoria and Paula were trafficked to the United States with the help of family friends and acquaintances. Victoria lived with her mother in a small village in Ghana. Rosemary, a friend from the village, stepped in when Victoria's mother became ill and money was scarce. Rosemary promised to take care of Victoria. She said she would give Victoria a "great opportunity." Rosemary brought Victoria to Chicago and Victoria ended in domestic servitude for several years, taking care of Rosemary's family. Victoria was not allowed to leave the house and both Rosemary and her husband physically and emotionally abused the girl. Rosemary's husband also sexually abused Victoria. Victoria said they made her feel "worthless." Sometime after arriving in Chicago, Rosemary told Victoria that her mother had died. This lie was supposed to make the girl believe that she did not have any kin to turn to for help. It worked; Victoria was afraid to pick up the phone to call the police or ask houseguests for help.

Upon finishing mandatory schooling at the age of fourteen, Paula decided to migrate to the United States from her native Honduras to contribute to her family's income. She needed assistance in planning the trip. Paula contacted a woman in the community she knew had helped other adolescent girls migrate to America. In fact, this woman had sent her own daughter to the United States just months before with the help of other family members. Paula's mother testified, when questioned by law enforcement, that she had no idea that this acquaintance was part of a kin network channeling young women to New Jersey bars to work as dance hall girls. The girls were held in debt bondage for as much as $20,000 in order to allegedly pay the costs of being brought to the United States, and they were forced to drink and dance with male customers to make roughly $250 a week. Interestingly, Paula's case was very similar to the plight of some of the girls mentioned earlier in this chapter, who did not identify as having been trafficked even though they were engaged in the same kind of work. Paula, on the other hand, felt deeply deceived and harmed.

Several children in this study were trafficked by "strangers." It is not incidental that I qualify this word. Unlike Amanda in the movie *Taken*, none of the children in this study were kidnapped or whisked away by people whom they had never met before. Traffickers who were not related to the youngsters they trafficked, or who were not long-term friends or acquaintances of the family, worked hard to gain the children's and their families' trust. In some cases, the men who intended to traffic particular girls seduced them and presented themselves as "boyfriends" who were enamored with their victims. Aida and Olivia, two teenage girls trafficked from Mexico, truly believed that they had meaningful romantic relationships with the perpetrators. The traffickers did everything to maintain this illusion and stayed in touch with them via mail and phone calls for quite some time, promising the girls they would join them in the United States and marry them.

In one large trafficking case for labor exploitation, the traffickers identified a group of Peruvian boys ranging in age from five to seventeen and used a simple ploy to initiate contact with the children. The traffickers set up a volleyball net in a public park in Lima in order to attract neighborhood kids and give them an opportunity to play. They scouted out boys that would make good workers in the United States and began making contacts. The traffickers were very familiar to the boys and their parents since they lived in the neighborhood. They were also objects of envy as they were quite well off; many residents of the neighborhood suspected that the money came from business dealings in the United States. Nobody, however, suspected that the source of the wealth was human trafficking. They promised the boys to take them to Disney World. They manipulated both the children and their parents; they sweet-talked the parents into signing affidavits giving them permission to travel with the kids to the United States. In a few cases, parents had signed over their property to the traffickers as collateral to pay for the trip to Florida. In some cases the parents went with the children. Prosecutors said the traffickers charged would-be immigrants up to $13,000 each. One father testified: "I had little to lose and lots to gain, so I agreed to mortgage my house and go with them." Several other families followed; some sold their houses to finance the scheme, others borrowed funds from moneylenders.

Although none of these traffickers were related to the children by blood or by law, their status as respected adults in the community or friends of parents and relatives gave them the necessary clout to be trusted or, at minimum, not to evoke suspicions on the part of the youth or their parents and guardians. In the case of Aida and Olivia romantic notions of love at first sight, cultural norms regarding mating rituals, and societal expectations that women marry and have children relatively young contributed to the level of trust the girls placed in their "boyfriends."

So were these traffickers benevolent, or did their kind words mask sinister intent? The youth definitely thought the people who smuggled them across international borders were helping them. Many youngsters understood that the *coyotes* and snakeheads were breaking the law, but at the same time did not think the smugglers had victimized them. If they felt wronged, it was by the "employers" who didn't pay them the promised rate, or didn't pay them at all. Unlike law enforcement and some service providers, who saw each trafficking case in black-and-white certainties, the girls and boys had a much more nuanced understanding of their experiences. As will be seen later in this chapter and in chapter 8, this tendency not to think in black-and-white, extreme categories was considered by the social workers to be an obstacle in adjusting to the rehabilitation program.

Criminals or "Helpers"?

Despite family members' involvement in different aspects of trafficking, many children did not condemn the actions of their relatives. Instead, they thought the parents, aunts, and uncles were helping them get an education or access to employment that would improve the family financial situation. This perception of relatives as "helpers" was often a conceptual challenge, both for the prosecutors and for social workers. The children's perception of relatives as facilitators of a better life in America and the resulting conceptualization of their trafficking as "work" sometimes interfered with prosecution team's gathering of information. The children were reluctant to provide law enforcement with details about their journey to the United States and identify their relatives as perpetrators of crimes. The notion that the traffickers were "helpers" and the trafficking experience was "work" made the girls' initial adjustment to rehabilitation services difficult in the eyes of the social workers. Several boys and girls, particularly the older adolescents, regarded themselves as labor migrants and thought that attending school and pursuing high school diplomas, as the rehabilitation programs required them to do, deprived them of the ability to make money, which was the main reason they wanted to be in the United States in the first place. They were reluctant to see themselves as victims and avail themselves of counseling services. Belen said: "I left school when

I was fourteen. I came here because, after my father committed suicide and my mother left Mexico, I had no one to support my brother and me. I still don't. If I don't work, I will have nothing." Seventeen-year-old Carlos refused to see a clinical social worker. "I don't have time," he said, "to waste talking about my experiences. I came here to work, as simple as that!"

Some girls who clearly understood that their parents wronged them were nevertheless ready to forgive and reconcile with their families. Ada, for example, said that she would very much like to go and visit her parents in Cameroon to tell them that she has forgiven them for sending her away. She is particularly keen "to hug her father, who did not want her to go to America because he thought she was too young to be living with strangers in a strange country." When asked whether she calls her parents often, she admitted that it is hard to have a close relationship with people whom she barely remembers after spending almost a decade in domestic servitude in the United States.

It was easier to vilify strangers, especially when sexual violence was involved. The smuggler who was helping Belen travel to the United States got her across the border without any incidents. However, when they got to the East Coast, he raped her and left her in a house described by Immigration and Customs Enforcement agents as a "house of prostitution." Belen escaped and was taken in by a woman she met in a supermarket. She soon found out that she was pregnant. Using someone else's Medicaid card, Belen went to a clinic and had an abortion. It is unclear how, but she learned about the Human Trafficking Hotline and called the number provided to have her rapist arrested.

Magdalena too wanted revenge on "the witches" who operated the brothel in New Jersey where the *coyote* hired by her "boyfriend," Jorge, dropped her off. Magdalena arrived at the brothel pregnant and was forced to abort the pregnancy. The brothel owners used herbs to help her abort. Magdalena criticized them for their poor skills and said that in her village women used better methods to terminate pregnancies. Following the abortion, Magdalena was put on a diet and forced to exercise in order to quickly regain her slim figure. Magdalena and the other young women in the brothel were forced to provide sexual services to several men every night. If they resisted they were beaten. The brothel owners beat the girls for rule infraction—talking to each other or to the clients—and verbally abused and demeaned them. Magdalena had no qualms talking about this abuse with the police and was ready to testify against her abusers.

Law enforcement saw all those involved in the youngsters' trafficking as part of an international mafia. These officials criminalized the children's families, regarding them as part of the trafficking chain regardless of what role, if any, they played in the trafficking ordeal. These perceptions about organized crime syndicates are pervasive in illegal migration despite the fact that empirical evidence points in a different direction. "While organized crime is certainly involved in many illegal human transfers," writes Raimo Väyrynen, "they can also take place without the criminal contribution. Moreover, many smuggling rings are more like small enterprises run by a group of relatives or acquaintances."[23]

Parents who smuggled their children across the border were described as greedy adults who sold their unsuspecting, innocent daughters into a life of prostitution. The persistent view of the trafficked girls as "sex slaves" was even more surprising since in many cases there was no evidence of sexual abuse. But stories about the irrevocable loss of sexual innocence are a particularly potent symbol that works well in many courtrooms.

Police officers and Immigration and Customs Enforcement agents alike often do not recognize that children and youth migrate or are smuggled partly to seek out economic opportunities to support their families. Marisa O. Ensor and I wrote about this issue in our book *Migrant Children*. Citing the work of other anthropologists, we concluded that "an excessive focus on migratory processes that are imposed, difficult, and traumatic may lead to the erroneous assumption that all forms of child migration are necessarily exploitative."[24] When law enforcement officials talked about migrant children, it was usually in the context of children migrating in the shadows of parents whom the police officers considered the primary migrants. They regarded the children and youth "exclusively as victims, 'lured' or 'duped' by the 'false promises' ostensibly made by traffickers of a better and more prosperous life elsewhere."[25] Yet, in order to engage more critically in debates about and analyses of child trafficking, the processes around child labor migration require a more careful examination. There is growing empirical research from many parts of the world on the reasons why children migrate, which should help dispel the notion that child labor migrants are always passive victims trafficked or forced to migrate because they are young, naïve, and don't know any better.[26] Karin Heissler posits that "given the emphasis on trafficking at the global policy level," the processes of facilitating child labor migration "are rarely seen as benign, especially when others reap material benefits."[27] Suppositional perceptions such as these have resulted in a certain ambiguity of the label "trafficker," which as a result is used to describe many different types of individuals who assist adolescents and young adults in crossing international borders and finding employment in the destination country.

Child advocates working with trafficked minors often forgot that the majority of the children were older adolescents, usually between fourteen and seventeen years of age. They have also disregarded the fact that the Fair Labor Standards Act of 1938 accords children between twelve and sixteen years of age the right to work in certain industries for limited number of hours per week. The Act also allows minors between the ages of sixteen and eighteen to be employed full-time in nonhazardous occupations. In the United States, many children work because they have to contribute to the family income, and many of those that don't have to support their families' livelihoods are encouraged to work to gain experience, acquire an appropriate work ethic, and learn how to manage money. It seems that the insistence that foreign-born children shouldn't work constitutes a double standard.

Conceptualizing children and adolescents exploited and abused by those who facilitated their migration to the United States as trafficked victims provides them with access to services and benefits, including immigration relief. However, extending this concept beyond the rights framework to other frameworks, particularly to the therapeutic one, is often counterproductive to their long-term integration into the new community. This topic will be further elaborated upon in chapter 8.

4

Not Chained to a
Bed in a Brothel

Sex sells in more ways than one. Images of underage sex slaves are often invoked when child trafficking is mentioned. As already emphasized, much of the writing about trafficked minors is based on sensationalistic media accounts. Pictures of sexually exploited girls summon more sympathy than descriptions of trafficked men toiling in the fields for a pittance to put tomatoes and lettuce in our salad bowls. Here's an example, from a blog post titled "How to Kick in a Brothel Door": "The man she met was a human trafficker, posing as a business owner. He drugged her, threw her in a van and slipped her across an international border. Now, she's locked in a room, possibly chained to a bed, with no phone or driver's license in a country whose language she doesn't speak."[1] While there is much literature about human trafficking, not enough of it is based on empirical research.[2]

In this chapter I analyze both the scant statistical information on foreign-born minors trafficked to the United States and present a range of narratives about trafficked children and youth's experiences in captivity. The stories illustrate different types of exploitation as well as the differential treatment of trafficked minors by their captors. The statistical data, together with the vignettes, is offered to expand knowledge about trafficked minors and present a more contextualized picture of their characteristics and experiences.

The Diversity of Trafficked Minors: Statistical Portrait

At conferences and meetings I am often asked, either directly or indirectly, to paint a portrait of children trafficked to the United States. Colleagues want to know what a trafficked child looks like. What are the characteristics of trafficked minors? What are their needs? "It is an impossible task," I answer. Some patterns are emerging, but more often than not it is the diversity of this relatively small cohort that is its most striking feature.

In the preceding chapters, I have already presented the general number of foreign-born minors trafficked to the United States since the passage of the TVPA of 2000. In this chapter, I return to the discussion of available statistical data. It is important to note that the information that is publicly available—mainly in the Office of Refugee Resettlement (ORR) and Department of Justice Annual Reports to Congress—is limited and missing crucial demographic indicators, such as age. In the following pages, I will present the publicly available data on minors trafficked to the United States, followed by information my research team and I compiled on the 142 minors in our original sample. Taken together, this data give a more accurate, if still partial, statistical portrait of trafficked children and youth.

From FY 2001 through FY2014,[3] the Anti-Trafficking in Persons Program in ORR issued 841 letters of eligibility to foreign-born trafficked minors. The number of all officially identified trafficked minors is slightly higher since ORR did not start recording the number of issued letters until late 2001. Also, minors who were trafficked with family members might have been served under different assistance programs, including the Per Capita Reimbursement program. Of the 1,969 foreign national survivors of human trafficking who received services from the Anti-Trafficking in Persons Program between 2007 and 2011 under the Per Capita program, seventy-eight were minors. Girls made up the majority of child survivors. The median age at the time of entry to the program was sixteen years for girls and fifteen years for boys.[4]

The ratio of females to males among the trafficked minors has changed over the years. Up until FY 2012, girls constituted the majority of trafficked minors. However, in FY 2012 the number of girls dropped to 39 percent. In FY 2013 and FY 2014 the percentage of girls went up slightly, hovering around 42 and 40 percent, respectively. Nonetheless, it was not near the 60 percent, or more, that it had been prior to FY 2012. This statistic single-handedly shatters the assumption that the majority of trafficked minors are girls. The table shows the number of minors who received eligibility letters and the number of adults who received letters of certification per fiscal year, starting in FY 2001.

Table 1

Number of Letters of Eligibility Issued to Trafficked Minors and Number of Certification Letters Issued to Trafficked Adults per Fiscal Year

Fiscal Year	Minors	Adults	Total
FY 2002	19	80	99
FY 2003	6	145	151
FY 2004	19	144	163
FY 2005	34	196	230
FY 2006	20	234	254
FY 2007	33	270	303
FY 2008	31	286	317
FY 2009	50	330	380
FY 2010	92	449	541
FY 2011	101	463	564
FY 2012	103	366	469
FY 2013	114	406	520
FY 2014	219	730	949
Grand Total	841	3,636	4,477

SOURCE: ORR Reports to Congress and personal communication with ORR staff.

Despite the emphasis on trafficking for sexual exploitation, the percentage of minors trafficked for sex in recent years has been relatively small. Thirty-one percent of the 219 minors who received eligibility letters from the Anti-Trafficking in Persons Program in FY 2014 were trafficked for sex: 24 percent of girls and 6.8 percent of boys. This represents an increase of 2 percent over FY 2013. In FY 2014, 65.6 percent of minors—13.6 percent of girls and 52 percent of boys—were trafficked for labor and an additional 3 percent for both labor and sexual exploitation.[5] This represents a 2.5 percent decrease in comparison with FY 2013. In FY 2012, 25 percent of the 103 minors who received eligibility letters were trafficked for sex. The percentage was slightly higher in previous fiscal years. In FY 2011, it reached 36 percent; in FY 2010 it was 29 percent, and in FY 2009 38 percent. At the same time, 72 percent (FY 2012), 57 percent (FY 2011), 62 percent (FY 2010), and 56 percent (FY 2009) of victims under the age of eighteen were trafficked for labor exploitation. Three, 7, 9, and 6 percent of minors were trafficked for both labor and sexual exploitation in these respective years.

In most cases of sexual exploitation, girls were not chained to a bed in a brothel, as popular depictions would have the concerned citizen imagine. Few actually worked in brothels at all, although law enforcement and child advocates often presented the bars and cantinas where the girls worked as houses of prostitution. In many instances, employers perpetrated sexual exploitation. In some situations, girls were encouraged to provide sexual favors to the bar customers and, if they agreed, received better treatment. They were allowed to keep more money for themselves or remit a portion of their earnings to families back home, and were showered with gifts and pretty clothing. In a few cases, however, there was brutal rape, often at the hands of smugglers en route to the United States. There were also a few pregnancies resulting from relationships with men the girls met in the cantinas where they worked. In the accounts of the social workers, these situations were always described as sexual exploitation or rape, at minimum statutory rape. The girls, however, often believed that they were in romantic relationships with the men who fathered their babies. Some kept the babies resulting from these unions.

I do not want to minimize the sexual violence against trafficked girls, but I also want to stress the differing views on sexual activity of adolescents expressed by law enforcement and service providers, on the one hand, and the youth, on the other. I also want to emphasize the diversity of experiences that are not fully captured by labeling the various trafficking trajectories above under the same category. In the girls' origin countries, the age of consent is often much lower than in the United States, and the local law, cultural customs of early marriage, and legal or common-law marriages stand in sharp contrast with the images of teenagers as innocent and devoid of sexuality held by police and service providers. Flora and Isa had boyfriends since they were thirteen years old. They said that most teen girls and boys they knew in Honduras were sexually active. Their mother had her first child when she was fifteen years old.

Research confirms these trends. According to the Ford Foundation, 11 percent of Honduran and 13.3 percent of Nicaraguan girls are married by the age of fifteen.[6] A UN Population Fund study suggests that Honduras has one of the highest "child marriage" prevalence rates in the world. On average, almost two out of five girls will be married before their eighteenth birthday. In 2006, about 39 percent of the women aged 20–24 were married/in union before age eighteen. In Choluteca, where Flora and Isa are from, the rate was 33 percent.[7] In some African countries the percentage is higher: 16.5 percent in Cameroon and 19.3 percent in Sierra Leone were married/in union by the age of fifteen, according to the Ford Foundation study cited above. The UN Population Fund indicates that, worldwide, 720 million women—10 percent of the world population—alive in 2010 were married before they turned eighteen years of age.[8] As much as we may want to prevent early marriage and teen motherhood, these patterns cannot be ignored. They provide evidence-based data to understand the cultural norms that affected the girls' understanding of their world.

ORR reports that every year trafficked minors hail from a wide range of countries and continents. Minors are trafficked to multiple states in the

United States. Therefore, there is not a single source country or a single destination. There are, however, countries that appear on the origin country list
every year. They include countries with a relatively close geographic proxim-
ity to the United States—Mexico, Honduras, and Guatemala—but trafficked
minors also come from faraway countries such as China. In FY 2013, the trafficked minors hailed from ten countries. The top three countries of origin of
trafficked minors included Honduras (38%), El Salvador (29%), and Guatemala (24%), followed by Mexico (10%), Nigeria with two minors, and Ecua-
dor, Ghana, Haiti, Nicaragua, and Peru with one minor each. There were no
minors from China, although China had figured on the list several times in
previous years.[9]

In FY 2012, trafficked adults and children came from forty-eight countries in the Americas, Africa, and Europe. They were trafficked to forty-one
states and the District of Columbia. The top five countries of origin of the 103
trafficked minors were Honduras (33), Mexico (29), El Salvador (15), Guatemala (14), and China (5). In FY 2011, trafficked adults and minors hailed
from fifty-five countries and were trafficked to thirty-eight states, the District
of Columbia, and the Northern Marianas. The top six countries of origin of
the 101 minors were Mexico (41), Guatemala (17), El Salvador (13), Honduras
(11), Cambodia (5), and China (5). A similar pattern was observed in FY 2010:
thirty individuals came from Mexico, twenty-seven from Honduras, twelve
from Guatemala, nine from El Salvador, and eight from China.[10]

Let me now turn to the cohort of the 142 minors I studied in the project
that served as a springboard for this book. The information I have on these
youngsters is more detailed than the data contained in ORR Reports to Congress. Two crucial pieces of information not included in the current ORR
reports are age at the time of trafficking and information on whether the
minors were accompanied by a parent or other legal guardian. Both are important in order to understand this group of young people and their prospects
for integration into U.S. society. One could hypothesize, for example, that
children who were trafficked with parents or other family members will have a
close-knit support system facilitating their adjustment to life after trafficking,
while minors who traveled on their own and do not have close family relatives
in the United States may face more challenges.

As already discussed, the label "children" is rather misleading. It frequently
brings to mind small children, preschoolers or even toddlers. While there
was one two year old and one three year old in my sample, the vast majority—83 percent—of the trafficked girls and boys were between fourteen and
seventeen years of age when they were trafficked and approximately two-thirds
were sixteen or seventeen years old at the time of trafficking. Not surprisingly,
the girls that traveled to the United States on their own were older on average
than those who were trafficked with other family members. The mean age of

the unaccompanied girls was sixteen, while the mean age of the accompanied girls was thirteen. All but four of the fifteen children who were younger than thirteen years of age came from Peru. This concentration, as well as the overall wide age range of the accompanied children, was largely a result of the Peruvian case.

While legally considered to be children, many of the older teens identified as adults. Several of the girls in the sample were mothers with children of their own. Some of these babies were the result of romantic relationships that the girls had back in their country of origin. The teen moms migrated because they needed to support their children. Conceptualizing these teenagers as on the brink of adulthood, instead of as helpless kids, is important not only in terms of self-identity but also in terms of the girls' and boys' wants and needs. They wanted to work instead of going to school, they wanted to emancipate rather than live in foster families, and they balked at curfews and limitations imposed on them by well-meaning—but often culturally misinformed—social workers that wanted the girls to "reclaim their childhoods."

Gabriela changed foster families three times. She blamed her foster mom for taking her away from her aunt and uncle's house—Gabriela's aunt and uncle were part of the alleged trafficking ring that brought Gabriela and her half-sister to the United States to work in their bar—and wanted to go back to live with her family. She did not understand why she couldn't speak to her family on the phone and why she couldn't go out on her own. These restrictions were part of Gabriela's "safety plan" devised by her caseworker. Gabriela felt that at nineteen she should be able to decide what she wanted to do and whom she wanted to call. "I am not a child," she kept on repeating.

The cohort of 142 trafficked minors was predominantly female, with girls comprising 83 percent and boys 17 percent. There was a substantial difference in the female to male ratio between the accompanied and unaccompanied minors. Among the accompanied minors, 33 percent were males. Boys constituted only 4 percent of the unaccompanied minors. Again, the single Peruvian case described above affected the gender distribution because over half of the accompanied males were part of that single case. The disproportionate distribution of females (96 percent among the unaccompanied and 67 percent among the accompanied) might indicate a higher vulnerability of teenage girls to trafficking. However, this characteristic might also be an artificial result of both the identification process and service eligibility determination. It is worth remembering that the group of minors I studied was identified in the early years after the passage of the TVPA when the focus of law enforcement was almost exclusively on women and girls and on sex trafficking. Indeed, 70 percent of the unaccompanied minors were classified as trafficked for sexual exploitation or a combination of sexual and labor exploitation. A much smaller percentage—24 percent—was trafficked solely for labor, including domestic servitude. The remaining cases were not categorized.

As I wrote at the outset of this section, the diversity of trafficked minors is the most striking characteristic of this population. The group I studied was no different. They hailed from four continents, represented several different ethnic and linguistic groups, and had a wide range of family and socioeconomic backgrounds. The group included girls born to middle-class educated parents as well as girls whose parents, especially mothers, had no formal schooling. There were girls and boys born in large metropolitan centers and girls from small villages and hamlets. The majority came from very poor families.

The highest number of girls in the study came from Mexico and Honduras, followed by India, Guatemala, and China. Law enforcement alleged that 60 percent were trafficked for sexual exploitation. However, many of the girls were adamant that they were neither involved in sex work nor sexually abused. One Immigration and Customs Enforcement agent told me: "Look, when I see young girls with lots of make-up wearing low-cut blouses and the shortest skirt you can imagine, of course, I am going to conclude that they were trafficked for sex. Maybe nothing happened yet, but whether they realize it or not, the intent was obvious." In interviews, the girls presented different assessment of the situation. They liked pretty and revealing clothing. Tight and low-cut blouses made them feel sexy and sophisticated, they said. I thought there was a lot of cultural misunderstanding, both on the part of the law enforcement and on the part of the girls, about what was age-appropriate attire and what was not.

Some children were trafficked by strangers, but family members and friends brought many of them to the United States. Some endured several years in the hands of their traffickers, but six of the unaccompanied girls were rescued before the exploitation actually occurred. All six of the preempted cases involved girls from China. Five of them were seventeen years old, but one was only thirteen. All five of the older girls were apprehended at the ports of entry: three in New York and two at the Mexican border. All five were put in removal proceedings and transferred to the Unaccompanied Alien Children program, formerly the Division of Unaccompanied Children's Services within the Office of Refugee Resettlement. After varying lengths of time—anywhere from three to twenty-one months—in Division of Unaccompanied Children's Services care, all of the girls were reclassified as trafficked minors. It took time to develop a rapport with the girls, understand the intricacies of their journey from China to the United States, and convince law enforcement that the girls were trafficked even though they were apprehended before they reached their final destination.

Diverse Experiences in "Captivity"

Learning details of the journey and in-depth descriptions of the trafficking experiences was not easy. Some girls and boys volunteered to narrate their exodus and their experiences while trafficked, but others did not, often because their parents and relatives were involved in smuggling them into the United States and the youth worried that talking about what happened would implicate their relatives even more.

Case file and court document reviews, as well as interviews with law enforcement and case managers, provided further insight into what the girls and boys endured at the hands of the traffickers. Frequently, service providers wished for more details from Immigration and Customs Enforcement agents regarding the border-crossing ordeals and the abuse the girls and boys experienced in "captivity." However, law enforcement was mum, citing ongoing investigations as a reason for not being able to share information. They did talk more openly about closed cases, though. Obviously, service providers were not motivated by sheer curiosity. They thought the more detailed description of the trafficking they had, the better treatment plan they could devise. On the other hand, fear that the girls would be retraumatized recalling the details of their trafficking ordeal prevented many social workers from pressing for details. In the end, many assumptions were made without the ability to verify them.

While some authors warn against the risk of retraumatizing survivors of trauma, especially women sexually abused in childhood,[11] others write about the healing power of the interviews and survivors' resiliency.[12] Working with torture victims and refugees, Derek Summerfield writes eloquently about the tendency to medicalize human suffering and the resulting fear that the slightest inquiry into the experiences of those who suffer would render them traumatized again.[13] John, a federal prosecutor who has worked with trafficked girls and adult women since the early 2000s, has always emphasized that "if done right, an interview or a testimony can be very empowering." I know this to be true from my experiences conducting research with and designing assistance programs for refugees.

Some service providers, however, avoided asking questions about the girls' trafficking experiences for fear that if the prosecution subpoenaed them, the traffickers' defense team might use this information. The nature of the profession places social workers in the difficult position of being obliged to maintain client confidentiality, provide for informed consent, and comply with the law. Unfortunately, there are no clear standards regarding when and under what circumstances a court might require a caseworker to waive the right to maintain privileged information undisclosed. However, the ethics of the social work profession and most state licensing laws "require that social workers resist releasing information unless clients waive privilege or until a court forces them to do otherwise after all legal forms of resistance have been exercised."[14] Regardless, this is a situation that service providers wanted to avoid. The fact that social workers might be subpoenaed to provide confidential information conflicted with their desire to know more about the ordeals experienced by the trafficked youth in their care.

Some girls' narratives were very inconsistent. The circumstances of Josefina's trafficking history, for example, were fuzzy from the very beginning. Apparently, her boyfriend brought her to the border and she crossed into California successfully on the first try. How she found herself in a brothel was much more difficult to establish. Josefina was very reluctant to share information about her trafficking with her caseworker. She made every effort, according to the program staff, to omit details despite the fact that those details would have been helpful in tailoring assistance to help her rebuild her life. When I met with her, a couple of years after she was extracted from the brothel, she said she didn't want to talk about what happened to her. "I wouldn't share my story with my Mom and I don't want to tell you either. You would both judge me," she said.

Belen's story was also very inconsistent. At some point she told her social worker that the smuggler was extorting money from her uncle, but on another occasion she was blaming her uncle for sending her to the smuggler. The details of her rape story were also conflicting; in one interview she told me her uncle raped her, but in an intake interview she claimed the smuggler violated her; she said that she was raped only once. Other girls were more forthcoming. Interestingly, some related to the young male researcher on my team—fluent in Spanish—much better than to the female members of the study team, regardless of these women's ages. Many girls living in a group home preferred male staff members as well. They were chattier and more relaxed around them.

My research team and I were hard-pressed to find two individuals that were very similar and would conform to the poster image of the trafficked victim promoted by the news media and popular writing. Trafficking for sexual exploitation is but one—and not necessarily the most common—form of child trafficking. Twelve girls in my sample came to the United States in the hope of pursuing educational opportunities, but ended up in domestic servitude, mostly in the homes of close family members. Five of them were also sexually abused. The girls in domestic servitude—even those that were not sexually violated—were still treated particularly badly. Their situation was exacerbated by the fact that they had no respite from their captors: their abusers watched them 24/7. They each spent several years in the homes of their captors, where verbal, physical, and psychological abuse was commonplace. One time when Fatima's uncle hit her face, her nose started bleeding and drops of blood fell on the light-colored carpet. Observing the situation, Fatima's aunt told her husband: "If you are going to hit her, hit her outside." Evelyn often speaks publicly about the plight of young children in domestic servitude. Given the prevalence of other countries' cultural norms regarding child domestic workers, it is surprising that this issue has not received more attention. Admittedly, it is hard to find young children that live with the family they work for and are never allowed outside to play or to go to school.

The majority of the girls I studied worked in bars and cantinas. The vice cops described the establishments as seedy holes in the wall, catering mainly to Latino men who wanted to have a good time on Friday nights. In several cases, relatives of the young women who worked there owned the cantinas. Most of the girls working in bars and cantinas worked long hours. Flora and Isa reported for work Thursday through Monday around 7:30 p.m. and worked until the bar closed at 2:00 a.m. They were off on Tuesdays and Wednesdays when they slept in at their mom's apartment, watched *telenovelas*, or went to the local mall. They were paid $120 a week. Working for their uncle, Flora and Isa had more flexibility and better financial arrangements then the other girls working in the cantina who could not claim a blood relationship to the bar owner. They were able to make their own schedules and were allowed to keep most of the money for themselves.

Several Mexican girls trafficked to a bar in Arizona were told at first that their smuggling debts were between eight and ten thousand dollars. As time went on, the smuggling debt kept growing since the traffickers added the cost of clothing, jewelry, and makeup they bought for the girls to make them look alluring to the bar clients. The traffickers also forced the girls to participate in a *tanda*, a form of revolving credit. The girls pooled their money weekly and then one of the 20 girls working in the bar would "win" some of the money back and the bar owners would collect the rest.

As the statistical data show, trafficking of minors for labor exploitation far outnumbers sex trafficking, especially in recent years. In the early 2000s, on the other hand, most of the girls identified as victims of trafficking were trafficked for sexual exploitation, although—luckily—in some cases the sexual exploitation had not commenced yet. The interesting fact remains: the zeal with which the Bush administration combated sex trafficking resulted in relatively quick rescue of victims of sex trafficking, while children in domestic servitude lingered for years behind closed doors. Recently, cases of teen boys, between fourteen and seventeen years of age, trafficked to be foot soldiers to smuggle people or drugs across the Mexico-U.S. border are surfacing more and more frequently.[15]

Part III

"Rescued"

Pastors, students, Good Samaritans, and vice cops are eager to rescue trafficked children. Helmed by such do-gooders, new projects are always springing up in different towns and cities. In 2004, the Rescue and Restore Campaign was launched. The federal government and its local partners vowed to leave no stone unturned until every victim of human trafficking was found. Over the years, the federal government funded forty-two antitrafficking task forces, which trained over eighty-five thousand law enforcement officers in identifying victims of human trafficking. A whole new rescue industry has been established.

Yet all these efforts have resulted in very few actual rescues. In 2006, at the time when this research began, only 142 youths had been identified as victims of child trafficking. In later years—despite increased funding—the results were equally meager. In Lee County, Florida, for example, of forty-two potential human trafficking cases, involving both adults and minors, referred to the Anti-Trafficking Task Force in 2008, none were confirmed as trafficking cases. During the previous three years, despite many investigations, there was not a single confirmed and certified trafficking case and only a handful of precertified victims. Yet at the same time Lee County received a further $250,000 in federal funds for the Task Force and the Office of Victims of Crime provided $260,000 to Catholic Charities for comprehensive victims' services for eighteen months (2008–10). Additionally, the Department of Health and Human Services funded victim awareness campaigns through its Rescue and Restore initiatives in the same area, often duplicating efforts with little communication or coordination with the task forces in the area.[1] This is but one example of money spent without any results. Eight years later, in 2014, the number of trafficked minors has increased but not drastically; 841 is a far cry from the supposed fourteen thousand to fifteen thousand minors trafficked to the United States every year. Over time, the number of American-born (domestic) victims of trafficking in the United States has surpassed the number of international victims by a margin of twenty to one.[2]

Why has this pattern emerged? The U.S. Department of Justice says that as many as three hundred thousand young Americans are victimized by some form of human trafficking each year. Service providers who have been working with foreign-born survivors of trafficking disagree. They argue that the shift in focus on domestic minor sex trafficking means that nobody is looking for foreign-born victims. In a recent interview, Walter, a director of a large social service agency in Texas, told me that his program is almost exclusively working with victims of domestic minor sex trafficking. "We used to call them the CSEC [commercially sexually exploited children] kids," he said, "now they are trafficked victims." "We no longer get any referrals of foreign-born victims," he added. Margaret, a director of children's services at a large agency serving trafficked children in the Mid-Atlantic region, indicated that in the last few years foreign-born victims have been identified mainly among apprehended unaccompanied children and youths in detention centers. "While the unaccompanied minors need and deserve protection and assistance, identification efforts should not be limited to detention centers," she added. At a meeting with representatives of the Department of Homeland Security, I learned that ICE is also focusing mainly on domestic victims. "We are pressured to meet our objectives," the ICE agent said. This piece of news was astounding. Why would immigration authorities be interested in CSEC kids? They are U.S. citizens, and thus outside ICE's mandate.

The only logical conclusion that can be reached is that they are the proverbial low-hanging fruit. It is easier to identify English-speaking, American teen sex workers or U.S. citizen youth engaged in survival sex than foreign-born youths in domestic servitude, exploitative labor, and forced into the sex industry. Currently, domestic victims garner the most attention from child advocates, antitrafficking activists, researchers, and funders. At a conference organized by the National Institute of Justice in Washington, DC, in May 2014, the number of grantees working with and studying domestic victims far outnumbered those interested in foreign-born victims. Among some eighty participants, only three were interested in foreign-born trafficked persons, and I was the only scholar studying foreign-born minors. When I attended similar conferences in early 2000s, virtually all of the presenters focused on cross-border trafficking of foreign nationals.

In this section, I look at the reasons for these outcomes and discuss the gaps in the apparatus established to identify foreign-born minors trafficked across international borders (chapter 5). I also analyze the prosecution of traffickers involved in child trafficking and explore the effects of collaboration with federal investigators and prosecutors on the well-being of trafficked children (chapter 6). Underage victims of child trafficking are not required to collaborate with law enforcement in order to qualify for federally funded assistance. However, some prosecutors have pressured survivors of child trafficking to provide testimonies and appear in the courtroom. For some victims, these requests resulted in additional trauma, while for others it was an empowering experience.

5

Hidden in Plain Sight

There are invisible victims found in nearly every industry, claims the Department of Homeland Security. As Attorney General Eric Holder stated, "In communities nationwide, human trafficking victims often are hiding in plain sight." Government agencies and service providers maintain that traffickers hold large numbers of individuals against their will, yet identifying them is difficult.[1] As discussed in chapter 1, the number of child survivors of human trafficking identified to date has paled in comparison with official estimates. Several different explanations for the low numbers of identified victims have been put forth. Some claim that lower-than-expected numbers of victims suggest that government officials could have done more to enforce the provisions of the TVPA and provided more resources for antitrafficking programming.[2] Others attribute the low numbers of victims identified to insufficient coordination among responsible federal agencies.[3] Still others argue that the low number of trafficking cases indicates that the phenomenon was never as large as politicians and advocates lobbying for the passage of the antitrafficking legislation have claimed.[4] Victim advocates, child protection experts, and social workers assisting survivors of child trafficking do not find the latter argument persuasive. They agree that identification is the greatest hurdle in the antitrafficking efforts, but never doubt that with increased efforts more victims will be found.[5]

The task of victim identification falls on Good Samaritans in local communities, social service providers, law enforcement, and other first-line responders who come in contact with trafficked children (and adults).[6] However, despite increased media coverage of the trafficking phenomenon and millions of dollars spent on antitrafficking campaigns, there is a perception that there still is a lack of awareness and inadequate provisions for public education and outreach aimed at understanding the human trafficking phenomenon and identifying victims.[7]

Some writers indicate that trafficked individuals are frequently not recognized as victims because Border Patrol and other law enforcement personnel view them as illegal immigrants.[8] Hepburn and Simon remind us that when Immigration and Customs Enforcement agents raided a meat packing plant in Pottsville, Iowa, in 2008, they found workers, including minors, in abysmal conditions. The case showed signs of labor trafficking, but there was no investigation. All workers were deported before anyone could talk to them.[9] Service providers are concerned about the number of persons who are found during raids, arrested, and deported without any further thought whether they might be victims of human trafficking.

My own assessment is that the Bush administration focused primarily on sex trafficking, a problem that the president called a "special evil" in his 2003 address to the UN General Assembly, because looking at labor exploitation outside the sex industry would upset his corporate backers and the religious Right. The Obama administration, instead of adopting its predecessor's myopic focus on sex trafficking, has expanded the definition of trafficking to include a wider variety of labor abuses than ever before and focused on force, fraud, and coercion more generally, whether in construction, the hospitality industry, agriculture, or elsewhere. However, these expanded criteria did not have the anticipated results either. As Denise Brennan writes, "the legacy of the Bush administration is clear. The anti-prostitution frame continues to dominate discussions on trafficking in the media and in policy-making."[10]

Amy Farrell and her colleagues suggest that existing research on law enforcement responses to trafficking is focused narrowly on high-profile trafficking investigations, and that less is known about how frequently police encounter human trafficking in its different incarnations and how well officers are prepared to pursue and handle trafficking cases.[11] A national survey of police agencies indicates that fewer than 10 percent of agencies identified victims of human trafficking between 2000 and 2006.[12] Many officers believe that calls for service agency and community tips could be a chief source of investigative leads, but there is not enough of this kind of information coming from community members. Officers report that trafficking cases are most frequently initiated as a corollary to other ongoing criminal investigations.[13]

Are actors outside the law enforcement system better equipped to identify trafficked victims? Some researchers maintain that "service providers are likely to encounter trafficking victims among clients of agencies that provide services related to child protection and child welfare, criminal justice, domestic violence, health care, homeless outreach and shelter, juvenile justice, and victim advocacy," but that they are ill-prepared to identify them. Little attention has been given to "developing protocols or guidelines to assist service providers in identifying sex-trafficking victims among their clients."[14] Even fewer attempts are made to identify children in domestic servitude and adolescents in forced labor, especially young males. Efforts to develop screening instruments to assist in identifying victims have been hindered by the dearth of empirical research on human trafficking.[15] Collaborative assessments and sharing of information are essential, but woefully lacking.[16]

The role of Good Samaritans in the antitrafficking efforts has been emphasized by many awareness-raising campaigns. *Look Beneath the Surface* was an appeal used by the U.S. Department of Health and Human Services's Rescue and Restore Campaign to encourage the public to take more careful notice of what they saw and heard in their neighborhoods and call a 1–800 call center established to assist the government in the process of identifying potential human trafficking victims.[17] While the call center concept was never formally evaluated, monthly tallies and incident reports were collected between June 2005 and mid-November 2007. During these twenty-nine months, the center received approximately 6,000 calls, with the highest average number of calls per month (239) in the first six months, and considerable decreases in subsequent time periods: 186 and 174 monthly calls in 2006 and 2007, respectively. The majority of the callers sought information about human trafficking, far fewer offered tips on possible victims, and the number of callers seeking assistance for a victim was negligible. A more recent report prepared by the Polaris Project indicates that the number of calls has increased since 2008. However, all indications point to the fact that the great majority of these calls are related to domestic victims. Seventy-three percent of the 1,488 victims who called the National Human Trafficking Resource Center between 2008 and 2012 were English speakers. Only 8 percent of the victims of sex trafficking were foreign nationals; the rest were U.S. citizens or legal permanent residents.[18] This lends further credence to the notion that domestic victims dominate the trafficked population.

While some praise Good Samaritans and award them medals for their efforts, others caution that the involvement of Good Samaritans can be dangerous for them and damaging for trafficked children. "Private actors and organizations meaning to help often do not have the experience or expertise to identify whether people have actually been trafficked, and they rarely have the capacity or expertise required to offer high-quality legal and social services to those who have been trafficked or who were caught in a raid."[19] Others say that there are no incentives for Good Samaritans to get involved, because without the backing of federal law enforcement, their tips are often not acted upon.

In the winter of 2005, Julia, a service provider at a national NGO working with trafficked children, recommended that I look into the identification issue. "We are very curious," she said, "to see where the system is not working." She suggested I interview a young victim named Analisa whose case "was illustrative of the cracks, gaps, and crevices in the system established to identify minors trafficked to the U.S." A couple of weeks later, I boarded a plane and headed to upstate New York. As we approached the airport, I saw a small town covered in downy snow. Bright lights flickered against the midnight blue sky. It resembled a winter wonderland. "I am glad," I thought to myself, "that a survivor of child trafficking is living in this tranquil place."

The evening was still young when I arrived at my hotel. I ordered a pot of tea and started rereading the notes from my conversation with Julia and the telephone interview with Analisa's caseworker. I remembered that she was from Tegucigalpa, Honduras, and was trafficked by her stepsister, Carmen. The next day, when I interviewed Analisa she reported having a warm and loving relationship with her grandmother. The same, however, could not be said about her relationship with her uncles, who had reportedly forced Analisa to work on a family farm since she was six years of age. Analisa did not like getting up at dawn to join her uncles and cousins to plant maize and beans. She found the backbreaking work unpleasant, but not unusual. "All the kids in the village helped on the farm," she told me. "My cousins worked as well." Analisa's work on the family farm did not interfere with her schooling. Child advocates opposing child labor often point out that working children are deprived of the opportunity to attend school. Analisa attended school for five years and is literate in Spanish. She also reported having been able to play with friends and having a good childhood.

The fact that Analisa farmed alongside her uncles did not shock me. Child labor is quite common in Honduras. According to a report prepared by the National Statistics Institute of Honduras, 15.5 percent of children between the age of seven and seventeen worked in 2002. The majority (69.2%) of the working children lived in rural areas.[20] The National Child Labor Survey conducted in the same year by the International Labor Organization reported that 9.2 percent of Honduran children between the ages of five and fourteen worked. Close to 4 percent of the working children did not attend school. The percentage is approximately four times higher for boys (6.1%) than for girls (1.5%) and children in rural areas are more likely to work without attending school than urban dwellers (5.5% vs. 1.5%).[21]

In 1998, when Analisa reached twelve years of age, her grandmother fell ill and sent her to live with her biological father and his wife. Analisa had not seen her father since infancy and reported feeling like a stranger in his household. Her stepmother was not happy to have to care for Analisa. When her adult daughter from a previous marriage, Carmen, came to visit from the United

States and offered to take Analisa back with her, Analisa's stepmother readily agreed. It is unclear what Analisa's father thought about this plan, but he did not object. Analisa reported wanting to take advantage of the opportunities Carmen presented: learning English, going to school, and getting a good job.

In the fall of 1998, Analisa traveled with her stepsister, Carmen, to a large metropolitan area on the U.S. West Coast. Analisa doesn't remember much about the trip except that it was long and involved a couple of plane rides and a car trip. They crossed the border by car, using fraudulent papers, seemingly without any difficulties. It became apparent later that Carmen had many aliases, which she used both to cross the U.S.-Mexican border and to find employment.

This is the first point at which the system failed Analisa. If there were established protocols in place at the U.S. borders to identify trafficking cases among the population of minors crossing the frontier in the company of adults who are not their legal guardians, Analisa might have been identified as a trafficked child at the time of border crossing. While it may not have been possible at this early stage to ascertain the grim situation Analisa was headed into, the circumstances of her entry into the country—traveling with fraudulent documents and accompanied by a woman she barely knew—certainly warranted a closer look.

Analisa's caseworker expressed surprise that Customs and Border Patrol did not ask any questions about the relationship between Carmen and Analisa. With U.S. immigration officials annually apprehending approximately 100,000 unaccompanied children at the borders, it is likely that a significant number of potential victims are being overlooked. By their own admission, with more than 42,000 frontline Customs and Border Patrol agents protecting nearly seven thousand miles of land border and 328 ports of entry—including official crossings by land, air, and sea—the Customs and Border Patrol is uniquely situated to deter and disrupt human trafficking. At the same time, to interview 100,000 minors every year is a daunting task.

Carmen, who manages a cleaning service, had two children of her own by different fathers: a boy named Mauricio and a girl named Sofia. Although the case notes indicated that Carmen forced Analisa to help her clean apartments, Analisa did not see anything unusual about needing to contribute to the income of the household. The neighbors, however, noticed that Analisa was at home when all other neighborhood children were at school and reported this information to the police. The police ordered Carmen to enroll Analisa in school. However, the girl attended the local school for only a few days.

This is the second point where the system failed Analisa. The police did nothing beyond ordering Carmen to enroll Analisa in school. They did not inquire why Analisa was being taken care of by a stepsister. They did not seem interested in whether Carmen had legal guardianship of Analisa and did not inquire about her biological parents. Whether their inaction was the result of a lack of training on issues of child trafficking or simply apathy is unclear. Analisa's case worker believes that the school asked for certain documents—including immunization records and birth certificate—to finalize her school enrollment. However, Carmen did not have any of the required documentation and Analisa did not return to school. After Carmen failed to produce the required documents, the school administration stopped checking on Analisa.

If the system worked properly, the police would have interviewed Analisa separately from her stepsister. Someone would have talked to her about why she was not in school, how she was spending her days, and how long she had been in the United States working. Her answers would certainly have raised red flags and may have warranted a call to Child Protective Services (CPS) to initiate an investigation of the stepsister and possible removal of Analisa from the home. Additionally, questions about whether she was being paid and how she ended up cleaning apartments would have revealed that she was not just working but was trafficked. This line of questioning by the law enforcement representatives Analisa encountered up to this point—border patrol and local police—could have led to a report of trafficking to federal law enforcement, a federal investigation, and ideally a referral for services and benefits. According to her caseworker, Analisa never mentioned speaking to the police. In a conversation with me, Analisa did mention the policewoman who questioned Carmen as to why Analisa was not in school. The officer, however, never included Analisa in the conversation.

Case file notes indicate that Analisa attended school only for a few days. She disappeared from the school shortly after enrollment. Neither the school administration nor the teachers reported her absence. The system failed Analisa for the third time. If the system worked correctly, the school would likely have attempted to contact Carmen and after a certain number of absences would contact a juvenile court, truancy officer, or other designated party. Indeed, an analysis of truancy policies in the state where Analisa resided at the time of this incident indicates that schools are obligated to contact the family of a truant child and after seven days must file a petition in juvenile court. It is unclear why the school did not follow-up. When I called the truancy office, I was told, "There are too many immigrant children missing school every day. We don't have the resources to check on every one of them."

Shortly after being forced by the police to enroll Analisa in school, Carmen, fearing discovery, decided to leave the West Coast and moved the family, including Analisa, to a large metropolitan area in the South. They lived there for about two years. Again Carmen found work managing a crew of workers cleaning local motels. Likewise, Analisa once again began to work for Carmen. While living in the South, the fourteen-year-old Analisa met Jorge. He was a native Spanish speaker, but it is unclear whether he was of Honduran origin.

Jorge was two or three years older than Analisa. Analisa said that both Jorge and his mother were very kind to her.

In the summer of 2002, Carmen was fired from her job and arrested for writing fraudulent checks. Carmen's children and Analisa were placed in the custody of CPS. Carmen's children, Mauricio and Sofia, were released to the custody of their respective fathers. Mauricio's father came from California to claim his son and Sofia's father came from the upper Northwest to claim his daughter. Mauricio's father volunteered to take Analisa with him as well, and she was released into his custody. The system failed Analisa again. Analisa's placement in CPS should have been the perfect opportunity for her to be identified as a trafficked child. If CPS were well versed in issues related to child trafficking they might have been more vigilant; not only would they not have released her to a stranger, they could have reported her case as trafficking to federal or local authorities and begun Analisa on the path to appropriate benefits and services.

It seemed that Analisa did not like living in California with her stepsister's former partner and ran back to the South to be reunited with Jorge, who wired money to Analisa to pay for her bus ticket. It is unclear what Analisa's plans were at this juncture. At some point she stated that she intended to stay with her stepsister's female friend in the South, who had been kind to her. Another time she indicated that she wanted to live with her boyfriend and his family. The money wire and the bus receipts suggested the latter. Whatever her plans, she did not succeed. Immigration officials apprehended Analisa when the bus she was traveling on was stopped at a random checkpoint on the way from California. Needless to say, Analisa did not have any identification documents and did not speak much English, so she ended up in an immigration detention center. She told me she was disoriented by her new circumstances and frightened by the detention center, which she perceived as a jail.

Here is another point where the system failed Analisa. The authorities at the checkpoint failed to identify Analisa as a victim of trafficking. While it might be somewhat unreasonable to expect the Border Patrol to identify trafficking victims at this point, it could be argued that they should be conducting more thorough interviews. They should have asked Analisa how long she had been in the United States, how she had supported herself during that time, and whether she had gone to school. Were Analisa willing to tell them the truth, they would have recognized that she may have been trafficked and reported it to Immigration and Customs Enforcement agents to follow up with an investigation and referral for benefits.

Analisa stayed in a detention center, a large institution ill-equipped to provide child-centered services. She remained there for about seven or eight months; during that time, the administration of the center was undergoing a transition from the Immigration and Naturalization Service to the Office of

Refugee Resettlement, which probably complicated things even further. An inquiry from the police to the regional juvenile coordinator at the local immigration office revealed that Analisa was in deportation proceedings and was scheduled to be deported within forty-five days. Yet again, the system did not work for Analisa. Despite having been at the detention center for months, it appears that the staff of the center, who would have had daily contact with her, were ill-prepared to recognize her as a trafficked victim. At the time, the intake interview did not include any questions related to possible trafficking.

The detention center where Analisa stayed had a good relationship with a local legal aid program. The program staff organized periodic "know your rights" training for the detained youth and provided them with a list of pro bono attorneys willing to represent them. Analisa took advantage of this opportunity. Her attorney interviewed her in order to file an asylum claim and suspected that she was a victim of human trafficking. This was the first time when the system actually worked. The attorney notified immigration authorities that there was a trafficking allegation. He also contacted the Civil Rights Division in the Department of Justice (DOJ), after which the Federal Bureau of Investigation (FBI) got involved. An FBI agent interviewed Analisa while she was in the detention center. Despite the fact that DOJ policy is to interview child victims of trafficking in the presence of an attorney who would be their advocate, the FBI interviewed Analisa without an attorney present. It is quite surprising that the FBI interviewed Analisa alone, especially since she had a pro bono attorney who could have been summoned. After a promising turn of events, the system stumbled once again.

Analisa's pro bono attorney worked to convince immigration officials to terminate the deportation order. They were reluctant to do so at first, because they would have to release her from their custody. At some point, however, immigration officials must have dropped their immigration case because there is evidence in the case files that the attorney initiated an application for a T-Visa. As already indicated, after the passage of the Homeland Security legislation in 2003, care of children in federal custody was transferred from immigration authorities to ORR. ORR agreed to release Analisa from their custody and new living arrangements were made for her.

Although foster care was available, Analisa was not referred for such services. Instead, she was released to a group of Catholic nuns in the South, with neither custody arrangements nor any financial support other than the sisters' charity. One of the nuns was on the board of directors of the legal aid agency that had assigned the pro bono attorney to Analisa. While living with the nuns, Analisa attended school. Her school counselor carried out several needs assessments, which proved to be very helpful when Analisa relocated to live with a foster family. While Analisa enjoyed living with the nuns, did not dislike attending school, and felt secure in her new surroundings, not all was well.

At this point, Analisa still had no access to benefits available to child victims of trafficking and had to rely on the generosity of the sisters. The foster care system was failing her, or at least working very slowly.

The FBI contacted the nuns to interview Analisa and they agreed. However, Analisa was again interviewed without an attorney present. This is yet another point where the system did not work: children should not be subjected to law enforcement interviews without an attorney present. They need the assistance of an attorney to help them understand what is happening and what is expected of them, as well as to protect their rights and advocate for them. While she was not afraid of the FBI agent—she described him as a nice person—Analisa said she did not understand his questions about being trafficked and about Carmen's illegal activities.

The Migration and Refugee Services at USCCB learned about Analisa and her case in March 2003. A staff member from the refugee resettlement program in the state where Analisa was residing contacted USCCB to find a way to provide Analisa with access to benefits. USCCB was concerned that Analisa did not have any benefits and advocated on her behalf with DOJ. Numerous phone calls and several weeks later, DOJ contacted ORR to request benefits for Analisa. In late May 2003, Analisa's attorney said he had notified DOJ's Civil Rights Division about the trafficking case "several months earlier." DOJ did not request benefits from ORR until approximately May 23, 2003. Under the TVPA, ORR can determine trafficked children to be eligible for federal benefits to the same extent as refugees. This means access to specialized, federally funded foster care through the Unaccompanied Refugee Minors program, eligibility for Medicaid, and other federal benefits. Generally, ORR grants benefits after receiving a request to do so from a federal law enforcement agency. Since this was an early case—discovered just a couple of years after the passage of the TVPA legislation—it took quite a long time to secure benefits for Analisa.

Almost a decade later, in 2014, the situation has improved dramatically. The Office of Refugee Resettlement is able to issue letters of eligibility for interim assistance without involving federal law enforcement. However, at the time when Analisa was seeking assistance, ORR had to receive a referral for benefits from federal law enforcement. Analisa had to wait until law enforcement had reviewed her case and gathered enough evidence to feel comfortable requesting benefits on her behalf. Were ORR able to grant benefits directly, they would have been able to do so after hearing the details of her story from her attorney. Analisa would then have been able to access benefits more quickly and her living situation could have been stabilized while law enforcement continued to investigate.

Once benefits were granted, USCCB and a URM program representative talked to Analisa and described available options. At this point, a plan was established to place Analisa in foster care. It was not easy to find a suitable Spanish-speaking foster family. For example, one Spanish-speaking family that wanted to take Analisa in was still in the process of being licensed. They could not get licensed until their adult son moved out of the house. A second family, originally from Puerto Rico, was selected. However, this family, the Sanchez family, was also awaiting completion of the licensing process. It took two months longer than anticipated for the foster family to be licensed. Analisa was safe and comfortable living with the nuns; resolving her living situation did not seem as urgent as it might have been if her living conditions were less stable. Had she been in a more tenuous situation, a new URM program that could place her more quickly would have been identified. The sisters were working with Analisa to prepare her to move to upstate New York; they talked to her about the town she was to live in, and prepared her for life in a foster family. In retrospect, this period of time allowed Analisa to get ready for a new phase in her life and to say good-bye to the sisters who had taken her in.

At the same time, the foster care program director stayed in telephone contact both with Analisa and the nuns to describe to them available services and to describe the foster family Analisa was going to live with. Plans were made for a female bilingual and bicultural worker to accompany her on a flight to her new place of residence and ease the transition to new living arrangements. The foster family was licensed in the summer of 2003 and assumed care of Analisa shortly thereafter. Analisa moved to her new foster home in August 2003. Analisa, with both her old and her new caseworker, spent several hours in the new foster home to get acclimated to her new surroundings. The program director also consulted with Analisa's original attorney to get his insights into her case.

There were several obstacles in obtaining a T-Visa for Analisa. Her original pro bono attorney, Mr. Orozco, applied for a T-Visa, but it is unclear if anyone filed a change of address for Analisa once she left the nuns and was placed in a foster family. It appears that Mr. Orozco remained the attorney of record. Unfortunately, he left the legal aid agency not long after Analisa moved to the East Coast. While the legal aid agency continued to represent Analisa during her T-Visa application process, with the departure of Mr. Orozco there was no consistency in the point of contact. The geographic distance between Texas and upstate New York was not helping either; it was impossible for Analisa to have direct contact with the legal aid agency.

Once Analisa resettled to the East Coast, she started working with a new pro bono attorney, Mr. Fitzgerald. Mr. Fitzgerald thought it would be confusing to change her attorney of record since the Vermont Service Center of the Immigration and Naturalization Service was already working on her T-Visa application. Unfortunately, Mr. Fitzgerald was not very accessible to Analisa or the foster parents. The county had custody of Analisa and decided to get her an attorney as well since the FBI was going to interview her again. This attorney was provided by the County Department of Social Services to safeguard her best interests during an interview with the FBI; his role was, however, limited to interaction with the FBI. A "law guardian" was also provided to advocate for and represent Analisa's interest in family court matters and proceedings. This is standard procedure in foster care cases. At the time of my research, Analisa's visa application was still pending, more than two years after it was first filed.

While Analisa was still living in the South, the DOJ became involved in trying to obtain permission for Analisa to stay in the country. Among many things, the process required fingerprinting Analisa. The legal aid agency asked one of the nuns to take Analisa to be fingerprinted. The nun reported a problem accomplishing this relatively simple task because Analisa did not have a government-issued identification document. Eventually, Analisa was able to get fingerprinted. However, almost a year later she still did not have an appropriate visa. USCCB contacted the DOJ to find out what needed to be done to get her continued presence. Continued presence (U-Visa or T-Visa) was necessary to issue an employment authorization document, which would allow Analisa to work part-time during the summer. Analisa had to be fingerprinted again, and again she did not have the required government-issued identification card. Eventually, however, she was granted continued presence. The case files are silent on the actual date, but the caseworker interviewed thought it was summer of 2004.

While the law provided for an identification system to be set up, the system was full of bureaucratic delays and formalities, which hindered Analisa's adjustment to post-trafficking life. Analisa's story illustrates the gaps and weaknesses in the system. Moreover, it exemplifies the consequences of the shortcomings that exist in the system. Analisa stayed in her exploitative situation for several years and was deprived of an opportunity to attend school and receive legal, financial, and social assistance. Eventually, she found her way into the system—with the help of many service providers, starting with her pro bono attorney—but the various programs charged with providing services she was entitled to were hindered in their mission by inefficiencies and oversights. It shouldn't be this hard for trafficked victims, especially minors, to get what they deserve and what the law provides for them.

Identification Challenges

Analisa is an example of a minor who should have been identified as a victim of human trafficking much earlier in the course of her journey to and within the United States if the authorities she came into contact with were properly equipped to identify child victims. Unfortunately, the fact that Analisa traveled to the United States on fraudulent papers in the company of a young woman who was neither her mother nor her legal guardian did not arouse any suspicion on the part of immigration officials at the U.S.-Mexico border. While the fraudulent papers might have been difficult to spot, the border patrol should have asked questions about the relationship between Analisa and Carmen. Later on, representatives of local police also did not seem to be overly concerned that a twelve-year-old girl did not attend school, nor did they ask about her legal guardians. They simply ordered Carmen to enroll Analisa in school and thought the matter resolved. When she stopped attending school, responsible officials did not follow up. Still later, authorities at a checkpoint on the road leading from California to a neighboring state also failed to identify Analisa as a victim of trafficking. Again, a minor traveling alone without any documentation was thought of as a child violating immigration laws, not as a possible victim of trafficking. Additionally, she spent several months in the custody of state Child Protective Services without being identified as a victim and was released to a stranger connected to her trafficker.

Analisa could also have been identified as a victim of child trafficking during the eight months she spent in the detention facility. This length of time should have given the staff ample opportunity to identify her as a trafficked minor, not a mere violator of immigration law. As a child detainee, it is likely that social services personnel interviewed Analisa at least a couple of times and asked about her family and migration experiences. The staff seems to have been ill-equipped to ask appropriate questions that could have led to proper identification of her trafficking circumstances. The detention center's personnel not only had more time but also more responsibility than the Border Patrol to assess her situation. It appears that they missed the problem entirely; perhaps because they were not well versed in the antitrafficking law and did not receive appropriate training in interviewing children and adolescents.

Experts suggest that first contact with unidentified child victims would most likely be made by one of the following groups: (1) immigration officials at or between ports of entry and at detention facilities, (2) local law enforcement, or (3) service providers such as educational, social service, and medical providers.[22] Improvements at the border have the most potential for increasing the identification of child victims of trafficking. At the time when Analisa traveled to the United States, there were no bilateral protocols in place at U.S. borders to identify trafficking cases at initial apprehension. The "gentlemen's agreement" between Mexico and the United States calls for returning all Mexican minors to Mexican authorities. At the time when Analisa was trafficked, Mexico did not have any antitrafficking legislation—the Mexican Congress passed the first national law on human trafficking in 2007—and it was unclear whether Mexican authorities made an effort to assess whether the unaccompanied or accompanied minors were smuggled or trafficked to the United States.

Immigration laws in many countries stipulate that the border patrol pays particular attention to children traveling abroad to make sure that they indeed travel with a parent or legal guardian.

The heightened sense of security post-9/11 has channeled governmental resources overwhelmingly toward combating terrorism. As a result, Border Patrol agents are not receiving enough training on trafficking issues. This is further complicated by the fact that identification of minors, especially females, at the border is difficult because oftentimes they present themselves as adults, and are subsequently classified as such. Analysis of fingerprint records at the border shows an unusually high number of female entrants who are twenty-one years old.[23] Trafficked girls are also coached to say that they are the spouses or relatives of the trafficker. Analisa was instructed to refer to Carmen as her sister despite the fact that they are not biologically related.

Furthermore, at the time of crossing or apprehension at the border, trafficked minors may not have suffered through the most terrible exploitation or even know that they are being trafficked. Analisa is a case in point. She was told by her stepmother to go to the United States with Carmen to ease the burden of her presence in her father's household. Analisa seemed to have been eager to avail herself of the opportunities this journey was supposed to provide. She had no way of knowing that Carmen would exploit her, force her to work, and not send her to school.

At the time she was apprehended at a checkpoint on the way from California back to Texas, she had certainly already been trafficked by Carmen. It appears, though, that Border Patrol agents did not identify her situation as trafficking. Even if the Border Patrol had suspected trafficking, there were no comprehensive procedures to ensure that information would always be passed on to ORR when the child is placed into federal custody. Even today, no such procedures exist. Border Patrol or Immigration and Customs Enforcement agents may have reason to believe that a minor was trafficked, but it is possible, even likely, that such information will not be conveyed to the federal facility that will be caring for the child. Awareness of such information is crucial to prevent deportation or release back to traffickers.

At the local level, training of law enforcement is essential to improving the identification of child victims of human trafficking. At present, the majority of local law enforcement contact with trafficking victims happens in an ad hoc manner; police officers usually encounter child victims during the course of their daily routines. Analisa was one of the very early cases of child victims identified in the United States and her contact with local law enforcement, as well as with CPS, predated the Rescue and Restore Campaign and associated training programs for law enforcement personnel, service providers, and the general public to become aware of human trafficking and to be better equipped to identify potential victims. The police, child welfare workers, and school administrators were ill equipped to make a proper assessment of her circumstances that might have resulted in an early identification.

The low number of trafficked children identified and receiving services vis-à-vis the number of estimated victims continues to plague the antitrafficking community. In July 2001, DOJ announced the issuance of regulations implementing Section 107(c) of the TVPA. One of the regulations under 107(c) requires the federal government to identify victims of severe forms of human trafficking. Although regulations have been released, the federal government has found it challenging to carry out their mandate. More recently, governmental and nongovernmental organizations have begun creating a complex system of collaboration in response to the TVPA. Governments, both federal and local, and nongovernmental agencies that must work together are frequently starting from scratch to design collaboration. Many of the actors in the current system are not used to working with each other. For instance, while foster care providers may be familiar with the courts and mental health care resources, they may not be used to working with federal law enforcement, and vice versa. Thus, the very complexity of the system sometimes defeats the goal of finding and serving trafficked children; the more pieces there are to a system, the more possible cracks there are for children to fall through. Despite the fact that virtually every federal agency has an antitrafficking initiative, the number of identified trafficked minors remains relatively small. It seems that either there are not as many trafficked children as initially thought or these initiatives are inefficient.

Closing the Gaps

In interviews conducted almost a decade after Analisa had been identified as a victim of child trafficking, child advocates and service providers spoke of continued challenges in identifying trafficked children. Fewer than seven hundred additional children have been identified since I first spoke to Analisa in 2006. Virtually all of the children identified in recent years have come from the cohort of migrant children who were already in federal custody. Service providers are surprised that no children are being referred to the Unaccompanied Refugee Minors program that traditionally served young victims of trafficking. One provider, who spoke on condition of anonymity, indicated that the federal government is scrambling to find child victims: "Some of the cases we see barely, if at all, meet the definition of child trafficking. NGOs are getting a lot of money from the federal government but there are no referrals from community members." Again, it remains an open question whether such low numbers of identifications are related to the "cracks" through which children are slipping or to the fact that fewer minors than anticipated have been victimized.

Advocates are adamant that many gaps remain. They also insist that not enough resources—human and financial—have been allocated to finding trafficked minors, especially at the southern border. They maintain that particular attention needs to be paid to children crossing borders in the company of adults who are not their legal guardians. There are calls for increased funding for ongoing comprehensive training programs for different actors—educators, child welfare personnel, and health-care providers—that might be in a position to identify trafficked minors. But first and foremost, antitrafficking advocates insist the identification of child victims of trafficking must be made a top priority by the government. It bears repeating that all these recommendations rest on the premise that there are large numbers of trafficked children and adolescents hidden in plain sight.

Victim identification is directly related to the prosecution of perpetrators of human trafficking. Without victims, especially victims who are willing and able to provide credible testimonies, prosecutors cannot file and try a case. The challenges involved in prosecuting perpetrators of child trafficking are the topic of the next chapter.

6

Jail the Offender,
Protect the Victim

Prosecution is a complicated issue. Traffickers use force, fraud, and coercion to compel children to follow them and should be punished for their manipulations, say antitrafficking advocates. On the other hand, many close family members are involved in the trafficking of children and adolescents and caution is warranted when mounting prosecution in such circumstances. Prosecutors need to balance the need to make those who broke the law accountable, while at the same time taking care not to adversely affect the well-being of the trafficked girls and boys.

The number of prosecutions is used to measure the efficacy of antitrafficking efforts. Yet, only a small fraction of trafficking cases have been prosecuted, claim antitrafficking advocates. Why so few? Trafficking cases are not easy to prosecute. They are resource-intensive, require coordination across different agencies, international fact-finding, interpreters, witness protection, and witness cooperation (in the case of adults). In one report, the Central Intelligence Agency pointed out that "low penalties and the long, complicated and resource intensive nature of trafficking cases tends to make them unattractive to many US attorneys."[1] Prosecutors, however, say that they are eager to bring forth trafficking cases despite these challenges because they are often high profile, bring good publicity, and the government has prioritized the fight against trafficking. "Effective prosecution is the linchpin to eradicating human trafficking," according to Cynthia Shepard Torg, former chief counsel for the Human Smuggling and Trafficking Center in the Department of Justice.[2] At the same time, prosecutors pursue only the cases they believe they can win.

In this chapter, I discuss the challenges in the investigation and prosecution of trafficking cases. I also tell the story of several girls who reacted very differently to the prosecution of their traffickers. Melinda and Pilar's unwillingness to cooperate with law enforcement was an obstacle in a potentially strong court case. This prompted federal investigators to pressure them to play a part in the investigation and court proceedings without regard for the law—which does not require underage victims to cooperate with law enforcement—and with a shallow concern for the potentially harmful emotional and physical effects of such participation on the girls. Julia, on the other hand, was eager to bring her trafficker "to justice" and bravely faced him in a court of law. I use the stories of Melinda, Pilar, and Julia to discuss the complications involved in prosecuting traffickers and the effects of prosecutions on survivors of child trafficking. I discuss both the potential adverse effects of collaboration with law enforcement and the empowering and healing aspects of such cooperation.

Prosecution, Sentencing, and Restitution

In the United States, trafficking cases are prosecuted under a variety of federal and, to a lesser extent, state laws. While the federal government keeps records of the DOJ criminal caseload and from time to time makes them available to the public,[3] there is no central data collection system that provides comprehensive statistics for all trafficking prosecutions.[4] The Human Trafficking Reporting System (HTRS), which was designed to measure the performance of federally funded task forces, is supposed to capture information on human trafficking investigations conducted by state and local law enforcement agencies in the United States. However, the task forces were not mandated to provide HTRS with data for several years. Only eighteen of the forty-two federally funded task forces regularly provided data before 2011. This situation will hopefully change; in 2011, participation in HTRS became a requirement of continued federal funding.[5] The existing data is not publicly available for independent analysis. Moreover, the HTRS reports that the quality of the data they do have is inadequate to draw meaningful conclusions.[6]

Given this state of affairs, piecing together a picture of trafficking prosecutions is like putting together a jigsaw puzzle and realizing that the pieces come from different sets. In some reports, the federal government provides information on suspected and confirmed cases of human trafficking (including the number of confirmed victims), while other reports include information on convictions. Distinguishing between cases related to foreign-born and "domestic" victims is also difficult, especially in identifying cases involving foreign-born minors. Some reports provide visa statuses, but they do not associate immigration statuses with age. In the following pages, I attempt to present the available data and discuss emerging trends and issues related to prosecution of trafficking cases before turning to the analysis of qualitative data I gathered on the prosecution of cases involving foreign-born minors.

The Bureau of Justice Statistics reported that between January 2008 and June 2010, federally funded task forces opened 2,515 suspected incidents of human trafficking for investigation. Further analysis identified 389 confirmed human trafficking incidents, including 488 suspects and 527 victims. Confirmed sex trafficking victims were overwhelmingly female (94 percent of victims). Of the sixty-three confirmed labor trafficking victims, twenty were male and forty-three were female. Confirmed labor trafficking victims were more likely to be older than confirmed sex trafficking victims. Sixty-two percent of confirmed labor trafficking victims were identified as twenty-five years of age or older, compared to 13 percent of confirmed sex trafficking victims, based on victims with known age. The vast majority of the victims were U.S. citizens (domestic victims); foreign-born accounted for 24 percent. It is not clear from this data how many minors were foreign-born.[7]

The Bureau of Justice Statistics report does not discuss prosecutions or convictions. However, it does mention the arrests of 144 suspects in confirmed human trafficking incidents open for at least a year during the study period, including 139 sex trafficking suspects and five labor trafficking suspects. It also mentions that of the eighty-seven foreign-born victims, twenty-one received T-Visas, while forty-six visa applications were still pending or had an unknown status.[8] T-Visa dispositions are a sign of victims' collaboration with law enforcement in mounting a case against perpetrators of human trafficking, thus providing another glimpse into the issue of prosecution of traffickers. However, T-Visa issuance is by no means a proxy for prosecution.

In an earlier period, between January 1, 2007, and September 30, 2008, 1,229 alleged incidents of human trafficking were recorded. However, only eighty-eight cases accounting for 269 victims were confirmed. Overall, 94 percent of victims in confirmed human trafficking incidents were female. Nearly 40 percent of victims in the thirty-six confirmed labor trafficking incidents were male. For confirmed sex trafficking incidents, almost all of the victims were female. Almost 60 percent of the confirmed victims in all cases were seventeen years of age or younger. A quarter of victims trafficked for sexual exploitation were seventeen years of age or younger. Over two-thirds of victims were foreign-born. All victims of labor trafficking were foreign-born and two-thirds of victims trafficked for sexual exploitation were foreign-born. Task forces reported arrest information for 216 of the 543 suspects in alleged human trafficking incidents. Sixty-eight percent of these suspects were arrested at the state level; 26 percent were arrested at the federal level. Task forces reported court adjudication information for 113 human trafficking suspects. For these suspects, over half were convicted of some offense, six suspects had their case dismissed, and forty-six suspects were awaiting adjudication at the time the report was published.[9]

Between 2001 and 2005, U.S. attorneys investigated 555 suspects in matters involving violation of federal human trafficking statutes. Fifty-eight percent of matters opened during this period were for offenses committed under the TVPA of 2000. A total of seventy-five of the seventy-eight defendants in cases terminated during this period were convicted under human trafficking statutes. Fifty-seven of the convicted defendants pled guilty and eighteen were found guilty at trial. It is impossible to calculate accurate conviction rates from available data simply because cases indicted in one fiscal year may not be resolved in the same year. Interviews with prosecutors and law enforcement suggest that it often takes years for a case to be closed.

According to William McDonald's calculations, based on the Attorney General's Reports to Congress, the federal government filed 238 trafficking cases, charged 644 defendants with human trafficking violations, and obtained 466 convictions from the passage of the TVPA until the end of fiscal year 2010.[10] The U.S. State Department indicated that in FY 2011, forty DOJ-led task forces reported over nine hundred investigations that involved more than 1,350 suspects. During the same fiscal year the Immigration and Customs Enforcement reported investigating 722 cases possibly involving human trafficking. At the end of FY 2011, the FBI had 337 pending human trafficking investigations with suspected adult and foreign minor victims. In FY 2011, DOJ charged forty-two cases involving human trafficking of adults by force, fraud, or coercion. Of these, half involved primarily sex trafficking and half involved primarily labor trafficking, although several involved both sex and labor trafficking. Including federal cases involving sex trafficking of minors, DOJ prosecuted 125 human trafficking cases in FY 2011. A total of 118 defendants were charged in FY 2011 in forced labor and adult sex trafficking cases, representing a 19 percent increase over the number of defendants charged in such cases the previous year. During the same period, DOJ secured seventy convictions in forced labor and adult sex trafficking cases. Of these cases, thirty-five were predominantly sex trafficking and thirty-five were predominantly labor trafficking, although multiple cases involved both. The combined number of federal trafficking convictions totaled 151, including cases involving forced labor, sex trafficking of adults, and sex trafficking of minors, compared to 141 such convictions in 2010.

While these numbers are not broken down by cases involving foreign- and native-born victims, the TIP report notes:

> Notable prosecutions included those of sex and labor traffickers who used threats of deportation, violence, and sexual abuse to compel young, undocumented Central American women and girls into hostess jobs and forced prostitution in bars and nightclubs on Long Island, New York. Based on a bilateral prosecution brought by U.S. and Mexican authorities against a transnational sex trafficking ring, Mexican authorities secured sentences of up to 37 years' imprisonment against three traffickers. DOJ also secured the conviction of a defendant in Chicago who used beatings, threats, and sexual assault to force Eastern European victims to work in massage parlors and prostitution.[11]

This quote suggests that the majority of these cases involved foreign-born victims.

In FY 2013, ICE reported opening 1,025 investigations possibly involving human trafficking, an increase from 894 in FY 2012. The FBI formally opened 220 human trafficking investigations concerning suspected adult and foreign child victims, a decrease from 306 in FY 2012, and additionally initiated 514 investigations involving the sex trafficking of children, an increase from 440 in FY 2012. DOJ initiated a total of 161 federal human trafficking prosecutions in FY 2013, charging 253 defendants. Of these, 222 defendants engaged predominately in sex trafficking and thirty-one engaged predominately in labor trafficking, although multiple defendants engaged in both. In FY 2013, DOJ's Civil Rights Division initiated seventy-one prosecutions involving forced labor and sex trafficking- of adults by force, fraud, or coercion. Of these, fifty-three were predominantly sex trafficking and eighteen predominantly labor trafficking; several cases involved both. During FY 2013, DOJ convicted a total of 174 traffickers in cases involving forced labor, sex trafficking of adults, and sex trafficking of children, compared to 138 such convictions obtained in FY 2012. Of these, 113 were predominantly sex trafficking and twenty-five were predominantly labor trafficking, although several involved both.[12]

I surmise that all of the labor trafficking cases most likely involved foreign-born individuals as labor exploitation of U.S. citizens has never been investigated under federal or state trafficking laws. On the other hand, the cases involving sexual exploitation of minors in all likelihood pertain to both foreign-born and "domestic" victims. Traffickers were also prosecuted under a myriad of state laws, but comprehensive data is not currently collected on state prosecutions and convictions.

It is also worth remembering that trafficking cases represent a small percentage of the total criminal investigations dealing with immigration. In 2005 the

Government Accountability Office studied smuggling operations using data from FY 2004 and part of 2005. Government Accountability Office researchers determined that for the then newly established federal Bureau of Immigration and Customs Enforcement, trafficking was but one element within a much larger focal area. ICE spent 71 percent of its investigative efforts—ten million investigative hours—on drug, financial, and criminal alien investigations and related probes, only 2 percent on human trafficking, and an additional 7 percent on smuggling.[13]

Prosecutions of traffickers are also limited at the state and local level. Using data from investigative case records and court files for 140 human trafficking cases in twelve counties, Amy Farrell, Coleen Owens, and Jack McDevitt found that the number of trafficking cases discovered, arrested, and prosecuted has been minimal at the state and local level.[14] Only a quarter of the studied cases involved foreign-born victims. The researchers concluded that the failure of state and local authorities to prosecute large numbers of human trafficking perpetrators does not suggest that human trafficking is a smaller problem than the public outcry would imply. Rather, they assert, the problem lies in legal, institutional, and attitudinal challenges inherent in using new human trafficking laws. Almost one-third of the suspects that Farrell and colleagues studied were not prosecuted on any charges, and the majority who were prosecuted were charged with related offenses, such as compelling prostitution or transport for purposes of prostitution.

Most studies analyze prosecutions of perpetrators of human trafficking vis-à-vis estimates of the number of trafficked victims. This is a risky proposition since the estimates are often based on murky methodologies. I have wondered about the rates of prosecutions versus the number of identified victims. How many of the traffickers implicated in crimes against minors officially acknowledged by the federal government to be victims of child trafficking have been indicted and tried or pled guilty? Has it been a majority? A small percentage? It is not easy to answer these questions given the lack of a centralized database. The perception is that only a small number of cases have gone to prosecution.

Let's look at the Human Trafficking Law Project[15] to analyze cases involving foreign-born minors that have been mounted and brought to a conclusion since the passage of the TVPA in 2000 through 2012. The Human Trafficking Law Project is a database[16] maintained by the Human Trafficking Clinic at the University of Michigan Law School to identify U.S. criminal and civil court cases.[17] Content analysis of the database reveals that sixty-four cases involving minors were investigated and adjudicated between 2000 and 2012. Cases involved a single minor, more than one minor, or both minors and adults. Almost 54 percent (thirty-five cases) involved sex trafficking, while 36 percent (twenty-three cases) involved labor trafficking. The remaining six cases involved both sex and labor trafficking. The largest number of cases involved trafficking victims from Mexico (sixteen cases), followed by Costa Rica (seven cases) and Cameroon (four cases).

The examined cases included approximately 1,978 victims. This data is somewhat skewed because of the United States v. Gouw case, which according to the database involved trafficking, smuggling, and immigration fraud of some 1,000 adults and minors.[18] Unfortunately, it is impossible to identify the number of minors in cases that included both adults and children as the database provides only a total number of victims in each case. Moreover, in some instances it is even less precise and indicates that there were fifteen-plus or twenty-plus victims. Cases that involve only minors accounted for approximately four hundred victims. In light of the number of minors who received eligibility letters from ORR—841 individuals—the number of minor victims involved in cases that were investigated and prosecuted is significant. The analyzed cases included 295 defendants. With two exceptions, the cases were tried in federal courts, with the vast majority (fifty-five cases) in criminal courts and the remaining seven in civil courts. The two cases tried in state courts were also criminal cases.[19]

Table 2

Cases Involving Minors

Year	# of Cases	Type of Trafficking	State	Country of Origin	Sex of Victims in the Cases
2000	5	Labor (5)	NY (1) MI (2) CA (1) MD (1)	Cameroon (3) India (1) Mexico (1)	Male (1) Female (3) Female and Male (1)
2001	5	Labor (1) Sex (3) Labor and Sex (1)	CA (2) MD (1) NJ (1) AK (1)	Unknown (1) Nigeria (1) Ukraine (1) Russia (1) Thailand (1)	Female (4) Female and Male (1)
2002	5	Labor (2) Sex (2) Labor and Sex (1)	CA (3) NJ (1) TX (1)	India (1) Egypt (1) Mexico (2) Honduras (1)	Female (4) Female and Male (1)
2003	6	Labor (1) Sex (4) Labor and Sex (1)	GA (2) NY (1) FL (1) TX (2)	Mexico (4) Costa Rica (1) Ecuador (1)	Female (6)

Year	Count	Type	State	Origin	Sex
2004	11	Sex (7) Labor (3) Labor and Sex (1)	FL (7) VA (1) MD (1) NY (2)	Costa Rica (6) Indonesia (1) Haiti (1) Peru (1) Cameroon (1) Mexico (1)	Female (10) Female and Male (1)
2005	5	Labor (3) Sex (1) Labor and Sex (1)	TX (3) WA (1) NJ (1)	Morocco (1) Mexico (2) Honduras (1) Central America unspecified (1)	Female (5)
2006	7	Labor (1) Sex (6)	NY (1) NJ (1) FL (2) CA (1) WY (1) TN (1)	S. Korea (1) Cambodia (1) Mexico (3) Guatemala (1) Multiple Latin American (1)	Female (7)
2007	6	Labor (3) Sex (3)	KY (1) CA (1) TX (1) MD (1) SC (1) FL (1)	South Asia and Africa (1) Russia (1) Mexico (3) Haiti (1)	Female (5) Male (1)
2008	2	Sex (2)	Guam (1) NC (1)	Micronesian (1) Honduras and unknown (1)	Female (2)
2009	3	Sex (3)	CA (1) TX (1) AL (1)	Mexico (3)	Female (3)
2010	6	Labor (3) Sex (2) Labor and Sex (1)	DC (1) NY (1) TN (1) TX (1) GA (1) FL (1)	Sudan (1) India (1) Unknown (1) Honduras (1) Nigeria (1) Mexico (1)	Female (6)
2011	2	Labor (1) Sex (1)	AZ (1) TX (1)	Vietnam (1) Mexico (1)	Female (1) Female and Male (1)
2012	1	Sex (1)	Puerto Rico (1)	Puerto Rico (1)	Female (1)
Total	64				

SOURCE: Author's analysis of the Human Trafficking Law Project database.

Analysis of the Human Trafficking Law Project database reveals that sentences varied from 556 months (forty-six years) to no prison time. In the case of the United States v. Abdenasser Ennassime, the defendant would have been eligible for a sentence of three to four years under federal sentencing guidelines. At the victim's request, however, the government agreed to ask for home detention. The average sentence was thirty-six months. Although in several cases damages were assessed there is no evidence that victims actually received any restitution. In one case involving Indian diplomats a restitution of $1.5 million was assessed, but the diplomatic couple left the country and there is no way to collect the money. As this analysis shows, while there is room for improvement in investigating and prosecuting trafficking cases, the picture is not as grim as it seems if prosecution outcomes are assessed against the number of officially identified victims instead of against unreliable estimates.

Table 3

Trafficking Cases Involving Minors by Type of Court

Year	# of Cases	Civil Federal	Criminal Federal	Civil State	Criminal State
2000	5	1	3	0	1
2001	5	0	4	0	1
2002	5	1	4	0	0
2003	6	1	5	0	0
2004	11	0	11	0	0
2005	5	0	5	0	0
2006	7	0	7	0	0
2007	6	2	4	0	0
2008	2	0	2	0	0
2009	3	0	3	0	0
2010	6	2	4	0	0
2011	2	0	2	0	0
2012	1	0	1	0	0
Total	64	7	55	0	2

SOURCE: Author's analysis of the Human Trafficking Law Project database.

Protect the Victims

Much has been written about the dangers of requiring trafficked victims to testify against their traffickers. Advocates and researchers alike bemoan the fact that cooperation with law enforcement is a requirement for adult victims to receive federally funded services, including T-Visas.[20] Child welfare experts rejoice that the trafficking law does not stipulate the same for minors, but caution that zealous prosecutors might want to secure testimonies from children and youth. Indeed, two girls in my study—Melinda and Pilar—were approached by law enforcement to testify against their trafficker, Melinda's mother. The story of Melinda and Pilar, while rare, is a cautionary tale of how things can go wrong if undue pressure is put on a young woman to collaborate with law enforcement post-trafficking.

Melinda and Pilar are both from Honduras. Melinda's father was a farmer and worked hard to support his family. Unfortunately, his ability to provide for the family got cut short when he lost a leg to diabetes complications. Melinda's parents were never well off but now their poverty was even greater. Melinda said that she often went to bed hungry. In 2003, at fourteen years of age, Melinda was smuggled from Honduras, through Mexico to Texas and eventually ended up in New Jersey. While they did not accompany Melinda on her trek through Mexico, her mother, grandmother, and aunts facilitated the smuggling operation and were later convicted of trafficking Melinda and several other girls and young women. Melinda described the journey as the worst part of the entire ordeal and revealed that she was sexually assaulted by one of the male smugglers en route. Once at her final destination in New Jersey, Melinda was put to work as a dance hall girl in a bar catering to Latino men. She worked there until January 2005 when ICE raided the bar and rescued Melinda along with several other young girls.

It is unclear whether Melinda and Pilar knew each other before coming to the United States, but they both made initial preparations for their journey with the assistance of Melinda's mother, grandmother, and aunts. A couple of months after Melinda and Pilar were placed in a foster care program, ICE enforcement officials sent a letter to the program requesting that two ICE agents, an assistant U.S. attorney, and a U.S. Department of Labor agent be allowed to interview Melinda and Pilar to aid their investigation of the traffickers.

The program staff fought these summons on the grounds that TVPA stipulations do not require minors to collaborate with law enforcement or testify in a court of law, but to no avail.[21] In the end, Melinda and Pilar did testify in front of a grand jury against Melinda's relatives. The experience was devastating. After returning from court, Melinda said she was going to kill herself. A couple weeks later, she followed through with these suicidal ideations, and swallowed a mixture of pills "to take away the pain." Her suicide attempt failed. Pilar too threatened to take her own life. Both Melinda and Pilar were placed in a residential treatment home and, while they showed some signs of progress, continued to struggle with depression, low self-esteem, and guilt. Melinda said she felt responsible for her mother and grandmother's incarceration in Honduras. Whenever she talked on the phone with family members in Honduras, she needed the reassuring presence of her therapist. While they are no longer in a psychiatric hospital, they continue to struggle with depression to this day, especially Melinda.

Melinda and Pilar's plight is a paradigmatic example of why the U.S. Congress excused trafficked minors from participating in investigations and testimony against their will. This case is particularly egregious because Melinda was forced to testify against her own family. Her testimony was instrumental in the incarceration of her mother, grandmother, and aunts in Honduras. As Micah Bump writes: "This is not to undermine the importance of apprehending, prosecuting, and sentencing traffickers; to the contrary, such activity is essential to the antitrafficking effort, but it should not be carried out at the expense of a child's emotional and physical well-being."[22]

I agree that caution is warranted. Not every survivor of child trafficking is able to face his or her trafficker. On the other hand, the potential therapeutic value of testimony that can lead to incarceration of the trafficker should also be considered, especially when the survivor of trafficking is a resilient older adolescent. Of course, the final decision belongs to the trafficked victim. Unfortunately, few trafficked girls and boys were given an opportunity to make this kind of decision. Most programs working with the trafficked youth were convinced that talking about their trafficking experiences would retraumatize the girls, full stop. Some programs cited the danger of retraumatization as the main reason of not wanting their charges to participate in research. And yet they sent them to therapy to repeatedly recount their experiences.

Julia was aware that she did not have to testify against her abusers. Nonetheless, she was adamant that she wanted to confront her trafficker in a court of law because it was "important for her as a person" to make sure "that man never hurts anyone again." Julia's acute sense of justice and duty drove her to testify. She said that she took time to participate in my research and risked discussing experiences that were painful in hopes that it would help other trafficked girls.

Julia was not isolated in her desire to testify in order to bring about justice. When I visited some of the girls, now young women, several years after our initial meeting, a number of them remarked that they wished they could confront their abusers—they wanted to look them in the eye. The motivations to do that varied; retribution played a role in some instances, but in most cases the girls wanted to reconcile with the family members accused of trafficking them or simply put closure to the trafficking experiences and begin their new lives. Evelyn had a chance to travel to Cameroon to challenge her mother and uncle who sold her into domestic servitude. The trip was cathartic and helped alleviate Evelyn's depression.

John, a federal prosecutor whom I met on several occasions, often talks about the therapeutic benefits of a witness testimony. Neither he nor I advocate pressuring minors (or adults) to provide testimonies against their will—far from it. In workshops and at conferences, John reminds participants that victims need to be well prepared—emotionally and practically—to narrate their experiences in a manner that would convince the jury that the perpetrator is indeed guilty as charged. I like to remind victim advocates that instead of stubbornly refusing to entertain any ideas about collaboration with the prosecution, they ought to reflect on the ways we have been preparing refugees, asylum seekers, and torture survivors to tell their stories. Granted, these victims do not have to confront their abusers, but neither do trafficked minors. Courts have been working with minors in a variety of contexts and have devised creative ways—through videotaping, for example—to obtain their input without needing to put them face-to-face with their abusers. If we want to increase prosecutions because we believe that it is an important element in the 4Ps framework deployed to fight human trafficking, we need to be open to the notion that adolescents are often very resilient and capable of making a decision of their own about whether to testify or not. Testimonies can be powerful tools in healing the wounded, a topic explored in the next chapter.

Part IV

"Restored"

Assumptions about an ideal childhood—a protected and safe space, a time of innocence and unsullied existence—and the evil of child trafficking have resulted in a rescue and restore movement aimed at rebuilding trafficked children's lost childhoods and intended lives. Almost every major city in America has a Rescue and Restore program or campaign.

As of 2014, there were twenty-six antitrafficking coalitions.[1] There are many more programs serving survivors of child trafficking. Some of these programs are faith-based, others are secular. Whether they cater to six year olds or seventeen year olds, they call them children. Most child advocates are saddened and shocked to find out that "children" are working instead of going to school, that they live with aunts and uncles rather than with parents, and that they support younger siblings instead of being lovingly cared for by their parents.

The chapters in this section interrogate these Western ideals about universal childhood and the resulting trauma-based assistance model. As will be discussed in chapter 7, in the United States the system of care for survivors of child trafficking has been developed within a framework based on middle-class Western conceptualizations of childhood as a time of dependency and innocence during which children are socialized by adults and become competent social actors. Adults generally mediate economic and social responsibilities so that the children can grow up free from the pressure of responsibilities such as work and childcare. Children who are not raised in this way are considered "victims" who have had their childhood stolen from them.

This framework views universal concern for children as transcending political and social divides. It also assumes a universally applicable model of childhood development and presupposes a consensus on what policies should be in place to realize the best interests of the child. Furthermore, it promotes a therapeutic model of service provision and assumes that child victims have universal needs, such as a need for rehabilitation.

The service model is grounded in the discourse of trauma, pathology, and vulnerability. The prominence of the discourse of "trauma" as a major articulator of the trafficked children's suffering is based on the premise that human trafficking constitutes a mental health emergency and results in post-traumatic stress. The system of care for trafficked children is based on the principle of the "child's best interests." This principle often seems to contradict the right of the child to participate in determining his or her best interests. The principles of participation and best interests are often said to represent two different perspectives: a rights-based approach and a protectionist approach. Chapter 8 presents narratives of service providers deciding on the child's best interest rather than advocating for her wishes and feelings. These narratives are juxtaposed with trafficked children's accounts of their trafficking experiences and service needs. Together, chapters 7 and 8 demystify the notion of a singular idealized childhood and "one size fits all" service programs.

7

Idealized Childhoods

Definitions and understandings of childhood in the West assume that a child is someone under the age of eighteen and is vulnerable, dependent, and innocent.[1] Interestingly, Western public discourses and legal frameworks conveniently omit the fact that the 1989 UN Convention on the Rights of the Child defines children as persons under the age of eighteen unless the laws of their country of origin set the legal age for adulthood younger. The latter part of the definition is hardly ever brought up when dealing with trafficked or migrant youth that hail from countries where seventeen or sixteen, or even fifteen, year olds are considered adults. U.S. antitrafficking laws definitely do not account for these diverse conceptualizations—legal or cultural—of who is a child and when one becomes an adult. The TVPA considers all victims who were trafficked prior to turning eighteen years of age as children.

Philippe Aries, a French philosopher and historian, claims that the concepts of "child" and "childhood" are fairly recent inventions. The concept of childhood as a distinct state in human development did not exist until a few hundred years ago. Instead, he writes in his influential book *Centuries of Childhood* published in 1960, there were two preadult life stages: the baby toddler stage—devoid of the ability to speak and walk properly—and the proto-adult stage—when a person is treated as a small and incompetent adult.[2] Historians have taken issue with the limited sources Aries relied on and the inferences that he drew from these sources.[3] While they found proof that the concept of "childhood" existed in ancient Egypt, in Middle Kingdom China, and in medieval times,[4] most historians and social scientists accept that "the attitudes, sensibilities, and experiences that we now think of as immanent to childhood are an invention of the modern period."[5]

There is also agreement among scholars that the notion of childhood has evolved over time. Contemporary American society views children as innocent cherubs. However, for much of human history, children have been seen as anything but cherubic, claims David Lancy. In many societies, during long periods of history, children were considered unwanted, inconvenient changelings, or desired but commoditized chattel.[6] Moreover, in reality the concepts of "child" and "childhood" have varied according to social, cultural, historical, religious, and rational norms as well as according to one's personal circumstances. There are tremendous differences between four year olds and seventeen year olds. There are also often considerable differences between two seventeen year olds, particularly individuals coming from different cultural, social, and economic backgrounds. Gender differences need to be accounted for as well. I have seen these differences in my study. Belen took the responsibility for caring for her younger brother when she was very young. When she turned fourteen, the Mexican court judged Belen old enough to be recognized as the sole owner of the family home.

Several girls in my study were mothers. The consensus among the social workers was that their babies were a product of sexual abuse or rape; this conclusion was drawn merely on the basis of the age of the young mother. However, the age of consent for sexual activity in some of the countries they came from was much lower than in the United States. In Honduras the age of consent is set at fifteen, in Cameroon at sixteen, and in China at fourteen, to give just a few examples. Both Catalina and Analisa indicated that their pregnancies were the result of consensual sex. Both also stressed that in their communities most sixteen- or seventeen-year-old girls were viewed as old enough to engage in sexual activities and have children. Many caseworkers, however, viewed them as incapable of making decisions about sexual activity, motherhood, and migration. As a result of such views, many programs struggled with allowing the girls to exercise their agency and participate in the decision-making process regarding their future post-trafficking.

In this chapter, I discuss the evolution of the concept of childhood. For a long time, scholars and child advocates have seen childhood as the embodiment of weakness and marked the child as a "passive and unknowing defendant" without the ability to make independent decisions, especially decisions regarding work and migration.[7] I unpack the notion that children are better off living at home than being on the move and engage with the issue of working children and adolescents. I close this chapter with some remarks on the heterogeneity of childhoods that slowly gives way to novel understandings of childhoods, children, and youth.

Lost Childhood and the Beginning of the Child Rescue Movement

The historical antecedents of the modern conceptualizations of childhood are rooted in the British child-rescue movement dating back to the second part of the nineteenth century. The origins of the child rescue movement can be found in the evangelical outreach to inner cities and the establishments of a wide range of institutions—the Ragged Schools Union (1844), Dr. Bernardo's Homes (1868), Wesleyan National Children's Homes (1869), the Anglican Waifs and Strays Society (1881), and the National Society for the Prevention of Cruelty to Children (1889)—aimed at rescuing children from "the 'modern Babylon' where children are forced into crime to survive; overcrowding, which forced children to 'perambulate the streets;' 'perpetuating and intensifying the evil' of child neglect; child vagrancy resulted from 'vicious and criminal parents' bringing up children 'ignorant of everything but evil'; premature wage earning; juvenile street trading, where children looking for freedom opted to work on the 'soul-destroying streets' unaware of the moral dangers involved."[8]

Romantic notions of childhood as a time of innocence and dependence were central to the nineteenth-century child rescue movement. Not unlike contemporary stories about trafficked children, the nineteenth-century accounts presented the neglected inner city children as "innocent, pure, helpless, and unprotected," who had "never tasted joys of childhood," were "defrauded" or "robbed" of the joys of real childhood.[9] Needless to say, these emotive images of "childhood lost" were highly effective in bringing supporters and resources to the cause the same way that contemporary media portrayals of trafficked children result in public outrage and financial support for the rescue industry. Similarly to contemporary abolitionists, the charismatic leaders of the nineteenth-century child rescue industry were able to attract many writers, artists, and poets who incorporated child rescue themes into their work.[10] In the twenty-first century, popular TV networks and actors have also joined the antitrafficking fight. On August 13, 2014, the USA network announced that the hit drama series *Graceland* and *Law and Order: Special Victims Unit* would be joining forces to help raise awareness of and stop human trafficking, especially trafficking of innocent children. They kicked off this effort with a ten-hour "End Human Trafficking" marathon, hosted by Graceland cast members Daniel Sunjata and Serinda Swan. The actress Mira Sorvino, who appeared in the movies *Human Trafficking* and *Trade of Innocents*, was appointed by the United Nations as a "goodwill ambassador" to combat human trafficking in 2009. She draws big crowds whenever she speaks about child trafficking.

Lydia Murdoch argues that the nineteenth-century philanthropic narratives served to demonize poor parents who were accused of not providing for their children's well-being, abandoning them, and selling them to strangers.[11]

There was never any critique of the society that allowed poverty to flourish: "Parental failure, rather than poverty or social inequality, was identified as the key enemy of childhood."[12] This is eerily reminiscent of the current discourse about parents and family members accused of trafficking their own children. Child advocates talk about abuse and neglect the trafficked children and youth experienced at the hands of their families. The girls talk about having warm and loving relationships with their moms and grandmothers. Scholars suggest that child trafficking is maintained by the silence of community members that look the other way when a young girl goes missing from a village.[13] The new abolitionists also condemn parents; few focus on the role of governments unable or unwilling to support poor families or insufficient international support for development projects. At best, parents are characterized as being duped and tricked by traffickers with promises of education, employment, and better livelihoods.[14] Organized crime is blamed for recruiting underage migrants without any discussion of why such crime is allowed to flourish.[15] Only the very brave are willing to write about the role the U.S. government played in creating the conditions that prompted the recent unprecedented exodus of Central American children and youth.[16] The dangers experienced at the hands of state actors who hold migrant children in detention centers for days or weeks[17] and treat them as criminals violating immigration laws, not as young labor migrants or trafficked children, are absent in public discourses. Analisa had spent quite some time in a detention center before her pro bono attorney identified her as a victim of child trafficking. Analisa considered herself lucky because she had legal representation and did not linger in detention as long as those children and teens unfortunate enough to lack legal representation.

The nineteenth century had also witnessed the export of these white middle-class Western notions about childhood to the rest of the world. Known as the "global model of childhood," this concept defined children as biologically and psychologically distinct from adults.[18] The appeal of this allegedly "universal model" of childhood is rooted in the idea that children possess qualities that are inferior to those of adults, largely due to biological and cognitive stages of development.[19] However, the global model of childhood is neither universal nor does it reflect the experiences of the majority of children and youth, especially in poor communities—whether in developing or developed countries. Empirical social science research provides ample proof of this assertion.[20] Yet the model still prevails, particularly in the antitrafficking discourse.

As will be seen in the next chapter, the childhoods imagined by the social workers assisting trafficked minors differed drastically from the lived experiences of the youth. The girls and boys in my study did not always share their lives with their biological parents, were expected to contribute to family livelihoods, and many did not go to school. Several of the girls became teen mothers. They had much greater economic and social responsibilities than the Western conceptualization of childhood ever envisioned and thus the Western framework may not be the most appropriate for the trafficked adolescents on the brink of legal adulthood.

Home versus the Dangerous World

The visions of "innocent" and "healthy childhoods" pair with essential perceptions of "home" as a safe haven and call for curbing the migration of children, because they are better off staying "at home." [21] Children who do not have a home and a family, or do not spend most of their time at home or in school, have often been considered deviant and "out of place." Catherine Panter-Brick's research on street children illustrates this point well: "the characteristics of street children—their tenuous links with families and independent activity—are the hallmark of a childhood distinct from the 'proper' childhood experienced by the urban middle-class."[22] As Brenda Oude Breuil suggests: "The legal definition of child trafficking . . . follows . . . these hegemonic ideas on children and their 'proper' place in the social order. Its normative character may make it useful as a legal document, but renders it less fit for analyzing and understanding child trafficking."[23]

As noted above, the living arrangements in the countries of origin of many of the trafficked minors I studied did not conform to middle-class Western ideals, where children live in nuclear families, experience childhood together with their siblings, and have access to resources provided by both biological parents.[24] Many of the trafficked minors I studied had never lived with both of their biological parents. Some lived with a single mom, many were raised by their grandparents, but others stayed with more distant relatives. Analisa's mom took her to be raised by her grandma when Analisa was six months old. She never saw her mother. Several of the girls I interviewed talked about unrelated children that lived in the households where they resided. Evelyn said that her mother has always had a couple of unrelated children living in the house. According to Evelyn, many families took in children to help out less fortunate relatives and friends.

Child fostering or child circulation is a long-standing cultural practice in many regions of the world, including the Latin American and African countries where the youngsters of my study were born.[25] As the anthropologist Jessaca Leinaweaver discovered, child circulation is the principal way in which Peruvian rural-to-urban migrants move children between houses as part of a common survival and betterment strategy in the context of social and economic inequality. Poverty and vulnerability shape Peruvian practices of kinship formation through child circulation. For the receiving family, child circulation represents strategic labor recruitment; for the sending household, it spells relief from the economic burdens of child rearing and constitutes a source of highly desirable remittances.[26]

Research shows that a considerable proportion of children in Mexico and Colombia were found to spend some time during childhood without a father. When births outside a union were included, one-fifth of Mexican and one-third of Colombian children were affected. An additional 5 percent of Mexican children and 9 percent of Colombian children did not live with their mothers.[27] This research focused on nonmigrant families. However, when migrant families are considered, rates of family separation are much higher. Carola Suarez-Orozco and colleagues studied 385 immigrant families and found that 85 percent of children in these families had experienced separation from immediate family members. Among Mexican immigrants, 42 percent of children were separated from their father only, 40 percent from both parents, and 2 percent were separated from their mother only. The study also found that 28 percent had been separated from siblings.[28] This does not mean that Mexican families do not try to maintain family unity,[29] but it does mean that children either live apart from their parents for prolonged periods of time or undertake risky journeys to *el Norte* to reunite with migrant parents living in the United States. Twin sisters Flora and Isa were separated from their mom for several years. The girls and the mother missed each other very much. The heartache they experienced prompted the mother to arrange for a *coyote* to bring the teens to the United States. She was trying to live up to the ideal of a good mother but instead was arrested for trafficking her daughters.

In the nineteenth and early twentieth centuries, children without a "proper" home were often stigmatized.[30] The anthropologists Nancy Scheper-Hughes and Daniel Hoffman show that in contemporary times street children are also subjected to processes of "othering" and stigmatization.[31] Trafficked children are treated with a lot more compassion. As Brenda Breuil asserts, "they are mainly considered 'in danger' and looked upon as victims."[32] They are often perceived as being forcefully torn away from their imagined safe homes. Finding them in environments envisaged as vile, dangerous, and exploitative— serving drinks to boozy men in cantinas and bars, scrubbing floors and changing dirty diapers under the watchful eye of evil traffickers, dancing in nightclubs, and selling sex—produces public outrage not just because we care about children, but because these scenarios invade our own social order.[33]

The powerful ideologies that placed childhoods in fixed and bounded spaces are contested by the realities of the lives of children on the move.[34] Most of the girls and boys I studied were affected by migration, either their own or that of their family members. Some of the girls migrated from rural areas to nearby towns before attempting to migrate across international borders. Others felt emboldened to embark on a migration journey because they wanted to be reunited with their mother (Flora and Isa), join an aunt (Lian), find better educational opportunities with a stepsister (Analisa), or get assistance finding a job from an uncle (Belen). Although girls like Lin or Belen made the decision to migrate on their own—by the time she was planning to join her uncle in Pennsylvania, Belen's father was deceased and her mother nowhere to be found—they were told by the U.S. law enforcement and child advocates that they were not capable of making independent decisions. After all, they were underage and in the eyes of the U.S. law did not have volition.

Agency: Deciding to Migrate and Work

Children are not imagined as being able to make independent, informed choices regarding decisions to engage in labor migration. Trafficked children are hardly ever seen as child migrants in search of better livelihoods or protection from violence, but rather as object-like, removed, transported, and put to use.[35] These notions persist despite growing empirical proof and enhanced theoretical understanding for the emerging, developing, and extending agency of children.[36] Child advocates—World Vision, Save the Children, UNICEF, and End Child Prostitution and Trafficking, among others—consider trafficked children to be destined for ruthless exploitation, and whether this takes place in the sex industry or another context, the consequences are always horrifying.[37] As Julia O'Connell Davidson observes: "'Trafficked' children win their place at the high table of child suffering, deserving of special and particular care and protection, because they are non-agential—they are 'unwilling or unknowing victims,' vacant, inert, innocent, entirely lacking in will or agency."[38]

Acknowledging that minors—especially older teens—possess agency does not take away from the suffering they experience at the hands of traffickers. However, depriving them of the recognition that they are rational human beings capable of making independent decisions perpetuates the myth that child development is solely based in biological and psychological structures that are fairly uniform across history, class, and culture. In contrast to the notion of the universal model of childhood, anthropological research shows that childhood and youth are social and cultural rather than biological constructs.[39]

Children and adolescents are people, and therefore they do have agency. Agency is an intentional action that encompasses both intended and unintended consequences, according to Anthony Giddens.[40] Trafficking was certainly an unintended consequence of the girls' decision to migrate in search of work. Had they known that they would be maltreated, insufficiently compensated, and isolated from the outside world, they most likely would not have agreed to leave even the most poverty-ridden native village. Without a crystal ball to show them the future, they made the best decisions they could under the circumstances. They owned these decisions even when they desperately wanted to leave the trafficking situation.

While many anthropologists theorizing agency[41] have a very celebratory view of the concept, Julia Meredith Hess and Dianna Shandy suggest that at the juncture of migrant children and the state, this view is more constricted.[42] The same can be said about trafficked children. The politics of compassion governing the lives of trafficked (and other unaccompanied) children tempered the agency of the trafficked girls and boys in my study. The decisions law enforcement and service providers were making were glossed over as "being in the best interest" of the youth.[43] Perhaps it was in the best interest to classify the trafficked girls and boys as "victims" in order to provide them with the legal assistance and social services they needed to stay in the United States. However, stripping them of decision-making abilities did not serve the youth well. How were they to make decisions about their future if they were not recognized as human beings with volition?

Nowhere are Western views on childhood more at odds with the reality experienced by the trafficked minors than on the issue of work. As Olga Nieuwenhuys observes, "the dissociation of childhood from the performance of valued work is considered a yardstick of modernity, and a high incidence of child labor is considered a sign of underdevelopment."[44] The fact that the girls and boys migrated to find work did not correspond with the service providers' ideals of childhood; they conceptualized the girls' and boys' work solely as forced labor and exploitation even when the young people insisted that they wanted to work and did not feel exploited by their own parents or relatives.

Exploitation, a politically contested concept, also varies across history and culture.[45] The International Labor Organization no longer considers all forms of child labor exploitation. It differentiates between children engaged in agricultural or domestic work, especially if they have reached the minimum working age, and hazardous or worst forms of child labor. I find it extraordinary that we encourage our own teens to seek employment—sometimes in the form of unpaid internships, but often in the form of waged employment—in order to gain experience and to learn time and money management, but deny children from outside our own society the same. In practice, migrant children's labor is commonly presented as "child trafficking."[46] The programs aimed at integrating the "rescued" girls and boys into American society shied away from discussing employment options and preferred to focus on formal schooling. The emphasis on education, on attending school regularly and getting good grades, corresponded well with the social workers' ideals about childhood. It is often said that the best course of action for children and youth is to remove them from the harsh reality of trafficking and "rehabilitate" them into their "traditional" roles.[47] I will return to this issue in chapter 8. Now, I want to briefly examine the changing landscape of "childhood studies" in the hope that the emerging paradigm shift will affect the ways we study and deal with trafficked minors.

Shifting the Paradigm

As Myra Bluebond-Langner and Jill Korbin observe, there has been a resurgence of interest in the study of children.[48] Scholars began to reexamine many commonly held ideas about children and "proper" childhoods in the 1990s.[49] New frameworks of "childhood studies" or the "anthropology of childhoods" grounded in empirical research started to conceptualize children as at once developing beings, in possession of agency, and to varying degrees vulnerable. It has been a hallmark of anthropological work to recognize that these attributes manifest themselves in different times and places, and under particular social, political, economic, and moral circumstances and conditions. Holistic approaches to the study of children in various sociocultural contexts acknowledge that childhood integrates both biological and social processes. Although biology shapes children's lives, especially in early childhood, the familial and cultural circumstances that affect their daily lives are eminently social.[50] Abject poverty, broken families, cultural expectations that adolescents earn their keep by contributing wages to the family livelihood, and motherhood shaped the lives of the girls and boys in my study much more than their chronological age.

Recent childhood studies scholarship is also providing novel theoretical tools for thinking about children's agency as spatially, temporally, and materially complex. Writing about child soldiers in different places and at different historical times—Sierra Leone, Palestine, and Eastern Europe during the Holocaust—David Rosen emphasizes that children are not always passive victims, but often make the rational decision that not fighting is worse than fighting: "child soldiers are rational human actors who have a surprisingly mature understanding of their predicament."[51] The children that Rosen writes about were in many instances younger than the girls and boys in my study. Michael Wyness writes: "As with other child-related issues, the problem with our understanding of child soldiers lies in the absence of accounts from the child soldiers themselves."[52] Indeed, the same is true about trafficked children and youth. With the exception of Jean-Robert Cadet,[53] who wrote about his experiences as a *restavec* (a child domestic servant) in Haiti, there are no other first-person accounts from trafficked children. This paucity of trafficked children's voices is what motivates Evelyn to speak publicly about her life as a trafficked child. The dearth of narratives by trafficked youth describing their experiences—not just in trafficking, but their lives prior to crossing international borders—does not inform the social work practice well. Social workers are supposed to "start where the client is," but often they do not really know the realities from where their young charges come. Law enforcement and attorneys rarely share the stories they elicited from the trafficked youth. When they do, these stories are supposed to pull at the heartstrings of immigration judges, federal officials, and the general public. They are rarely collected to help case managers devise a service plan for the trafficked youth in their care. Without understanding the full story, service providers rely on textbook norms.

Although the field of childhood studies is moving in new and exciting directions, policies and programs based on normative ideas of a good childhood and the best interest of the child still dominate the child trafficking field. This reliance on normative concepts runs the risk of being unproductive for children whose reality does not correspond with the image of childhood as "a time to grow, learn, play and feel safe" with access to "essential services such as hospitals and schools" and protection of family and community.[54] "As a society," observes Kate Price of Putting Children First, "we often seem to care more about protecting our cultural ideal of childhood innocence than about meeting the actual needs of real-life children."[55]

In the next chapter, I explore further the differences between the trafficked girls' and boys' accounts of their experiences and the service providers understanding of child trafficking. I discuss the tensions between the normative ideas of "the best interest of the child" and the needs and wants expressed by the trafficked minors.

8

Healing the Wounded

In the Northern Hemisphere, migration of young people under the age of eighteen is often conceptualized—both through interventions and research—within legal and child protection categories such as "child trafficking," "unaccompanied minors," and "child exploitation."[1] These frameworks are based on the principle of the "best interest of the child" but frequently fail to understand the mix of vulnerability and resiliency of young migrants in its full complexity. This, in turn, ends up further exacerbating their vulnerability. The protectionist narratives of child advocates and service providers stand in sharp contrast with the narratives of the youth that emphasize their own agency and resiliency.

Let me turn back to the twin sisters Flora and Isa, introduced earlier in this book. Flora and Isa never thought they were trafficked. They came to the United States to join their mother, who managed a bar owned by one of her brothers. The girls ended up working in the bar as well. On a tip from a local resident, Immigration and Customs Enforcement agents raided the bar and Flora and Isa, along with several other girls, were "rescued" and referred to a foster care program to begin a process of restoration and rehabilitation. Prosecutors said that the young women were subjected to long and dangerous smuggling routes and that at least one was raped during the journey. Some of the defendants and their attorneys disputed the forced labor allegations, saying it was more a situation of poor people helping poor relatives affected by a hurricane. "If it was a family business," Assistant U.S. Attorney Richard Roper said, "it was a hell of a way to treat your family; smuggling them through dangerous routes, misrepresenting to them what they were going to do here."

Shortly after the raid, Special Agent George Ramirez, formerly with the Immigration and Naturalization Service, testified in court that the smuggling ring, called the Molina Organization, forced some of the young women into prostitution to pay off smuggling fees. The young ladies, however, did not corroborate this view, saying, "Wearing a low-cut dress does not a sex slave make." Prosecutors and defense attorneys offered sharply differing opinions about accusations of forced labor and prostitution. According to defense attorney Mick Mickelsen, who represented the accused family members, "There were fifty-two girls interviewed, and there was only one that said anything about prostitution." Flora and Isa consistently emphasized that they were not pressured to provide sexual services to any of the bar clients or, for that matter, to any of the men that smuggled them from Honduras through Guatemala and Mexico to Texas. In the end, the twenty-four-count indictment returned on September 10, 2002, did not mention any prostitution allegations. Assistant U.S. Attorney Roper said that the allegations were dropped because the victims did not want to testify. Without their cooperation, he said, the allegations would have been impossible to prove to a jury. Eighty-eight people, including Flora and Isa's mother, were detained, mostly on immigration violations.

Flora did not want to be placed in foster care; she wished to return to Honduras. Her pro bono attorney counseled Flora that it was not in her best interest to return home. Some of the relatives involved in her trafficking were deported to Honduras and might try to traffic her again. Flora did not think her uncles posed a threat, but did concede that it might be best to stay in the United States. She was mainly afraid of the poverty she would face if she returned to Honduras.

Flora also decided to stay because she wished to visit her mother, who was in a California jail on charges of smuggling underage girls. It is unclear from Flora's narrative why her mom was in prison in California and not in Texas. Again, Flora was counseled against visiting her incarcerated mother. Flora's caseworker told her that it was not in her best interest to see her "abuser." Despite the advice, Flora kept in touch with her mom through letters and phone calls. Persistence paid off and in the end she and Isa, accompanied by their caseworker, did travel to California. A note in Flora's file described the trip as very successful: "The trip went well. The girls' mother was supportive, encouraging, and very appropriate with her daughters during the visit. She encouraged her daughters to work hard in school and put Christ first in their lives." The caseworker was able to talk to the mother and upon hearing more of her story she determined that, despite the mother's involvement in her daughters' trafficking, "contact with the mother was not detrimental to the girls' safety."

While in foster care, Flora's "best interests" were determined mainly by her middle-class, non-Spanish-speaking foster mother who thought that an obedient child should stay home and study, not go out with friends or watch TV. Flora's caseworker sided with the foster mother. However, the foster mother's dissonant views on the "proper behavior" of a seventeen-year-old young woman led to even more rebellion on Flora's part. Flora thought she should have fun. She wanted to have a boyfriend and she started dating a young Latino man. When she became pregnant, she left her foster family to live with the baby's father and moved into a group home after they broke up. Whether the pregnancy was a conscious choice to have a baby or a result of unprotected sex is unclear. What was obvious was Flora's dedication to her son. As her situation changed—from being in the care of a foster mother to being responsible for herself and her baby in a group home—the social worker's assessment of Flora changed as well. The caseworker noted: "Flora is a very outgoing and confident young woman. Very strong-willed and determined. Though these traits created difficulties when she was in foster care, she now is applying them to planning for the future and is showing much more understanding of living independently and using the responsibilities she has." It seemed that the social worker had a complete change of heart, from denying Flora's ability to make her own decisions by supporting the foster mother's rules to advocating for Flora's rights to determine her own best interests and the interests of Alejandro, her infant son. Flora welcomed this change in attitude, but could not articulate the reason for this transformation. The social worker put it simply: "I was wrong. I should have listened more carefully to Flora."

Best Interests and the Rights of the Child: A Necessary Tension?

The "best interest" standard is a widely used ethical, legal, and social basis for policy and decision making involving children.[2] The origins of the "child's best interests" principle date back to the late nineteenth century when the European public became aware of the plight of exploited, abused, and neglected children through popular novels such as those penned by Charles Dickens. In addition, influential lobbies—composed of members of the women's movement, the new specialty of pediatrics, and the nurses' home health programs—began to form at the turn of the twentieth century to seek protection of children from neglect, cruelty, and exploitation by setting legally enforceable thresholds of acceptable parenting.[3] In 1989, the principle became part of the Convention on the Rights of the Child. In the intervening years the notion of "best interest" has come under attack as self-defeating, individualistic, unknowable, vague, dangerous, and open to abuse.[4] Attempts have also been made to defend the principle as a threshold for intervention and judgment, an ideal to establish policies regarding prima facie duties, and as a standard of reasonableness.[5]

Despite criticisms, the best interest principle remains the dominant legal standard in actions concerning children, including migrant and trafficked children. Attorneys, social workers, and therapists working with trafficked youth frequently and fervently invoke the concept. However, because the concept is broad and rarely defined, it is open to idiosyncratic interpretations.[6] Flora's caseworker, for example, has changed her opinions about what was in Flora's best interest several times, eventually realizing that Flora's independent decision making was in the girl's best interest. These subjective assessments can result in an inconsistency in service provision, and may hamper postmigration transition efforts. Moreover, the best interest principle sometimes seems to contradict the right of the minor to participate in determining what is best for her. The question, thus, remains: Who determines the best interests of the trafficked minor, and how? How does the determination of the child's best interests correspond with the child's right to express her wishes? There is consensus in the literature that Western policymakers and caretakers tend to prioritize the children's perceived best interests over the children's right to express their wishes and feelings.[7] In the course of this research, I have seen many examples of service providers deciding the child's best interest rather than advocating for her wishes and respecting her feelings.

Victimhood and Vulnerability

The criteria used by foster parents and service providers for determining a child's best interests were based on a culture-specific understanding of children as "nurtured" by their caretakers. As indicated earlier, the TVPA does not distinguish between four and seventeen year olds. It does, however, make a clear distinction—ideological, strategic, and operational—between children and adults. Taking issue with this dichotomy, Jyoti Sanghera explains: "This distinction is based on the principle that the development of children as human beings is a process and is not complete as long as they are minors. Children are deemed 'innocent' and in need of special protection and assistance in making decisions. It is believed that minors cannot be expected to act in their own best interest as their ability to exercise full agency is not yet entirely developed."[8] These attitudes produce the system that ignores the voice of the minor, the system in which "all persons under the age of eighteen constitute a homogenous category—children, devoid equally of sexual identity and sexual activity, bereft equally of the ability to exercise agency and hence in need of identical protective measures."[9]

My research team and I did not question the legal framework, which classifies children as trafficked whether they were forced or coerced into following their traffickers or willingly accompanied their parents and relatives. We accepted the young people's assertion that they wanted to come to the United States while recognizing that, at the time of making the decision to migrate, they might have had no idea about the abuse and exploitation they would face once they crossed the border, and consequently might not have agreed to come to the United States had they known. The bigger challenge was related to where "to draw a line between coercion and consent for young people under the age of 18 and how best to promote their rights and agency while still protecting them."[10] The dilemma was whether to treat them as vulnerable victims—the way U.S. law does, stipulating who is a victim and thus who is eligible for services—or as young people with a great deal of resiliency to overcome the adverse circumstances and hardships, or both. Identifying vulnerabilities is important in order to facilitate access to appropriate services. However, a focus on vulnerability and victimhood without recognition that many of these minors were survivors with a great deal of resiliency is detrimental to recovery, as it creates unnecessary dependency on support programs.

Understanding youth's perception of the trafficking experiences as victimization and their identity as victims plays an important role in post-trafficking adjustment, according to social workers and clinicians working with the young people. However, this understanding is widely contested, especially by social and behavioral scientists wanting to understand subjects—adults and minors—as agentive, sensuous, and intentional.[11] Given the programmatic importance of these frameworks, let me unpack and contextualize them both within the theoretical frameworks and the narratives put forth by the youth and the service providers in this study.

We have seen a surge in victim-oriented politics in the last few decades.[12] Theorists such as Diana Meyers identify at least two kinds of victims: heroic and hapless.[13] The first category encompasses "martyrs and heroes, who, through their own agency, choice, or strength, are made into victims in the service of a greater good." Descriptions of these hero victims can be found in both revolutionary and religious discourses.[14] Evelyn, whom we met in the prologue, has embraced her own suffering to become an advocate. She often shares very painful memories, publicly hoping that her story will serve a greater good and will highlight the plight of children in domestic servitude. The victims of the second category are often seen as passively suffering bodies, and this view is especially prevalent in discourses of humanitarianism, forced migration studies, and discussions of trafficking of women and children for sexual exploitation. "Humanitarian victimhood is produced as a host of different agents, such as donors of international aid, clinicians,[15] and social movements and NGOs, and deploy the victim as a way to forge solidarities and relatedness across different social and geographical spaces."[16] The martyr is often perceived as a much more agentive victim, who takes it upon herself to become a victim, than the hapless victim of humanitarian disaster or the victim of human rights violations.

It is noteworthy that victim status gives priority of concern to certain sufferers over others, argues James Bayley.[17] The youth identified as victims of child trafficking by the federal government were indeed given a special status. Equipped with "letters of eligibility" from the Office of Refugee Resettlement, they could now access immigration relief—apply for T-Visas—and other forms of assistance, including education, health care, social services, and counseling. At the same time, Central American minors fleeing violence and poverty in Honduras, Guatemala, and El Salvador and arriving in the United States in large numbers as I write this book are considered to be undocumented migrants and put in detention centers.[18] It remains to be seen if any of them will be identified as trafficked minors. Trafficked children are conceptualized as wronged by others, duped by smugglers and traffickers, while unaccompanied children are thought of as criminals breaking the law. Looking at the demographics of these two groups of minors, the only difference is gender. The majority of the minors trafficked to the United States are girls, while the majority of the unaccompanied minors are boys.

By judging some sufferers as victims we risk the paternalistic devaluation of these individuals by transforming self-managing and agentive actors into dependent and hapless people.[19] As indicated above, the girls and boys in this study did not identify as victims. Admittedly, they may not have been living in the most idyllic conditions, but many did not see themselves as abused or taken advantage of. It is worth remembering that faced with poverty and lack of opportunities to improve their livelihoods the youngsters were not very happy back at home either. In imagining childhoods spent in tropical climates among extended family members, some service providers thought otherwise. The girls did speak about the natural beauty of their native lands, but in the same conversations often narrated the abject poverty that left them going to bed hungry and unable to feed their babies. Living in multigenerational families provided emotional comfort, but often meant that there were many more mouths to feed. While child advocates vilified parents who sent or brought their children and teens to the United States, the youngsters saw their experiences as labor migration undertaken voluntarily and their parents as helpers, not villains.

The girls' and boys' lack of identity as victims was closely related to their expectations about coming to the United States. Almost all of the youth were highly motivated to migrate to the United States in the hope of earning money, as many had compelling reasons to send remittances, such as sick parents and younger siblings or their own babies to support. They did not equate labor migration with victimhood. Save the Children suggests that the analysis of children's mobility—both within their countries of origin and across international borders—as a form of trafficking has downplayed the reasons why and how minors migrate and conceptualized the young migrants as devoid of agency.[20] Daniela Reale does not negate the existence of vulnerability, especially among unaccompanied children, but calls for a more nuanced understanding of the multidimensional movement of children that can have both positive and negative outcomes. These analyses are parts in the newly developing paradigm for understanding child migration, one that rights the balance between a victimized view and an appreciation of the agency of children and youth.

Typically, the youngsters' desire to earn money did not change once they were rescued. Several of the Peruvian boys wanted to stay with the same employer, but hoped that service providers would be able to ensure that the boss paid them what he promised, gave them cigarette and lunch breaks regularly, and treated them with respect. When Angela stripped in a bar in New Jersey, she earned good money—about $400 or $500 a night. She paid her *coyote* half of the $15,000 she owed him for bringing her from Honduras to New Jersey and was still able to send money home to her family. The million Honduran lempira, approximately $48,000, she sent to her grandparents allowed them to build a nice house. When *la migra* (immigration) "rescued" Angela, she had a few thousand dollars in savings, but the money was confiscated. Angela was very angry that the money was gone. "It would have come in handy," she said, "especially now that I am pregnant." She couldn't understand why she was being punished when she had earned the money fair and square. Frankly, neither could I. Yes, the money was earned performing a job that perhaps law enforcement does not approve of for a seventeen year old, but it was still Angela's money. Moreover, the antitrafficking law provides for restitution to victims of trafficking, but few survivors receive what is rightly theirs. Angela didn't, either. She did not think her financial interests were taken into consideration at all by law enforcement that claimed to be helping her.

The desire to get a job and make money conflicted with the programs' focus on formal schooling. Following U.S. laws requiring minors to attend school, the programs assisting trafficked youth focused more on education and less on employment. Social workers cited regulations defining the age of employment, the number of hours minors are allowed to work, and rules about work permits whenever the youth asked for assistance with finding work. These restrictions ran counter to the goals of many of the youth and resulted in adjustment challenges; they affected the girls' commitment to education and their desire to remain in care. Cecilia, for example, told her caseworker she didn't want to go to school: "I need money! How am I going to support myself?" After much persuading, Cecilia stayed in school, but kept on asking whether she could leave high school and enroll in a vocational program that would give her tangible skills. "What am I going to do with all this reading and writing?," she kept on asking. "I need to be able to do something concrete to get a job." In her junior year, when her academic adviser mentioned college, Cecilia again rejected the idea. She told me: "How many years do they think I have to wait to get a good job?" Without access to decent jobs, and indeed requirements that restricted their ability to find work, the youth did not see the assistance as helpful.

Flora and Isa did not vilify their mother. They felt she had done nothing wrong and did not understand why she had been arrested. Many other girls whose parents arranged their travel to the United States thought the parents were facilitating access to education or employment, not committing a human rights violation. When considering their immigration to and employment in the United States, the youth argued that mothers and fathers would have equally helped their offspring find paid employment back at home. Matilde suggested that if there was work in Guatemala—in the village or in the nearby town—her mom would have assisted her in finding a job, but since work was scarce and poorly paid, her mom arranged for Matilde to come to the United States. "This is what good parents do," she said. "They help their children."

The children's perception of their relatives as facilitators of a better life in the United States and the resulting conceptualization of their trafficking experiences as "work" interfered with gathering information by the prosecution. The youths were reluctant to provide law enforcement with details about their journey to the United States and to identify their relatives as perpetrators of crimes. Some children who clearly understood that their parents wronged them were nevertheless ready to forgive and reconcile with their families. Evelyn's trip to Cameroon is a particularly powerful example of her need to reconcile with her mom.

The girls' reluctance to adopt the label "victim" stood in sharp contrast with the service providers' perceptions. Similarly to law enforcement, many social workers saw the girls and boys in their care as victims because the antitrafficking law treated them as victims. They also saw the girls as extremely vulnerable. Similarly to the "best interest principle," "vulnerability" is a "broad and often contested term," but is commonly used to mean "being exposed to the possibility of being harmed, either physically or emotionally. Within the trafficking discourse it is a term that is inherently gendered and linked not only to civil-political and socio-economic constraints but also with dominant perceptions of child trafficking 'victims' being mainly for sexual exploitation and female."[21] While the girls in this study experienced many forms of trafficking—including labor exploitation and domestic servitude—the sexual trafficking story, so popular in the media, often overshadowed the true narratives of young migrants and trafficking victims in the eyes of social workers, therapists, and mental health counselors.[22] With relatively few boys being identified as survivors of trafficking, the "victim" was more often than not portrayed as an extremely vulnerable and sexually exploited girl. Service providers regularly dismissed these girls' stories of their experiences in favor of the imagined story of trafficking.

Service providers tended to focus on the traumatic experiences, especially when they suspected or imagined that sexual exploitation was involved. Some therapists were convinced that exposure to the brutality of child trafficking would render the youth traumatized for life and that many survivors would need skilled care to help them cope with these traumatic experiences.[23] Girls who cooperated with the perpetrators or enjoyed aspects of their experiences (such as clothes, freedom, boyfriends, drugs or alcohol) may have been, in the words of the social workers, "more susceptible to trauma," but also more resistant to therapy. Thus, their self-identity, understanding of their situation, and subsequent goals—to get on with life, get a job, and integrate into American society—often conflicted with the goals of service providers who wanted their young charges to attend counseling, go to school, and not venture outside the safety of the foster home.

Trauma and Treatment

The contrast between the programs' perceptions of the youth's best interests and the girls' own personal wishes was strongest surrounding the psychological consequences of trafficking and culturally appropriate responses. Most programs used the Western concept of "trauma" both as the basis to imagine the trafficked children's experiences and to promote a therapeutic model of rehabilitation services despite the fact that a relatively small number of girls met the criteria of post-traumatic stress disorder. Some girls presented no psychological disturbance, while others exhibited symptoms of depression. Indeed, depression was the most common diagnosis noted in case files.[24] To mitigate the psychological consequences of trafficking, the girls were offered a wide range of mental health services: individual or group therapy, counseling by a torture treatment specialist, and art therapy.

Initially, the majority of the youth refused to avail themselves of psychological services, but program staff was persistent. Caseworkers tried many different tactics to convince the girls about the efficacy of mental health counseling. Angela, for example, was told that if she did not go to counseling and did not take her medication—she was prescribed Zoloft, an antidepressant—she would be separated from her baby son. This threat did not have the desired consequences. Instead of complying, Angela became hostile and was seen by the staff of the group house where she lived as verbally aggressive. What the staff perceived as aggression, Angela described as frustration. She compared the group house to a prison and the manager to a prison warden. She commented she was not used to asking permission for everything and keeping to a schedule. She also felt isolated and frightened as a result of being separated from the other four girls she was with when immigration raided the bar where they worked. Immigration and Customs Enforcement told the girls they had to cooperate with law enforcement or be deported. Angela and her friends were unsure as to what was going to happen to them. Communication barriers exacerbated Angela's frustration. She was told that the program staff was bilingual but when she arrived at the group house nobody spoke Spanish. Although Angela did not think she spoke English well and preferred to be interviewed in Spanish, her spoken English was actually quite good when we interviewed her. When left alone with a monolingual English-speaking researcher, she was able to communicate complicated and emotionally laden information regarding relationships and opinions. Nonetheless, the staff's lack of Spanish competency had proven problematic, especially during house meetings. Angela revealed she often did not understand the subjects that were brought up in the meetings because they revolved around "a whole bunch of papers."

Truth be told, Angela could have used a better support system—one more linguistically and culturally appropriate, especially when she first entered the program. She came to the group house four months' pregnant. The pregnancy was emotionally difficult for her. The father of the baby was a customer in the bar where Angela worked. She described him as the only man she was "involved with." While she liked him, upon discovering she was pregnant, she immediately distanced herself from him and never told him about the baby. "I have money," she said. "I will take care of the baby myself." However, despite pronouncing that she was capable of having the baby on her own, Angela was at first ambivalent about motherhood and said she was "afraid of being a mom." She shared that she was drunk on the night the baby was conceived. She also said: "I would rather chop my hand off than have a baby right now," and "I would have committed suicide before becoming pregnant." At some point she also expressed anxiety about having a son. She considered leaving the baby with her parents in Honduras. As her pregnancy progressed, Angela seemed calmer about the impending motherhood, but when the baby boy was born she became quite upset when the attending nurse suggested she hold him. Later she relayed her opinion that mothers don't hold their babies before they are cleaned and taken care of by a midwife. Angela's reaction—interpreted by her social worker as distress—was an appropriate response within her native culture.

Things improved considerably when Angela was introduced to a caseworker fluent in Spanish. After a couple of months working with the Spanish-speaking staff member and being reunited with one of the girls she had worked with in the bar, her mood improved. A note in her case file described her as "sensitive, friendly, and resilient" with "a good sense of humor." Offers of counseling and therapy were withdrawn.

While Angela was no longer pressured to see a mental health professional, other girls continued to be enticed to seek psychological help. Social workers' persistence often broke the girls' resistance and they succumbed to therapy. Many programs clearly wanted all children to participate in therapy and were convinced about the benefits of counseling. Some followed their agency's protocol as to the appropriate use of therapy and the girls' interest and willingness to attend sessions, but the pressure was on the youth to participate in counseling. Eventually, most youth were in treatment. Again, the service providers' assessment of what was in the girls' best interests prevailed.

Two girls with suspected sexual victimization were referred to a bilingual counselor; they participated in five counseling sessions, but refused to continue. Several other girls were concerned that going to therapy would stigmatize them further and label them as "crazy." Adina joked that she was "too lazy to go to counseling every week." She also added that she did not know what she would talk about in the sessions. Caseworkers often commented that the "girls went into therapy kicking and screaming," but mental health services were considered in the children's best interests, despite the fact that for some therapy proved "retriggering." Catalina reported having nightmares after her sessions. Upon consultation with a different clinician, a decision was made not to ask questions that did not relate to concrete aspects of the present, as such discussions reopened the pain of the trafficking experience. The therapist instead engaged with Catalina around an art project, thinking this approach would be less threatening. However, Catalina was still reluctant to participate.

Marianna was very averse to seeing a mental health professional at first. A Mexican girl who was raped by a trafficker and brutalized in a brothel, she was forced to have an abortion, beaten for talking to other girls working in the brothel, and verbally abused and demeaned. In the end, she decided that she needed to talk to someone. At first she found the sessions "very boring and uncomfortable, but after you start talking it gets better." Marianna went to psychotherapy for two years and found it helpful. She said: "I was dead before—I wasn't living—but now I can see myself having a family one day."

Programs did not consider indigenous healing strategies, social justice, or human rights approaches; for most programs, cultural competence was limited to finding a Western-trained therapist who could communicate with the survivor in her native language. Despite the fact that many of the assistance programs were operated by faith-based organizations, religion and spirituality were rarely considered as coping strategies, perhaps for fear of being accused of proselytization or perhaps not to bring on any more accusations that religion dictated whether programs provided reproductive health services or not.[25] The Peruvian boys, and their families, who insisted on seeing a Catholic priest, were an exception; the local Latino congregation embraced them and provided necessary support. Hua, a Chinese girl, also found solace and support at a local Protestant church; the youth ministry group, which provided her with an opportunity to socialize, was especially helpful.

The push for mental health services was consistent with strategies employed to deal with other victimized populations. The number of programs established to provide psychological help to refugees, victims of wartime violence, and more recently trafficked victims has grown exponentially.[26] The expansion of such programs indicates the prominence of mental health concepts in the forced migration and antitrafficking field. Particularly prominent is the discourse of "trauma" as a lens through which human suffering is viewed.[27] This approach is based on the premise that trafficking, ethnic cleansing, war, and civil strife constitute mental health emergencies and result in post-traumatic stress. In turn, this has led to the liberal application of treatment modalities based on the Western biomedical model in a diverse variety of circumstances. This expansion of trauma programs is directly related to what Arthur Kleinman calls the "medicalization of human suffering."[28] At the same time, other models, building on the victims' own resilience, indigenous coping strategies, and spirituality, are not being explored as much as they could be or should be.

Undeniably, most of the youth in this study suffered incredible ordeals and, without safe environments in which to recover, they were at risk for further exploitation. Indeed, there were a couple of instances where their traffickers, pretending to be relatives, contacted the girls. Marianela was one of those girls. Her abuser called her on the phone in the convent where she was staying awaiting placement in a group house. They arranged to meet in a nearby park and Marianela never came back to the program. The vigilance of the staff at their rehabilitation programs protected the youth from revictimization. The programs' unprecedented dedication to the protection of the girls in their care was admirable. At the same time, by focusing so much on the girls' vulnerability, the programs often lost sight of their resiliency. Preoccupied with Western standards of child welfare, staff did not have adequate resources to tap into culturally relevant healing strategies, emphasizing the youth's agency and resiliency.

Toward Solutions and Resolutions

Studies of children and childhoods increasingly see children as "at once developing beings, in possession of agency, and to varying degrees vulnerable."[29] Developments occurring in the field of childhood studies parallel developments in women's studies, which consider women as social actors and contextualize them in theories of behavior, culture, and society. Unfortunately, the discourse on child trafficking still focuses mainly on the vulnerability and victimization of trafficked children, even though recognition of the coexistence of agency and vulnerability is particularly important in the child trafficking domain. As Diane M. Hoffman, who studied *restavek* children in southwest Haiti, observes: "Recognizing their agency is not denying that they suffer; nor is it to sanction the social structural inequalities that make the *restavek* system possible in the first place. Rather, it is to point the way to a reconceptualization of the *restavek* child in a more positive light, to portray the child *as a person* who has real capacities, skills, intelligence, and personal fortitude that can make him or her an asset to the society, rather than a victim or a drain on a society that is itself in chaos."[30]

I recognize the legal necessity to use the term "victim"—the services the trafficked youth were eligible for were paid with money earmarked for "victims of crimes" and adjustment of their immigration status was also linked to being victimized. I am, however, opposed to extending this label beyond the legal realm and eligibility criteria. Therapeutically speaking, assigning the identity of "victim" is often counterproductive to the young people's integration into American society or reintegration into their home country, should they choose to return. Moreover, data show that children and youth exhibit a great deal of resiliency and are capable of recovering from trafficking experiences as much as adults. In a current study I am conducting, involving seventy-eight trafficked minors—fifty-seven girls and twenty-one boys ranging in age from six to seventeen—minors and adults recorded similar results in terms of stability outcomes, with 50 percent of adults and 51 percent of children improving stability. Given the size of the sample, this difference is not statistically significant. However, the outcome suggests that children and youth are just as resilient as adults. In relation to the speed of recovery, in the first five months of service, 52 percent of children and youth recorded improvement in stability, compared to 40 percent of adults over the same period of time.

Recognition of the coexistence of vulnerability and resiliency influences the way we conduct research with trafficked children and affects our ethical responsibilities to the studied youngsters. This recognition is important because it affects—or should affect—institutional responses to survivors of trafficking. While there is no denying that trafficked children and youth have often been severely abused and exploited, one must also consider questions of agency and resiliency while analyzing this phenomenon, designing services for trafficked minors, crafting policy responses aimed at preventing child trafficking, and prosecuting perpetrators. Well-informed rehabilitation approaches must consult children's voices, experiences, and perspectives to explicitly inform and shape policy decisions and programmatic responses. Listening to the voices of children has become a powerful mantra for activists and policymakers worldwide. Yet, despite such pronouncements, many of the trafficked girls and boys found their voices silenced or ignored in the name of their "best interests." "They never listened to what I wanted," said Fatima. Angela chimed in: "The social workers want feedback but when we express our desires for different house rules or for schedules that accommodate our babies' routines, we are ignored. I am tired of sitting on the house meetings; they don't accomplish anything." The Federal Strategic Action Plan for Victims of Human Trafficking in the United States: 2013–2017 emphasizes victim-centered approaches that include agency, but at the same time it advocates solely for trauma-informed approaches without even a nod toward any other strategies.[31]

Programs need to be flexible. The youth's perception of the nature of their experiences and their families' involvement in trafficking may be at odds with the opinions held by law enforcement and service providers. However, despite these differences, it is essential that law enforcement and service providers are flexible enough to allow the trafficked youth to have a unique, and perhaps differing, assessment of what happened to them and who wronged them. Flora's case manager admitted that it was in the girl's "best interest" to go and visit her mom in prison. Flora and Isa had a much better time adjusting to the program after they saw their mother. Flora repeatedly said how glad she was that her case manager changed her mind. "I didn't want her to think that my mother was some sort of a monster," she told me.

Programs need to enhance their cross-cultural competencies. Language barriers and cultural differences contribute to survivors' isolation from the larger community. However, it is not enough to have bilingual or multilingual staff members. Linguistic capabilities are necessary but understanding cultural conceptualizations of children, childhoods, helpers versus traffickers, culturally appropriate aesthetics and dress codes, as well as indigenous solutions to traumatic experiences is of equal import. Cross-cultural awareness is imperative for meaningful social work practice with survivors of human trafficking. Paradigm shifts away from the Western treatment modalities toward indigenous interventions and support groups—which "recognize oppression when working with people of low economic status and low power"—have been noted as key to working with immigrant and refugee victims. [32]

Minors should also be educated about their rights and about U.S. and international conventions protecting children. "Know your rights" sessions are commonplace for migrant children in detention centers; similar training should be provided for trafficked minors, especially adolescents. Trafficked minors need to be educated about the way the law views certain actions of adults as criminal. This kind of training should focus on the legal aspects of child trafficking, not moral assessments of the parents' actions. Hopefully, a rights-based service model taking into account the young people's resiliency and agency will empower them sufficiently to continue rebuilding their post-trafficking lives long after they leave assistance programs. In the epilogue we will get a chance to revisit some of the girls to see how they are doing several years after their trafficking experiences.

Epilogue

Everyday Struggles

In the early 2000s when I first began to study child trafficking, service providers did not have much experience working with trafficked children and adolescents. Many programs had one or two girls in their care and not much to compare their approaches to as they strived to integrate them into American society. Despite the fact that none of the girls were diagnosed with severe mental illness, fear that the trauma of trafficking was serious enough to affect them for a long time to come overshadowed other issues. Several social workers repeatedly emphasized that until the girls fully recover from the trafficking trauma, they will be unable to get on with their lives. As discussed in the final chapter, mental health counseling was thought of as the number one remedy.

In addition, the girls' adjustment to the fairly strict rules and regulations of the foster care programs and group houses was often problematic. As discussed throughout this book, the girls and boys, by and large, did not identify as children, but rather as young people on the brink of adulthood. Their experiences needing to contribute to their families' livelihoods at an early age made them grow up fast. Their migration and trafficking experiences hardened them even further. Many of the girls were used to making decisions for themselves and were used to certain freedoms. Upon entering the foster care programs, they were suddenly expected to behave like children, adhere to rules imposed on them by well-meaning foster parents and program staff, and reclaim their "lost childhoods." Both the caseworkers and the girls talked about adjustment difficulties. Narratives in case files often begun with the following sentence: "[Name] adjustment to the program was very difficult."

Angela was originally placed in an all-girls home, but did not like it there and was happy to leave and move to an apartment. However, in the independent living setting she felt "abandoned" and moved to a different group house a few weeks before our interview. She remembered arriving late and not feeling comfortable with the girls looking at her and her baby. She thought, "Why are they staring at me like this, I am the same [as them]." Things improved when Angela befriended Matilde, one of the other girls in the program. Matilde helped out with Angela's baby and was good company for Angela.

However, beyond the here and now, it was difficult to get Angela talking about her future plans. She said she wanted her son to "get bigger, go to school and know that he is worth something." As for her own future, she could not articulate any plans or dreams. She seemed overwhelmed by the demands of motherhood and had a hard time coping with her responsibilities. While childbirth classes were offered before her son was born, Angela was not referred to classes aimed at enhancing her parenting skills or support groups for teen moms. Several years later, Angela continues to struggle combining her parental responsibilities with work. She hopes that when her son goes to school things will become easier.

Belen, who witnessed her father's suicide, had a rocky adjustment to the foster care program. She was described in her case file as "sick, depressed, and often scared." Belen entered the program with a diagnosis of PTSD and was prescribed antipsychotic medication. Belen attended therapy sessions every two weeks and saw a psychiatrist once a month. She continued to see her therapist for several months. Belen often presented herself in the nurse's office complaining of stomachaches and migraines. She also suffered from skin allergies and asthma.

After changing group homes and foster families a few times, Belen was finally placed in a very supportive family. In our interview she said, "I now have a very strong support group around me." Belen developed a good relationship with her foster sisters. She compared her foster home to the home she had when her father was alive, "full of friendly people, laughing and sharing, and talking." She wants to stay in school and attend college. Belen would like to study nursing, because "there are always jobs for nurses."

Hoping to revisit some of the girls several years after I last talked to them, I contacted a few of the programs that participated in my study. Program staff were happy to chat, but it soon became clear that most had lost touch with the girls once they left their services. Funding was scarce and human resources stretched, which did not bode well for the programs' ability to follow up. The girls did not seem to call their caseworkers or seek referrals to other services once they left foster care. Social workers thought that meant the young women were self-sufficient and did not need to relay on outside assistance any more. Perhaps that was true. On the other hand, Evelyn told me she wished she could get help with finding a job. When I suggested she go and visit with the program that had originally assisted her, Evelyn did not have much faith that they would be able to help with employment. Evelyn was assisted by an agency that has been resettling refugees for a very long time and is well equipped to provide employment services. However, Evelyn knew only the antitrafficking program and was not aware that other support was available as well. Then again, Evelyn is now a U.S. citizen and no longer eligible for services for trafficked children.

Interestingly, the programs that had much more contact with their charges after the girls emancipated and lived independently were the agencies that provided legal aid. One social worker remarked, "It's very satisfying to see my former clients come back to meet with our staff attorney in order to finalize their T-Visa applications or even later to adjust their immigration status and get a green card. Some come to work with the attorney to reunite with the children they left behind or with their parents."

Generally speaking, program staff indicated that many factors affected the future prospects of the trafficked girls and boys, including the severity of the trafficking experience, length of time in captivity, and satisfaction and compliance with offered services. Background characteristics—such as levels of education and ability to speak or learn English quickly—were also of importance, according to program staff. It seemed to me that the success of the girls was also related to their personality traits: motivation to overcome integration challenges, perseverance, and levels of resiliency.

Magdalena had fairly good prospects for a bright future from the very beginning. At nineteen, she lived by herself in a nicely furnished apartment and had a part-time job at a fast food restaurant in a local mall. At the time of our first meeting, she wanted to get a driver's license, but had yet to pass the learning permit test. She spoke openly about being illiterate in Spanish and having difficulty reading and writing in English. These challenges notwithstanding, her spoken English was improving rapidly and she took every opportunity to practice English. She specifically asked to be interviewed in English despite having an option to converse with the research team in Spanish.

Over several months, as I checked with her periodically, Magdalena completed a cosmetology course offered through a vocational training program at a local community college. She passed the state practical cosmetology exam, but it took her an additional couple of years to pass the written test. She worked in salons catering to Spanish speakers, but later moved on to shops serving an English-speaking clientele. Magdalena dreams of owning a salon, but that dream has not materialized yet. She remains hopeful though and continues to save money. Although certainly not affluent, Magdalena is nevertheless economically self-sufficient. She attributes her financial independence to being frugal and saving money. Magdalena believes that other girls in her situation have not been able to be economically self-sufficient because they spent the money they earned too quickly. She lost touch with some of the girls that were in the same program as everybody changed phone numbers numerous times. She reported seeing Marta a month or so before our last meeting, but it was more of a chance meeting than a planned get-together.

Magdalena has made new friends, mostly through work. She has a boy-friend, Jamie, who has been with her for over four years. Jamie is a twenty-two year old from Honduras and has been in the United States for five years. He works at the mall where Magdalena's salon is located. Jamie is here with his father and his brothers, while his mom and sisters are still in Honduras. Magdalena worries a little when Jamie says he might want to return to Honduras, but at the same time does not want to marry Jamie to formalize their relationship and his legal status. She told me she wouldn't want to move to Honduras, not knowing the cultural norms.

Magdalena is comfortable living in the United States, she said, because women here have more freedom, more opportunities, and more protection. In Mexico, she remarked, police are often corrupt, men can hit you for no reason at all, and women worry about safety all the time. Here she travels on her own without giving it a second thought. When we last talked she was excited to go and visit with her cousin in California in a few weeks. This would be her second trip to see her family. While she tells Jamie where she travels and how long she will be gone, she does not ask him for permission. "In Mexico," she said, "a woman cannot go anywhere without her husband's permission." Magdalena and Jamie share chores whenever he comes to eat or spend the night at her place. His friends tease him about it, but he does not care.

Similarly to Evelyn, Magdalena speaks to other trafficked youth. She tells the girls what worked for her, how important learning English was, and how working outside the home has helped her to forget the bad things that happened to her. She is particularly grateful to her ESL teachers for helping her with learning English. She took English classes at a local community college and loved the "university atmosphere and that people took me seriously." Magdalena also took some life skills courses at the community college and learned how to budget time and money, how to find an apartment, and what to ask about when signing a lease. She takes pride in her new life and is looking forward to the future.

Without exception, all the Peruvian boys are doing really well. Several finished high school and went on to college. Alberto and Diego obtained engineering degrees, are both happily married, and have children. Joaquin served in the U.S. Army and works as a helicopter mechanic. His service in the army earned him U.S. citizenship. Several others obtained their green cards and are on a path to citizenship as well. Most reunited with their parents and siblings and are living in a tight-knit Spanish-speaking community. The program director attributed these extremely positive outcomes to the presence of two strong female leaders in the Peruvian community. They mothered the boys when they were still in the trafficking situation together. One of these women broke free and tipped off law enforcement about the trafficking situation. She has gained the boys' eternal gratitude. The women continue to provide support to the group and keep in touch with the antitrafficking program that helped the group find housing, employment, and educational resources.

However, not all trafficked youth are doing as well as Evelyn, Magdalena, Alberto, and Diego. Many continue to struggle, especially economically. Much has been written about poverty as a root cause of trafficking, but there is virtually no discussion about the economic self-sufficiency of survivors of trafficking, especially children. Denise Brennan's book *Life Interrupted* is a rare exception. Focusing on adult women in their post-trafficking lives in the United States, Brennan calls attention to the needs of the workers themselves rather than the moralities mobilized by well-intentioned rescuers.

As indicated throughout this book, much attention and accompanying resources are spent on "rehabilitating" trafficked minors and on "healing" the trauma resulting from the trafficking experiences. However, the economic well-being of these young people garners a lot less attention. The fact that these young people are now green card holders or U.S. citizens with access to legal employment does not mean that they are not discriminated against in the labor market. Similarly to other migrants—documented and undocumented—they face language barriers, wage exploitation, and lack of upward mobility. The antitrafficking field needs to rethink easy charity and focus on labor force participation as a source of both economic stability and healing.

Notes

Prologue

1   This is Evelyn's real name. Her story was written up on the front pages of many newspapers and Evelyn insisted that I use her real name. The name of her trafficker is also in the public domain; therefore, I use it here. All other names in this book, however, are pseudonyms.

2   See "Survivors of Slavery Speak Out," http://survivorsofslavery.org/.

Introduction: Researching and Writing about Child Trafficking

1   Laura María Agustín, *Sex at the Margins: Migration, Labor, Markets, and the Rescue Industry* (London: Zed Books, 2007).

2   See Denise Brennan, "Methodological Challenges in Research on Human Trafficking: Tales from the Field," *International Migration* 43, nos. 1–2 (2005): 35–54; Denise Brennan, *Life Interrupted: Trafficking into Forced Labor in the United States* (Durham: Duke University Press, 2014).

3   Elizabeth Bernstein, "Militarized Humanitarianism Meets Carceral Feminism: The Politics of Sex, Rights, and Freedom in Contemporary Anti-Trafficking Campaigns," in "Feminists Theorize International Political Economy," ed. Kate Bedford and Shirin Rai, a special issue of *Signs: Journal of Women in Culture and Society* 36, no. 1 (2010): 45–71.

4   Julia O'Connell Davidson, *Children in the Global Sex Trade* (Cambridge: Polity, 2005); Julia O'Connell Davidson, "Moving Children? Child Trafficking, Child Migration and Child Rights," *Critical Social Policy* 31, no. 3 (2011): 454–477.

5   Pardis Mahdavi, *Gridlock: Labor, Migration, and Human Trafficking in Dubai* (Stanford: Stanford University Press, 2011).

6   Svati Shah, *Street Corner Secrets: Sex, Work, and Migration in the City of Mumbai* (Durham: Duke University Press, 2014).

7   Carol S. Vance, "States of Contradiction: Twelve Ways to Do Nothing about Trafficking while Pretending To," *Social Research* 78, no. 3 (2011): 933.

8   See Elżbieta M. Goździak, "On Challenges, Dilemmas, and Opportunities in Studying Trafficked Children," *Anthropology Quarterly* 81, no. 4 (2008): 903–923;

Elżbieta M. Goździak, "Challenges, Dilemmas and Opportunities in Studying Trafficked Children in the United States," in *Course Reader eBooks* (Belmont: Wadsworth Cengage Learning, 2012).

9 Allison James, "Giving Voice to Children's Voices: Practices and Problem, Pitfalls and Potentials," *American Anthropologist* 109, no. 2 (2007): 261–272.

10 Brennan, "Methodological Challenges in Research with Trafficked Persons," 35–54.

11 The term "studying up" comes from an influential 1972 essay written by Laura Nader, "Up the Anthropologist: Perspectives Gained from Studying Up." What Nader suggested in her essay was that anthropologists should also point their ethnographic eye *up*, to people who wielded power: corporations, the government, the wealthy, scientists, the police, and so on.

12 Research funds continue to be limited, especially for studies of minors and adults trafficked to the United States. The National Institute of Justice remains the sole federal funder for this type of research. The State Department provides funding mainly for evaluating antitrafficking programs overseas.

13 See Dina Bowman, "Studying Up, Down, Sideways and through: Situated Research and Policy Networks," https://www.tasa.org.au/wp-content/uploads/2015/03/Bowman-Dina.pdf. See also Rachel Stryker and Roberto Gonzalez, eds., *Up, Down, and Sideways: Anthropologists Trace the Pathways of Power* (Oxford: Berghahn Books, 2014).

14 Brennan, "Methodological Challenges in Research with Trafficked Persons," 35–54.

15 Denise Brennan, "Methodological Challenges in Research with Trafficked Persons"; Joanna Cook, James Laidlwa, and Jonathan Mair, "What if There Is No Elephant? Towards a Conception of an Un-sited Field," in *Multi-sited Ethnography: Theory, Praxis and Locality in Contemporary Research*, ed. M-A Falzon (Farnham: Ashgate, 2009), 73–85.

16 Jeremy MacClancy, *Exotic No More: Anthropology on the Front Lines* (Chicago: University of Chicago Press, 2002), 6.

17 See Frank Laczko and Elżbieta M. Goździak, eds., "Data and Research on Human Trafficking: A Global Survey," special issue of *International Migration* 43, nos. 1–2 (2005); Elżbieta M. Goździak and Micah N. Bump, *Data and Research on Human Trafficking: Bibliography of Research-Based Literature*, Report to NIJ, October 2008; and Elżbieta M. Goździak, forthcoming.

18 "Minimum Age Convention, 1973," ILO Convention 138, 58th ILC Session (Geneva, 1973); "Worst Forms of Child Labour Convention 1999," ILO Convention 182 (Geneva, 1999).

19 Samuel Vincent Jones. "Human Trafficking Victim Identification: Should Consent Matter?" *Indiana Law Review* 45 (2012): 482–511; Carol Allais, "The Profile Less Considered: The Trafficking of Men in South Africa," *South African Review of Sociology* 44, no. 1 (2013): 40–54.

20 As a practicing anthropologist whose livelihood depends on research grants and contracts, I simply did not have the resources to spend weeks at a time with a particular survivor or program. Moreover, the program staff was too busy to spare more than a couple of hours with my research team and me.

21 Brennan, "Methodological Challenges in Research with Trafficked Persons," 35–54.

22 Erdmute Alber, Jeannett Martin, and Catrien Notermans, eds., *Child Fostering in West Africa: New Perspectives on Theory and Practices* (Leiden, The Netherlands: Brill Publishers, 2013).

Part I   Moral Panics

1   See Deborah Gorham, "The Maiden Tribute of Modern Babylon Re-examined: Child Prostitution and the Idea of Childhood in Late-Victorian England," *Victorian Studies* 21 (1978): 353–379; Vivienne E. Cree, Gary Clapton, and Mark Smith, "The Presentation of Child Trafficking in the UK: An Old and New Moral Panic?" *British Journal of Social Work Advances* (2012): 1–16.

2   Stanley Cohen, *Folk Devils and Moral Panics: The Creation of the Mods and Rockers* (London: Routledge, 2011).

3   "IOM Marks One Year of *Lilya 4-Ever* in Moldova: Information Campaign Reaches More Than 60,000," November 16, 2004. International Organization for Migration. http://www.iom.md/materials/press_161104.html.

4   See Gretchen Soderlund, *Sex Trafficking, Scandal, and the Transformation of Journalism, 1885–1917* (Chicago: University of Chicago Press, 2013); Roger N. Lancaster, *Sex Panic and the Punitive State* (Berkeley: University of California Press, 2011).

5   Lancaster, *Sex Panic and the Punitive State*; Denise Brennan, *Life Interrupted: Trafficking into Forced Labor in the United States* (Durham: Duke University Press, 2014).

6   Author's calculations based on Office of Refugee Resettlement Reports to Congress and personal communication with Office of Refugee Resettlement staff (2014).

7   Richard J. Estes and Neil Alan Weiner, "The Commercial Sexual Exploitation of Children in the U.S., Canada and Mexico," University of Pennsylvania, September 18, 2001.

Chapter 1   "Tidal Waves" of Trafficking

1   These regulations focused on the duties and responsibilities of all federal law enforcement, immigration, and State Department officials to identify trafficking victims and investigate or prosecute traffickers.

2   At the time of our meeting, it was assumed that the 15,000 referred to the number of children trafficked into the United States. In a revised version of the original report, Estes and Weiner suggested the number referred to children at-risk for trafficking (2001 meeting on identification of trafficked children).

3   Micah N. Bump et al., "Second Conference on Identifying and Serving Child Victims of Trafficking," *International Migration* 43, nos. 1–2 (2005): 343–363.

4   Department of Justice, "Attorney General's Annual Report to Congress and Assessment of U.S. Government Activities to Combat Trafficking in Persons," Department of Justice, Office of the Attorney General, Fiscal Years 2002–12.

5   Mike Dottridge and Ann Jordan, "Children, Adolescents and Human Trafficking: Making Sense of a Complex Problem," Issue Paper 5, Center for Human Rights and Humanitarian Law, Washington College of Law, American University, Washington DC, 2012.

6   Annuska Derks, "Combating Trafficking in South-East Asia: A Review of Policy and Programme Responses," prepared for the International Organization for Migration, 2000, 14.

7   Gerison Lansdown, "The Evolving Capacities of the Child" (Florence, Italy: UNICEF Innocenti Research Center and Save the Children, 2005).

8   Julia O'Connell Davidson, "Moving Children? Child Trafficking, Child Migration and Child Rights," *Critical Social Policy* 31, no. 3 (2011): 457.

9   Ibid.; R.B.C. Huijsmans and S. Baker, "Child Trafficking: Worst Form of Child Labour, or Worst Approach to Young Migrants?," *Development and Change* 43, no. 4 (2012): 919–946.

10   Wendy Chapkis, "Trafficking, Migration, and the Law: Protecting Innocents, Punishing Immigrants," *Gender & Society* 17 (2003): 923–937.

11   Juan Louis Cadena-Sosa and several of his family members conspired to smuggle girls and young women to the United States from Mexico and hold them in involuntary servitude in brothels owned and operated by his family. He was sentenced on September 3, 2008, to fifteen years in prison, followed by three years of supervised release, and ordered to pay $964,175 jointly with his codefendants in restitution to the victims.

12   In July 1997, the U.S. Immigration and Customs Enforcement and the government of Mexico initiated an investigation of an organization involved in the smuggling and trafficking of fifty-five deaf and mute Mexican nationals and nine U.S. citizen children. The organization forced the victims through violence and intimidation to work long hours begging and selling trinkets on the streets or in the subways in New York City. The victims were found at two residences in Jackson Heights, New York, after four of them sought help from police and led authorities to the Jackson Heights houses. Defendants Paoletti-Lemus and Paoletti-Moreda, both Mexican citizens, were arrested in August 1997. After serving their Mexican sentences, Paoletti-Lemus and Paoletti-Moreda were extradited to the United States to face U.S. charges. After a jury trial each of them was ordered to pay a total of $1.4 million in restitution, to be shared out among the victims, and they were sentenced to long prison terms. In addition, eighteen members of the investigated organization were convicted in the United States and received sentences varying from one to fifteen years.

13   Anthony DeStefano, *The War on Human Trafficking: U.S. Policy Assessed* (New Brunswick, NJ: Rutgers University Press, 2008), 9.

14   Richard J. Estes and Neil Alan Weiner, "The Commercial Sexual Exploitation of Children in the U.S., Canada, and Mexico," University of Pennsylvania, September 18, 2001.

15   Mia Spangenberg, "International Trafficking of Children in New York City for Sexual Purposes," ECPAT-USA, 2002.

16   Amy O'Neill Richard, "International Trafficking in Women to the United States: A Contemporary Manifestation of Slavery and Organized Crime," Center for the Study of Intelligence, April 2000. https://www.cia.gov/library/center-for-the-study-of-intelligence/csi-publications/books-and-monographs/trafficking.pdf.

17   In a footnote Richard cited a CIA briefing on "Global Trafficking in Women and Children: Assessing the Magnitude" as her source. Later on, it was discovered that the Central Intelligence Agency estimates were methodologically flawed.

18   "Trafficking Statistics Project," UNESCO, cited in DeStefano, *War on Human Trafficking*, 13.

19   Jerry Markon, "Human Trafficking Evokes Outrage, Little Evidence," *Washington Post*, September 23, 2007.

20   "Attorney General's Annual Report to Congress and Assessment of U.S. Government Activities to Combat Trafficking in Persons," Department of Justice, Office of the Attorney General, Fiscal Year 2005.

21   "Human Trafficking: Better Data, Strategy, and Reporting Needed to Enhance U.S. Antitrafficking Efforts Abroad," United States Government Accountability Office

Report to the Chairman, Committee on the Judiciary and the Chairman, Committee on International Relations, House of Representatives, Washington DC, 2006.

22 Jay S. Albanese, cited in Tom Coburn, "Blind Faith: How Congress Is Failing Trafficking Victims" (Washington, DC: Office of Tom Coburn, U.S. Senate, 2011), 15.

23 "2007 Trafficking in Persons Report" (Washington, DC: United States Department of State, June 2007).

24 A content analysis of the 2013 TIP report reveals that in some countries less than a handful of victims have been found during the reporting period, and prosecutions were also rare. In Nepal, for example, two nongovernmental organizations reported supporting 960 trafficking victims in 2012; at least 189 of them were trafficked for labor exploitation. The offenders in all of the 189 cases were prosecuted. However, the Nepali government did not provide information on sentences or confirm the number of convictions. In Cameroon, only three prosecutions have been initiated during the time frame reported in the 2013 TIP report: "2013 Trafficking in Persons Report" (Washington, DC: United States Department of State, June 2013).

25 Coburn, "Blind Faith: How Congress Is Failing Trafficking Victims."

26 For difficulties in measuring, see Frank Laczko and Marco A. Granmegna, "Developing Better Indicators of Human Trafficking" (Geneva: International Organization for Migration, 2003); Sheldon Zhang, "Beyond the 'Natasha' Story: A Review and Critique of Current Research on Sex Trafficking," *Global Crime* 10, no. 3 (2009): 178–195; Louise Shelly, *Human Trafficking: A Global Perspective* (Cambridge: Cambridge University Press, 2010); Elżbieta M. Goździak and Elizabeth A. Collett, "Research on Human Trafficking in North America: A Review of Literature," *International Migration* 43, nos. 1–2 (2005); Goździak, "On Challenges, Dilemmas, and Opportunities in Studying Trafficked Children." For calls for improved methodologies, see Guri Tyldum and Anette Brunovskis, "Describing the Unobserved: Methodological Challenges in Empirical Studies on Human Trafficking," *International Migration* 43, nos. 1–2 (2005): 17–34.

27 In 2006 the National Institute of Justice supported the Vera Institute to create a screening tool to identify possible victims of trafficking and an accompanying guide for the tool's administration. In 2011 the Vera Institute received further funding from the National Institute of Justice to validate this tool in the field. In 2008 and 2009, ICF International published reports based on their assessment of programs, supported by the U.S. Department of Health and Human Services, serving victims of trafficking, in which they attribute difficulties in identifying victims to the hidden nature of the crime: fear of law enforcement and fear of retaliation; feelings of shame and disgrace; and lack of self-identification as a victim. See Heather J. Clawson et al., *Prosecuting Human Trafficking Cases: Lessons Learned and Promising Practices* (Fairfax, VA: ICF International, 2008), 94. See also Clawson et al., *Study of HHS Programs Serving Human Trafficking Victims* (Washington, DC: U.S. Department of Health and Human Services, 2009), 74. So far, none of these studies have resulted in better identification outcomes.

28 Coburn, "Blind Faith: How Congress is Failing Trafficking Victims," 3–4.

29 Kevin Bales, *Understanding Global Slavery* (Berkeley: University of California Press, 2005).

30 "ILO Global Estimate of Forced Labour: Results and Methodology," Special Action Programme to Combat Forced Labour (Geneva: International Labour Office, 2012).

31 Ibid.

32 Personal communication with Cortland Robinson of Johns Hopkins University, 2012.

33 Tyldum and Brunovskis, "Describing the Unobserved."

34 "2014 Trafficking in Persons Report" (Washington, DC: United States Department of State, June 2014).

35 "Counter Trafficking and Assistance to Vulnerable Migrants" (Annual Report of Activities, International Organization for Migration, 2011).

36 See Jane Morse, "Resources, Better Coordination Needed to Fight Human Trafficking: Mobilization Just Beginning to Tackle the Problem, U.N. Official Says," *USINFO*, April 25, 2007; Janine Zeitlin, "Groups Push State to Fight Human Trafficking," *Naples* (Florida) *Daily News*, February 26, 2006.

37 Government Accountability Office, *Human Trafficking: Monitoring and Evaluation of International Projects Are Limited, but Experts Suggest Improvements* (Washington, DC: GAO, July 2007).

38 Amy Farrell, Jack McDevitt, and Stephanie Fahy, "Where Are All the Victims? Understanding the Determinants of Official Identification of Human Trafficking Incidents," *Criminology & Public Policy* 9, no. 2 (2010): 210.

39 See Laura María Agustín, *Sex at the Margins: Migrations, Labour Markets and Rescue Industry* (London: Zed Books, 2007); William F. McDonald, "Traffic Counts, Symbols and Agendas: A Critique of the Campaign against Trafficking of Human Beings," *International Review of Victimology* 11 (September 2004): 143–176; Ronald Weitzer, "The Social Construction of Sex Trafficking: Ideology and Institutionalization of a Moral Crusade," *Politics Society* 34 (2007): 447.

40 See Judith Walkowitz, *Prostitution and Victorian Society: Women, Class and State* (Cambridge: Cambridge University Press, 1980); Edward J. Bristow, *Prostitution and Prejudice: The Jewish Fight against White Slavery 1870–1938* (Oxford: Clarendon Press, 1982); Ruth Rosen, *The Lost Sisterhood: Prostitution in America, 1900–1918* (Baltimore: Johns Hopkins University Press, 1982); Alain Corbin and Alan Sheridan, *Women for Hire: Prostitution and Sexuality in France after 1850* (Cambridge, MA: Harvard University Press, 1990); Donna J. Guy, *Sex and Danger in Buenos Aires: Prostitution, Family, and Nation in Argentina* (Lincoln: University of Nebraska Press, 1991), quoted in Jo Doezema, "Loose Women or Lost Women? The Re-emergence of the Myth of White Slavery in Contemporary Discourses of Trafficking Women," *Gender Issues* (Winter 2000): 25–26.

41 Doezema, "Loose Women or Lost Women?," 16.

42 UN High Commissioner for Refugees, *Findings and Recommendations Relating to the 2012–2013 Mission to Monitor the Protection Screening of Mexican Unaccompanied Children along the U.S.-Mexico Border* (Washington, DC: June 2014).

43 Amy Thompson, *A Child Alone and without Papers: A Report on the Return and Repatriation of Undocumented Children by the United States* (Austin, TX: Center for Public Policy Priorities, 2008).

44 Personal communication with Office of Refugee Resettlement staff. The Office of Refugee Resettlement has indicated that they had released 53,518 unaccompanied children and youth to family and community members between October 1, 2013, and September 30, 2014 (FY2014) and an additional 3,310 in FY 2015 (October 1, 2014–January 22, 2015).

45 UN High Commissioner for Refugees Regional Office for the United States and the Caribbean, *Children on the Run: Unaccompanied Children Leaving Central America and Mexico and the Need for International Protection* (Washington, DC, 2014).

46 Elżbieta M. Goździak and Micah N. Bump, "The Care of Unaccompanied Undocumented Children in Federal Custody: Issues and Options," *Protecting Children* 23, no. 1 (2008): 67–84.

47 Personal communication with USCCB staff, 2007.

48 DeStefano, *The War on Human Trafficking*, 12.

49 Kimberly Kotrala, "Domestic Minor Sex Trafficking in the United States," *Social Work* 55, no.2 (2010): 181–187.

50 These figures conflate cross-border trafficking with internal trafficking and do not distinguish between trafficked children and those *at risk* for trafficking. The Ashton Kutcher–Demi Moore Foundation invoked the already-cited report by Estes and Weiner without realizing that the authors were actually writing about children who are at risk for sexual exploitation not only in the United States but also in Canada and Mexico.

51 Richard Curtis, Karen Terry, Meredith Dank, Kirk Dombrowski, and Blial Khan, *The Commercial Sexual Exploitation of Children in New York City* (New York: Center for Court Innovation, 2008).

52 Liz Kelly and Linda Regan, "Stopping Traffic: Exploring the Extent of, and Responses to, Trafficking in Women for Sexual Exploitation in the UK," *Police Research Series Paper* 125 (London: Home Office, 2000).

53 Nick Davies, "Prostitution and Trafficking—the Anatomy of a Moral Panic," *Guardian*, October 19, 2009.

54 Ibid.

55 Jo Doezema, *Sex Slaves and Discourse Matters: The Construction of Trafficking* (London: Zed Books, 2010), 7.

56 International Labour Organisation, *Unbearable to the Human Heart: Child Trafficking and Actions to Eliminate It* (Geneva: ILO Publications, 2002). http://www.unicef.org/violencestudy/pdf/2002_traff_unbearable_en.pdf. Accessed August 14, 2014.

57 Marjan Wijers and Lap-Chew Lin, *Trafficking in Women Forced Labour and Slavery-Like Practices in Marriage, Domestic Labour and Prostitution* (Utrecht, Netherlands: Foundation against Trafficking in Women, 1997), 15.

58 Andrea Lange, "Research Note: Challenges in Identifying Female Human Trafficking Victims Using a National 1–800 Call Center," *Trends in Organized Crime* 14 (2011): 47–55.

59 Personal communication, 2013.

60 Ronald Weitzer, "New Directions in Research on Prostitution," *Crime, Law & Social Change* 43 (2005): 211–235.

61 See Jyoti Sanghera, "Globalization, Labor Migration, and Human Rights: Unpacking the Trafficking Discourse," in *Trafficking and Prostitution Reconsidered*, ed. Kamala Kempadoo, Jyoti Sanghera, and Bandana Pattanaik (Boulder, CO: Paradigm Publishers, 2005), 13.

62 See Weitzer, "New Directions in Research on Prostitution"; Gayle Rubin, "Thinking Sex: Notes for a Radical Theory of the Politics of Sexuality," in *Pleasure and Danger*, ed. C. Vance, 267–319 (Boston: Routledge, 1984); Gayle Rubin, "Misguided, Dangerous, and Wrong: An Analysis of Antipornography Politics," in *Bad Girls and Dirty Pictures*, ed. A. Assiter and A. Carol (London: Pluto, 1993), 18–40; Jo Goodey, "Human Trafficking: Sketchy Data and Policy Responses," *Criminology and Criminal Justice* 8 (2008): 421; Weitzer, "Social Construction of Sex Trafficking:" 447; Doezema, *Sex Slaves and Discourse Matters*.

63 See Janice C. Raymond, "Prostitution as Violence against Women: NGO Stone-walling in Beijing and Elsewhere," *Women's Studies International Forum* 21, no. 1 (1999): 1–9; Janice G. Raymond, "Prostitution on Demand: Legalizing the Buyers as Sexual Consumers," *Violence Against Women* 10, no. 10 (2004): 1156–1186; D. Hughes, *Myths and Realities concerning Child Trafficking* (Brussels: Fafo Institution for Applied International Studies, 2005); D. Hughes, *The Demand for Victims of Sex Trafficking* (Washington, DC: U.S. Department of State, 2005).

64 Weitzer, "New Directions in Research on Prostitution."

65 Goździak, "Challenges, Dilemmas, and Opportunities in Studying Trafficked Children."

66 Ronald Weitzer, "Sex Trafficking and the Sex Industry: The Need for Evidence-Based Theory and Legislation," *Journal of Criminal Law and Criminology* 101, no. 4 (2007): 1347.

67 See Stephanie Hepburn and Rita J. Simon, "Hidden in Plain Sight: Human Trafficking in the United States," *Gender Issues* 27 (2010): 1–26; Stephanie Hepburn and Rita J. Simon, *Human Trafficking around the World: Hidden in Plain Sight* (New York: Columbia University Press, 2013); see Kathryn Farr, *Sex Trafficking: The Global Market in Women and Children* (Portland, OR: Worth Publishing, 2005), for inflated statements.

68 Julia O'Connell Davidson, *Children in the Global Sex Trade* (Cambridge: Polity Press, 2005).

69 Iman Hashim, "Discourse(s) of Childhood," paper presented to Child Abuse and Exploitation: Social, Legal and Political Dilemmas Workshop, International Institute for the Sociology of Law, Onati, May 2003.

70 Ibid.; O'Connell Davidson, *Children in the Global Sex Trade.*

71 Karin A. Heissler, "Rethinking 'Trafficking' in Children's Migratory Processes: The Role of Social Networks in Child Labor Migration in Bangladesh," *Children's Geographies* 11, no. 1 (2013): 89.

72 Ann Whitehead, Iman M. Hashim, and Vegard Iversen, "Child Migration, Child Agency and Inter-generational Relations in Africa and South Asia," Working paper T24 (Brighton: University of Sussex, Development Research Centre on Migration, Globalisation and Poverty, December 2007); Tanja Bastia, "Child Trafficking or Teenage Migration? Bolivian Migrants in Argentina," *International Migration* 43, no. 4 (2005): 57–89; K. H. Riioen, A. Hatloy, and L. Bjerkan, *Travel to Uncertainty: A Study of Child Relocation in Burkina Faso, Ghana and Mali* (Oslo: Fafo Institute for Applied International Studies, 2004).

73 Heissler, "Rethinking 'Trafficking' in Children's Migratory Processes," 90.

74 Weitzer, "Social Construction of Sex Trafficking," 448.

75 For the homeless, see Malcolm Williams and Brian Cheal, "Can We Measure Homelessness? A Critical Evaluation of the Method of 'Capture-Recapture,'" *International Journal Social Research Methodology* 5, no. 3 (2001): 239–254. For street children, see R. Q. Gurgel, J.D.C. da Fonseca, D. Neyra-Castaneda, Geoff Gill, and Luis Cuevas, "Capture-Recapture to Estimate the Number of Street Children in a City in Brazil," *Archives of Disease in Childhood* 89, no. 3 (2004): 222–224. For prostitution, see A. Brunovskis and G. Tyldum, "Crossing Borders: An Empirical Study of Transnational Prostitution and Trafficking in Human Beings" (Oslo: Fafo Research Institute, 2004).

76 Jeffrey Passel, "The Size and Characteristics of the Unauthorized Migrant Populations in the U.S.: Estimates Based on the March 2005 Current Population Survey,"

Pew Hispanic Center, March 7, 2006; Jeffrey S. Passel, "Unauthorized Migrants: Numbers and Characteristics," background briefing prepared for Task Force on Immigration and America's Future, Pew Hispanic Center, June 14, 2005. George Borjas, "Immigration and Self-Selection," in *Immigration, Trade, and the Labor Market*, ed. John M. Abowed and Richard B. Freeman (Chicago: University of Chicago Press, 1991); George Borjas, "Does Immigration Grease the Wheels of the Labor Market?," *Brookings Papers on Economic Activity* (2001).

Chapter 2   The Old and New Abolitionists

1   Laura María Agustín, *Sex at the Margins: Migration, Labor Markets and the Rescue Industry* (London: Zed Books, 2007).

2   Kimberly Kay Hoang and Rhacel Salazar Parreñas, eds., *Human Trafficking Reconsidered: Rethinking the Problem, Envisioning New Solutions* (New York: IDEBATE Press 2014), 14.

3   Hebah Farrag, Richard Flory, and Brie Loskota, "Evangelicals and Human Trafficking: Rescuing, Rehabilitating, and Releasing One Individual at a Time," in *Human Trafficking Reconsidered: Rethinking the Problem, Envisioning New Solutions*, ed. Kimberly Kay Hoang and Rhacel Salazar Parreñas (New York: IDEBATE Press, 2014), 118.

4   Alicia Peters, "Challenging the Sex/Labor Trafficking Dichotomy with Victim Experience," in *Human Trafficking Reconsidered: Rethinking the Problem, Envisioning New Solutions*, ed. Kimberly Kay Hoang and Rhacel Salazar Parreñas (New York: IDEBATE Press, 2014), 30–40.

5   See Elizabeth Bernstein, "The Sexual Politics of the New Abolitionism," *Journal of Feminist Cultural Studies* 18, no. 3 (2007): 128–151; Jacqueline Berman, "The Left, the Right, and the Prostitute: The Making of the U.S. Anti-trafficking in Persons Policy," *Tulane Journal of International and Comparative Law* 14 (2006): 269–295; Jennifer Block, "Sex Trafficking: Why the Faith Trade Is Interested in the Sex Trade," *Conscience* 25, no. 2 (2004): 32–35; Gretchen Soderlund, "Running from the Rescuers: New U.S. Crusades against Sex Trafficking and the Rhetoric of Abolition," *NAWSA Journal* 17, no. 3 (2005): 64–87.

6   Eileen Boris and Heather Berg. "Protecting Virtue, Erasing Labor: Historical Responses to Trafficking," in *Human Trafficking Reconsidered: Rethinking the Problem, Envisioning New Solutions*, ed. Kimberly Kay Hoang and Rhacel Salazar Parreñas (New York: IDEBATE Press, 2014): 19–40.

7   Annuska Derks, "From White Slaves to Trafficking Survivors: Notes on the Trafficking Debate," Working paper 00–02 (Princeton: Center for Migration and Development, Princeton University, 2000.)

8   Jo Doezema, "Who Gets to Choose? Coercion, Consent, and the UN Trafficking Protocol," *Gender and Development* 10, no. 1 (2002): 20–27.

9   Vern Bullough and Bonnie Bullough, *Women and Prostitution: A Social History* (New York: Prometheus Books, 1987).

10   Doezema, "Who Gets to Choose?"

11   Marjan Wijers and Lin Lap-Chew, *Trafficking in Women: Forced Labor and Slavery-Like Practices in Marriage, Domestic Labor and Prostitution* (Amersfoort, Netherlands: La Strada International, 1997).

12   Ibid.; Doezema, "Who Gets to Choose?"

13   Elizabeth Kelly and Linda Regan, "Stopping Trafficking, Exploring the Extent of,

and Responses to, Trafficking in Women for Sexual Exploitation in the UK," *Police Research Series* 125 (London: Home Office, 2000).

14 Other relevant international instruments followed, including the International Labor Organization Convention Concerning the Prohibition and Immediate Action for the Elimination of the Worst Forms of Child Labor and the Protocol to the Convention of the Right of the Child on the Sale of Children, Child Prostitution and Child Pornography.

15 Jo Doezema, "Now You See Her, Now You Don't: Sex Workers at the UN Trafficking Protocol Negotiations," *Social & Legal Studies* 14 (2005): 61–89.

16 Eric Goldscheider, "Prostitutes Work, but Do They Consent?" 2000. http://departments.bloomu.edu/crimjust/pages/articles/sex_tourism.htm.

17 Human Rights Caucus, "Recommendations and Commentary on the Draft Protocol to Prevent, Suppress and Punish Trafficking in Persons, Especially Women and Children, Supplementing the United Nations Convention against International Organized Crime." Available at UN Office on Drugs and Crime website, https://www.unodc.org/documents/middleeastandnorthafrica/organised-crime/ UNITED_NATIONS_CONVENTION_AGAINST_TRANSNATIONAL_ ORGANIZED_CRIME_AND_THE_PROTOCOLS_THERETO.pdf. Accessed August 31, 2015.

18 Elżbieta M. Goździak and Elizabeth A. Collett, "Research on Human Trafficking in North America: A Review of Literature," *International Migration* 43, nos. 1–2 (2005): 99–128.

19 United Nations, *UN Protocol to Prevent, Suppress, and Punish Trafficking in Persons, Especially Women and Children* (2000).

20 Louis Shelly, *Human Trafficking: A Global Perspective* (Cambridge: Cambridge University Press, 2010), 16.

21 Kamala Kempadoo, ed., *Trafficking and Prostitution Reconsidered: New Perspectives on Migration, Sex Work and Human Rights* (Boulder, CO: Paradigm Publishers, 2005), 109.

22 Pardis Mahdavi, *Gridlock: Labor, Migration, and Human Trafficking in Dubai* (Stanford: Stanford University Press, 2011); Christien Anker and Ilse van Liempt, eds., *Human Rights and Migration: Trafficking for Forced Labour* (Hampshire, England: Palgrave, 2012.)

23 Shelly, *Human Trafficking: A Global Perspective.*

24 See Barbara Limanowska, "Trafficking in Human Beings in South Eastern Europe," UN Children's Fund (UNICEF), March 2005; Rutvica Andrijasevic, "The Differences Borders Make: (Il)legality, Migration and Trafficking in Italy among Eastern European Women in Prostitution," in *Uprootings/Regroundings: Questions of Home and Migration*, ed. Sara Ahmed, Claudia Casteneda, Anne-Marie Fortier, and Mimi Sheller, 251–272 (New York: Berg, 2003); Rebecca Surtees, "Traffickers and Trafficking in Southern and Eastern Europe: Considering the Other Side of Human Trafficking," *European Journal of Criminology* 5, no. 1 (2008): 39–68.

25 Mahdavi, *Gridlock*, 13.

26 Kempadoo, *Trafficking and Prostitution Reconsidered*, ix.

27 Hania Zlotnik, "The Global Dimensions of Female Migration," 2003. Migration Information Source. http://www.migrationinformation.org/feature/display. cfm?ID=109. Accessed August 31, 2015.

28 Kempadoo, *Trafficking and Prostitution Reconsidered.* 29.

29 Anker and van Liempt, *Human Rights and Migration*, 8.

30 Ratna Kapur, "The Tragedy of Victimization Rhetoric: Resurrecting the 'Native' Subject in International/Postcolonial Feminist Legal Politics," *Harvard Law Review* 15 (2002): 1–37; Wendy Chapkis, "Trafficking, Migration and the Law: Protecting Innocents, Punishing Immigrants," *Gender and Society* 17, no. 6 (2003): 923–937; Nadita Sharma, "Anti-Trafficking Rhetoric and the Making of a Global Apartheid," *NWSA Journal* 17, no. 3 (2005): 88–111.

31 Soderlund, "Running from the Rescuers," 73.

32 Ibid.

33 Anna-Louise Crago, "Unholy Collaboration," *Rabble*, May 15, 2003. http://rabble.ca/news/unholy-collaboration.

34 Soderlund, "Running from the Rescuers," 67.

35 Allan D. Hertzke, *Freeing God's Children: The Unlikely Alliance for Human Rights* (Lanham, MD: Rowman and Littlefield, 2004), 331. Cited in Soderlund, "Running from the Rescuers."

36 Chuck Neubauer. "Top Human Traffickers Need Not Fear Obama," *Washington Times*, July 29, 2012.

37 Anthony M. DeStefano, *The War on Human Trafficking: U.S. Policy Assessed* (New Brunswick, NJ: Rutgers University Press, 2008), xix.

38 Adult victims who want to avail themselves of publicly funded assistance programs must be willing to cooperate with law enforcement. Minors under the age of eighteen are exempt from this requirement.

39 Trafficking Victims Protection Act of 2000, P.L. 106–386 (2000). Trafficking Victims Protection Reauthorization Act of 2003, P.L.108–193 (2003).

40 Tom Coburn, "Blind Faith: How Congress is Failing Trafficking Victims" (Office of Tom Coburn, U.S. Senate, 2011).

41 Benjamin E. Skinner, *A Crime So Monstrous: Face-to-Face with Modern-Day Slavery* (New York: Free Press, 2008), 45.

42 Personal communication, September 2013.

43 Elizabeth Bernstein, "The Sexual Politics of the 'New Abolitionism,'" *Differences: A Journal of Feminist Cultural Studies* 18, no. 3 (2007): 128–151.

44 DeStefano, *War on Human Trafficking*, 106–107.

45 Ibid., 113.

46 Ibid., 125.

47 I had a small subcontract from Westat, the main J/TIP contractor, to carry out several process and outcome evaluations, including an evaluation of an antitrafficking program in Doha, Qatar, funded by the State Department. The results of the evaluation were not as favorable as both the funder and the program hoped for and my report was never released.

48 "Partnerships." Office to Monitor and Combat Trafficking Persons (J/TIP), U.S. Department of State. http://www.state.gov/j/tip4p/partner/index.htm. Accessed August 15, 2014.

49 See Hoang and Parreñas, *Human Trafficking Reconsidered*, 10–11, for a list of federal departments involved in antitrafficking activities.

50 See Annual ORR Reports to Congress at http://www.acf.hhs.gov/programs/orr/resource/annual-orr-reports-to-congress.

51 Andrew Schoenholtz, "Refugee Protection Post-September 11," *Columbia Human Rights Law Review* 36 (2005): 323–364.

52 See Mark Greenberg's testimony on unaccompanied children before the Committee on Homeland Security and Governmental Affairs, July 9, 2014,

http://www.acf.hhs.gov/programs/olab/resource/testimony-from-mark-green
berg-on-unaccompanied-children.

53 Ibid.

54 Wendy Young, *The Struggle between Migration Control and Victim Protection: The UK Approach to Human Trafficking* (Washington, DC: Women's Commission for Refugee Women and Children, 2005).

55 *STOP Programme, Article 18: Protection of Victims of Trafficking and Fight against Crime (Italy and the European Scenarios)*. Research Report. 2002. On the Road Edizioni. http://lastradainternational.org/doc-center/1199/article-18-protection-of-victims-of-trafficking-and-fight-against-crime-italy-and-the-european-scenarios-research-report. Accessed August 31, 2015.

56 Alison Siskin and Liana Sun Wyler, *Trafficking in Persons: U.S. Policy and Issues for Congress* (Washington, DC: Congressional Research Service, 2013).

57 Gregory Zhong Tian Chen, "Elian or Alien? The Contradictions of Protecting Undocumented Children under the Special Juvenile Statute," *Hastings Constitutional Law Quarterly* 27 (2000): 597–666.

58 ORR has never funded any research or evaluation of their antitrafficking efforts. In May 2002, ORR did issue a request for proposals "(a) To determine the extent of community awareness regarding the problem of human trafficking among both the general United States population and the organizations that serve victims; and (b) to better understand the successful approaches that might encourage victims to come forward for identification and assistance. The resultant information will be used as the basis for an array of culturally appropriate Public Service Announcements designed to increase the number of victims identified and encourage the development and implementation of additional programs intended to protect and care for victims of severe forms of trafficking" (Federal Register, May 24, 2002). However, this funding stream was cancelled as a result of a campaign led by the Protection Project and other service providers who insisted that every federal dollar should be spent on direct services to trafficked persons and not on research.

59 Mindy Loiselle, Margaret MacDonnell, Julianne Duncan, and Mary Ellen Dougherty, "Care for Trafficked Children." United States Conference of Catholic Bishops, April 2006. http://www.brycs.org/documents/upload/CareForTraffickedChildren.pdf. Accessed August 31, 2015.

60 Greta Lynn Uehling, "International Smuggling of Children: Coyotes, Snakeheads and the Politics of Compassion," *Anthropological Quarterly* 81, no. 4(2008): 833–871.

61 Juan Lizama, "Did Catholic Charity Help Teen Get Abortion?" *Richmond Times Dispatch*, June 19, 2008. http://www.timesdispatch.com/entertainment-life/did-catholic-charity-staff-help-teen-get-abortion/article_1f18d4b3-f28c-5222-a367–902f39818685.html?mode=jqm.

62 See Joan Frawley Desmond, "HHS Ends Contract with Church Program for Trafficking Victims, Stressing Need for Contraception," *National Catholic Register*, October 17, 2011. http://www.ncregister.com/daily-news/hhs-ends-contract-with-church-program-for-trafficking-victims-stressing-nee/; Jerry Markon, "Health, Abortion Issues Split Obama Administration and Catholic Groups," *Washington Post*, October 31, 2011. http://www.washingtonpost.com/politics/health-abortion-issues-split-obama-administration-catholic-groups/2011/10/27/gIQAXV5xZM_story_1.html.

Chapter 3 Snakeheads, Coyotes, and . . . Mothers

1 Victor Malarek, *The Natashas: Inside the New Global Sex Trade* (New York: Arcade Publishing, 2004).

2 Sverre Molland, "'I Am Helping Them': 'Traffickers,' 'Anti-traffickers' and Economies of Bad Faith," *Australian Journal of Anthropology* 22 (2011): 237.

3 United Nations Office on Drugs and Crime, *Trafficking in Persons: Global Patterns* (UNODC, 2006), https://www.unodc.org/pdf/traffickinginpersons_report_2006-04.pdf (accessed September 6, 2015); Louise Shelley, *Human Trafficking: A Global Perspective* (New York: Cambridge University Press, 2010).

4 For those who emphasize the organized crime link, see Alexis Aronowitz, Gerda Theuermann, and Elena Tyurykanova, *Analyzing the Business Model of Trafficking in Human Beings to Better Prevent the Crime* (Vienna: Organization for Security and Cooperation in Europe, 2010); Shelley, *Human Trafficking: A Global Perspective.*

5 Christine Bruckert and Collette Parent, *Trafficking in Human Beings and Organized Crime: A Literature Review* (Ottawa: Research and Evaluation Branch, Canadian Mounted Police, 2002).

6 John Salt, "Trafficking and Human Smuggling: A European Perspective," *International Migration* 38, no. 3 (2000): 31–56.

7 Rebecca Taibly, "Organized Crime and People Smuggling/Trafficking in Australia," *Australian Institute of Criminology* 208 (2001): 1–6; Judith Juhasz, "Migrant Trafficking and Human Smuggling in Hungary," in *Migrant Trafficking and Human Smuggling in Europe: A Review of Evidence with Case Studies from Hungary, Poland, and Ukraine,* ed. Frank Laczko and David Thompson, 167–232 (Geneva: International Organization for Migration, 2000); Aronowitz, Theuermann, and Tyurykanova, *Analyzing the Business Model of Trafficking in Human Beings*; and Shelley, *Human Trafficking: A Global Perspective.*

8 *Trafficking in Persons Report* (Washington, DC: United States Department of State, June 2003–2007).

9 Sarah Shannon, "Prostitution and the Mafia: The Involvement of Organized Crime in the Global Economy," in *Illegal Migration and Commercial Sex: The New Slave Trade,* ed. Phil Williams (London: Frank Cass, 1999); Bruce Caldwell, Idrani Pieris, Barkat-e-Khuda, John Caldwell, and Pat Caldwell, "Sexual Regimes and Sexual Networking: The Risk of an HIV/AIDS Epidemic in Bangladesh," *Social Science and Medicine* 48, no. 8 (1999): 1103–1116.

10 Maggee Lee, *Trafficking and Global Crime Control* (London: Sage Publication, 2011), 90.

11 Dick Hobbs and Colin Dunningham, "Local Organised Crime: Context and Pretext," in *The New European Criminology,* ed. Vincenzo Ruggiero, Nigel South, and Ian Taylor (London: Routledge, 1998); Jef Huysmans, "The European Union and the Securitization of Migration," *Journal of Common Market Studies* 38, no. 5 (2000): 751–777; James Finckenauer and Yuri A. Voronin, "The Threat of Russian Organized Crime," *Issues in International Crime* (Washington, DC: National Institute of Justice, June 2001); James Finckenauer and Yuri A. Voronin, "The Threat of Russian Organized Crime," *Issues in International Crime* (Washington, DC: National Institute of Justice, June 2001); Ian Loader, "Policing, Securitization and Democratization in Europe," *Criminal Justice* 2, no. 2 (2002): 125–153; Michael Levi, "Organised Crime and Terrorism," in *The Oxford Handbook of Criminology,* ed. Mike Maguire, Rod Morgan, and Robert Reiner (Oxford: Oxford University

Press, 2007); Dick Hobbs, "The Firm: Organised Crime on a Shifting Terrain," *British Journal of Criminology* 41 (2001): 549–560.

12 Lee, *Trafficking and Global Crime Control*, 91.

13 Rowena Fong and Jodi Berger Cardoso, "Child Human Trafficking Victims: Challenges for the Child Welfare System," *Evaluation and Program Planning* 33 (2010): 311–316; Kathleen Fitzgibbon, "Modern-Day Slavery? The Scope of Trafficking in Persons in Africa," *African Security Review* 12, no. 1 (2003): 81–89.

14 See Deborah A. Boehm, *Intimate Migrations: Gender, Family, and Illegality among Transnational Mexicans* (New York: University Press, 2012).

15 "The Terrible Truth about the Ship of Slaves," by James Astill, *Guardian*, April 21, 2001, http://www.theguardian.com/world/2001/apr/21/jamesastill. Accessed September 4, 2015.

16 Phil Williams, "Trafficking in Women: The Role of Transnational Organized Crime," in *Trafficking in Humans: Social, Cultural and Political Dimensions*, ed. Sally Cameron and Edward Newman (Tokyo: United Nations University Press, 2008).

17 Karin Heissler, "No One Comes on Their Own: The System of Child Labor Migration in Bangladesh," *COMPAS Working Paper* no. 72 (2009): 11. COMPAS Center on Migration Policy and Society, https://www.compas.ox.ac.uk/fileadmin/files/Publications/working_papers/WP_2009/WP0972%20Karin%20Heissler.pdf.

18 Marcel Mauss, ed., *The Gift, the Form, and Reason for Exchanges in Archaic Societies*, trans. W. D. Halls (London: Routledge, 1990); Carol Vance, "Negotiating Sex and Gender in the Attorney General's Commission on Pornography," in *Uncertain Terms: Negotiating Gender in American Culture*, ed. Faye Ginsburg and Anna Lowenhaupt Tsing (Boston: Beacon Press, 1990).

19 Lynellyn D. Long, "Anthropological Perspectives on the Trafficking of Women for Sexual Exploitation," *International Migration* 42, no. 1 (2004): 5–30.

20 Anuja Agrawal, "Kinship and Trafficking: The Case of the Bedia Community," *Canadian Women's Studies* 22, nos. 3–4 (2003): 131–135.

21 Jessaca Leinaweaver, "Informal Kinship-Based Fostering around the World: Anthropological Finding," *Child Development Perspectives* 8, no. 3 (2014): 131–136.

22 Court Notes, University of Michigan Human Trafficking Database, https://www.law.umich.edu/clinical/HuTrafficCases/Pages/searchdatabase.aspx. Accessed September 6, 2015.

23 Raimo Väyrynen, "Illegal Immigration, Human Trafficking, and Organized Crime," Discussion Paper No. 2003/72 (Geneva: United Nations University, 2003).

24 Marisa O. Ensor and Elżbieta M. Goździak, eds., *Children and Migration: At the Crossroads of Resiliency and Vulnerability* (London: Palgrave Macmillan, 2010).

25 Ratna Kapur, "Migrant Women and the Legal Politics of Anti-Trafficking Interventions," in *Trafficking in Humans: Social, Cultural and Political Dimensions*, ed. Sally Cameron and Edward Newman (Tokyo: United Nations University Press, 2008), 119.

26 Ann Whitehead and Iman Hashim, *Children and Migration: Background Paper for DFID Migration Team* (Brighton: University of Sussex, Development Research Center on Migration, Globalization and Poverty, 2005).

27 Karin A. Heissler, "Rethinking 'Trafficking' in Children's Migratory Processes: The Role of Social Networks in Child Labor Migration in Bangladesh," *Children's Geographies* 11, no. 1 (2013): 90; Julia O'Connell Davidson, *Children in the Global Sex Trade* (Cambridge: Polity Press, 2005); Michael Bourdillon, "Children and

Work: A Review of Current Literature and Debates," *Development and Change* 37, no. 6 (2006): 1201–1226; Peter Hopkins and Malcolm Hill, "Pre-flight Experiences and Migration Stories: The Accounts of Unaccompanied Asylum-Seeking Children," *Children's Geographies* 6, no. 3 (2008): 257–268; Oude Breuil and Brenda Carina, "'Precious Children in a Heartless World'? The Complexities of Child Trafficking in Marseille," *Children & Society* 22, no. 3 (2008): 223–234; Madeleine Dobson, "Unpacking Children in Migration Research," *Children's Geographies* 7, no. 3 (2009): 355–360.

Chapter 4 Not Chained to a Bed in a Brothel

1   Erin Kirk, "How to Kick in a Brothel Door," *Going to the Sea* (blog), December 7, 2012, http://goingtothesea.com/2012/12/07/how-to-kick-in-a-brothel-door/.

2   Elżbieta M. Goździak and Micah N. Bump, *Data and Research on Human Trafficking: Bibliography of Research Based Literature* (Washington, DC: Institute for the Study of International Migration, Georgetown University, 2008).

3   As I write this book in the summer of 2014, neither ORR nor the Department of Justice has released their FY 2013 and FY 2014 Reports to Congress. However, ORR program staff has been gracious enough to provide me with an aggregate number of minors that received eligibility letters in FY 2013 and FY 2014.

4   Data received from USCCB.

5   FY 2014 data comes from ORR staff ahead of the publication of the 2014 Annual ORR Report to Congress.

6   See "Child Marriage. Annual Report 2011," Ford Foundation, http://www.ford-foundation.org/2011-annual/youth-sexuality-and-rights/map/#/married-by-15/ Niger. Accessed August 31, 2015.

7   See a fact sheet prepared by the UN Population Fund, "Child Marriage Profile," http://www.devinfo.info/mdg5b/profiles/files/profiles/4/Child_Marriage_Country_Profile_LACHND_Honduras.pdf. Accessed August 31, 2015.

8   See "Fact Sheet on Child Marriage Numbers," October 2014, http://girlsnotbrides. theideabureau.netdna-cdn.com/wp-content/uploads/2014/10/GNB-factsheet-on-child-marriage-numbers-Oct-2014.pdf.

9   Information provided by ORR, 2014.

10   "Annual ORR Reports to Congress," Office of Refugee Resettlement, Department of Health and Human Services, 1980–2012.

11   Victoria L. Banyard, Linda M. Williams, and Jane A. Siegel, "Retraumatization among Adult Women Sexually Abused in Childhood: Exploratory Analyses in a Prospective Study," *Journal of Child Sexual Abuse* 11, no. 3 (2003): 19–48.

12   Terry Coonan, "Human Trafficking: Victims' Voices in Florida," in *International Sex Trafficking of Women and Children: Understanding the Global Epidemic*, ed. Leonard Territo and George Kirkham (New York: Looseleaf Law Publications, 2010); Edward A. Walker, Elana Newman, Mary Koss, and David Bernstein, "Does the Study of Victimization Revictimize the Victim?," *General Hospital Psychiatry* 19 (1997): 403–410; James W. Pennebaker, *Opening Up: The Healing Power of Expressing Emotions* (New York: Guilford Press, 1997).

13   Derek Summerfield, "The Impact of War and Atrocity on Civilian Populations: Basic Principles for NGO Intervention and a Critique of Psychosocial Trauma Projects," Relief and Rehabilitation Network Paper 14 (London: Overseas Development Institute, 1996); Derek Summerfield, "The Invention of Post-Traumatic Stress

Disorder and the Social Usefulness of a Psychiatric Category," *British Medical Journal* 322 (2001): 95.

14 Susan Sarnoff, "Social Workers and the Witness Role: Ethics, Laws, and Roles," *Journal of Social Work Values & Ethics* 1, no. 1 (2004).

15 I serve as an independent consultant to ORR to provide advice on such cases. Without exception, in 2015 I have seen only cases of teen males allegedly captured by cartels to take part in smuggling operations.

Part III   "Rescued"

1 Johnny E. McGaha and Amanda Evans, "Where Are the Victims? The Credibility Gap in Human Trafficking Research." https://maggiemcneill.files.wordpress. com/2011/10/the-credibility-gap-in-human-trafficking-research.pdf. Accessed August 31, 2015.

2 See http://www.freedomyouthproject.org/p/human-trafficking-facts.html.

Chapter 5   Hidden in Plain Sight

1 Denise Brennan, "Competing Claims of Victimhood? Foreign and Domestic Victims of Trafficking in the United States," *Sexuality Research and Social Policy* 5, no. 4 (2008): 45–61.

2 Jane Morse, "Resources, Better Coordination Needed to Fight Human Trafficking: Mobilization Just Beginning to Tackle the Problem, U.N. Official Says," *UNINFO*, April 25, 2007; J. Zeitlin, "Groups Push State to Fight Human Trafficking," *Naples* (Florida) *Daily News*, February 26, 2006.

3 Government Accountability Office, *Human Trafficking: Monitoring and Evaluation of International Projects Are Limited, but Experts Suggest Improvements* (Washington, DC: GAO, 2007).

4 Laura María Agustín, *Sex at the Margins: Labor Markets and the Rescue Industry* (London: Zed Books, 2007); William F. McDonald, "Traffic Counts, Symbols and Agendas: A Critique of a Campaign against Trafficking in Human Beings," *International Review of Victimology* 11, no. 1 (2004): 143–176; Ronald Weitzer, "The Social Construction of Sex Trafficking: Ideology and Institutionalization of a Moral Crusade," *Politics & Society* 35, no. 3 (2007): 447–475.

5 Carole Angel, "Immigration Relief for Human Trafficking Victims: Focusing the Lens on the Human Rights of Victims," *University of Maryland Law Journal of Race, Religion, Gender & Class* 7, no. 1 (2007): 23–36.

6 Seri E. Izarola, et al., *Trafficking of U.S. Citizens and Legal Permanent Residents: The Forgotten Victims and Survivors* (Washington, DC: ICF International, 2008).

7 News accounts of human trafficking in the United States have grown from "a handful of articles to more than 3,750 stories . . . in 2008 alone." Amy Farrell, Jack McDevitt, and Stephanie Fahy, "Where Are All the Victims? Understanding the Determinants of Official Identification of Human Trafficking Incidents," *Criminology and Public Policy* 9, no. 2 (2010): 201–233. For prosecutions, see Mark J. Kappelhoff, "Federal Prosecutions of Human Trafficking Cases: Striking a Blow against Modern Day Slavery," *University of St. Thomas Law Journal* 6, no. 1 (2008): 9–20.

8 Jane Nady Sigmon, "Combating Modern-day Slavery: Issues in Identifying and

Assisting Victims of Human Trafficking Worldwide," *Victims and Offenders* 3, nos. 2–3 (2008): 245–257.

9 Stephanie Hepburn and Rita J. Simon, "Hidden in Plain Sight: Human Trafficking in the United States," *Gender Issues* 27, nos. 1–2 (2010): 1–26.

10 Denise Brennan, *Life Interrupted: Trafficking into Forced Labor in the United States* (Durham: Duke University Press, 2014), 66.

11 Farrell, McDevitt, and Fahy, "Where Are All the Victims?"; Heather Clawson, Nicole Dutch, and Megan Cummings, *Law Enforcement Response to Human Trafficking and the Implications for Victims: Current Practices and Lessons Learned* (Washington, DC: ICF International, 2006); Michael Shively et al., *Survey of Practitioners to Assess the Local Impact of Transnational Crime, Task Order Final Report* (Washington, DC: National Institute of Justice, U.S. Department of Justice, 2007); Deborah G. Wilson, William F. Walsh, and Sherilyn Kleuber, "Trafficking in Human Beings: Training and Services among US Law Enforcement Agencies," *Police Practice and Research* 7, no. 2 (2006): 149–160.

12 Farrell, McDevitt, and Fahy, "Where Are All the Victims?"

13 Amy Farrell, Jack McDevitt, and Stephanie Fahy, *Understanding and Improving Law Enforcement Responses to Human Trafficking: Final Report* (Washington, DC: U.S. Department of Justice, National Institute of Justice, 2008).

14 Rebecca J. Macy and Laurie M. Graham, "Identifying Domestic and International Sex-Trafficking Victims during Human Service Provision," *Trauma, Violence & Abuse* 13, no. 2 (2012): 60.

15 Michelle R. Kaufman and Mary Crawford, "Sex Trafficking in Nepal: A Review of Intervention and Prevention Programs," *Violence against Women* 17, no. 5 (2011): 651–665; Rebecca J. Macy and Natalie Johns, "Aftercare Services for International Sex Trafficking Survivors: Informing U.S. Service and Program Development in an Emerging Practice Area," *Trauma, Violence & Abuse* 12, no. 2 (2011): 87–98.

16 Paul Rigby, "Separated and Trafficked Children: The Challenges for Child Protection Professionals," *Child Abuse Review* 20, no. 5 (2011): 324–340.

17 The campaign focused primarily on outreach to those individuals who most likely encounter victims on a daily basis, but may not recognize them as victims of human trafficking. A critical component of the Rescue and Restore campaign was the creation of the National Human Trafficking Resource Center, a telephone hotline: 1 (888) 373–7888. The hotline is operated by a nongovernmental organization and connects victims of trafficking to organizations who can help them in their local area.

18 Polaris Project, *Human Trafficking Trends in the United States: National Human Trafficking Resource Center 2007–2012* (Washington, DC: Polaris Project, 2013).

19 Melissa Ditmor and Juhu Thukral, "Accountability and the Use of Raids to Fight Trafficking," *Anti-Trafficking Review* 1 (2012): 136.

20 María del Carmen Ayes Cerna, *An In-Depth Analysis of Child Labor and Poverty in Honduras* (San Jose, Costa Rica: International Labor Organization, 2003).

21 International Labor Organization, *Honduras Child Labor Data Country Brief* (Geneva: ILO-IPEC, 2002).

22 Micah N. Bump and Julianne Duncan, "Conference on Identifying and Serving Child Victims of Trafficking," *International Migration* 415 (2003): 201–218.

23 Ibid.

Chapter 6   Jail the Offender, Protect the Victim

1   Kathryn Farr, *Sex Trafficking: The Global Market in Women and Children* (New York: Worth, 2005), 22.

2   Cynthia Shepherd Torg, "Human Trafficking Enforcement in the United States," 14 *TUL. J. INT'L & COMP. L.* 503 (2006).

3   Anthony DeStefano, *The War on Human Trafficking: U.S. Policy Assessed* (New Brunswick, NJ: Rutgers University Press, 2008).

4   William F. McDonald, "Explaining the Underperformance of the Anti-trafficking Campaign: Experience from the United States and Europe," *Crime, Law and Social Change* 61, no. 2 (2014): 125–138.

5   Duren Banks and Tracey Kyckelhahn, *Characteristics of Suspected Human Trafficking Incidents, 2008–2010* (Washington, DC: Bureau of Justice Statistics, 2011), http://www.bjs.gov/content/pub/pdf/cshti0810.pdf.

6   Interview with HTRS staff member, summer 2013.

7   See Banks and Kyckelhahn, *Characteristics of Suspected Human Trafficking Incidents, 2008–2010.*

8   Data in this report are from the Human Trafficking Reporting System, which was designed to measure the performance of federally funded task forces. This report is the second in a Bureau of Justice Statistics series about the characteristics of human trafficking investigations, suspects, and victims. It reports case outcomes, including suspect arrests and visa status of confirmed victims, and describes the characteristics of incidents entered into the HTRS prospectively by the task forces beginning in 2008.

9   Tracey Kyckelhahn, Allen J. Beck, and Thomas H. Cohen, *Characteristics of Suspected Human Trafficking Incidents, 2007–08* (Washington, DC: Bureau of Justice Statistics, 2009), http://www.bjs.gov/content/pub/pdf/cshti08.pdf.

10   McDonald, "Explaining the Underperformance of the Anti-Trafficking Campaign."

11   United States Department of State, *2012 Trafficking in Persons Report* (Washington, DC: United States Department of State), 361.

12   United States Department of State, *2014 Trafficking in Persons Report* (Washington, DC: United States Department of State), 398.

13   DeStefano, *War on Human Trafficking*, 130.

14   Amy Farrell, Coleen Owens, and Jack McDevitt, "New Laws but Few Cases: Understanding the Challenges to the Investigation and Prosecution of Human Trafficking Cases," *Crime, Law and Social Change* 61, no. 2 (2014): 139–168.

15   See University of Michigan School of Law, "Human Trafficking Database," http://www.law.umich.edu/CLINICAL/HUTRAFFICCASES/Pages/searchdatabase.aspx. Accessed July 15, 2014.

16   The creators of the database acknowledge hurdles to data collection, namely access to information on state cases, and the frequency with which defendants accept plea bargains to avoid trial.

17   There is no publicly available data on ongoing cases.

18   Hans Gouw was the leader of a company that recruited women from Indonesia to come to the United States to work as prostitutes and strippers. The women (including teenage girls) were forced to work for at least a year. The victims' travel documents and identification were confiscated. Additionally, they were closely monitored while living in a house under the control of Gouw. Gouw pled guilty to conspiracy to commit sex trafficking, immigration fraud, and identification document fraud on April 26, 2005. He was sentenced to five and a half years in prison.

An additional defendant was sentenced to one year and one day in prison, with a $50,000 forfeiture.

19 Two Cameroonian cases in 2000 were related: State of Michigan v. Joseph Djoumessi and the corresponding United States v. Joseph Djoumessi case. Similarly, two Indian cases, United States v. Lakireddy and Jane Doe v. Lakireddy, were related.

20 U.S. Congress created both "T" and "U" visas to encourage victims of certain serious crimes to cooperate with law enforcement officials who are prosecuting criminal offenders. Only certain types of crimes will qualify the victim for a T or U visa, but both T and U visas include the qualifying crime of human trafficking.

21 Micah N. Bump, a member of my research team, published a longer paper about this issue: Micah N. Bump, "Treat the Children Well: Shortcomings in the United States' Effort to Protect Child Trafficking Victims," *Notre Dame Journal of Law, Ethics, and Public Policy* 23 (2009): 73–107.

22 Ibid.

Part IV   Restored

1 The coalitions funded by the Office of Refugee Resettlement are listed on the webpage, "Office of Refugee Resettlement," US Department of Health and Human Services Website, http://www.acf.hhs.gov/programs/orr/resource/contact-information-for-coalitions.

Chapter 7   Idealized Childhoods

1 Jessica Schafer, "The Use of Patriarchal Imagery in the Civil War in Mozambique and Its Implications for the Reintegration of Child Soldiers," in *Children and Youth on the Front Line: Ethnography, Armed Conflict and Displacement*, ed. Jo Boyden and Joanna de Berry (Oxford: Berghahn Books, 2004).

2 Philippe Aries, *Centuries of Childhood* (New York: Alfred A. Knopf, 1962).

3 Richard T. Vann, "The Youth of Centuries of Childhood," *History and Theory* 21, no. 2: 279–297. Cited in Karen Wells, *Childhood in a Global Perspective* (Cambridge: Polity, 2009).

4 See, for example, John C. Sommerville, "The Rise and Fall of Childhood," *Sage Library of Social Science Research* 140 (1982); Barbara A. Hanawalt, *The Ties That Bound* (Oxford: Oxford University Press, 1986); and Shahar Shulaminth, *Childhood in the Middle Ages* (London: Routledge, 1990).

5 Wells, *Childhood in a Global Perspective*, 5–6.

6 David F. Lancy, *The Anthropology of Childhood: Cherubs, Chattel, Changelings* (Cambridge: Cambridge University Press, 2008).

7 Pia Christensen and Allison James, eds., *Research with Children: Perspectives and Practices* (London: Falmer Press, 2000). Chris Jenks, *Childhood* (New York: Routledge, 1996).

8 Surlee Swain, "Sweet Childhood Lost: Idealized Images of Childhood in the British Child Rescue Literature," *Journal of the History of Childhood and Youth* 2, no. 2 (2009): 198.

9 Ibid., 201.

10 Ibid.

11 Lydia Murdoch, *Imagined Orphans: Poor Families, Child Welfare, and Contested Citizenship in London* (New Brunswick, NJ: Rutgers University Press, 2006).

12 Swain, "Sweet Childhood Lost," 208.

13 See Sankar Nair Sen, *Trafficking in Women and Children in India* (New Delhi: Orient Langman, 2005).

14 Rowena Fong and Jodi Berger Cardoso, "Child Human Trafficking Victims: Challenges for the Child Welfare System," *Evaluation and Program Planning, Child Welfare and the Challenge of the New Americans* 33, no. 3 (2010): 311–316.

15 Alexis A. Aronowitz, "Smuggling and Trafficking in Human Beings: The Phenomenon, The Markets That Drive It and the Organisations That Promote It," *European Journal on Criminal Policy and Research* 9, no. 2 (2001): 163–195; Raimo Väyrynen, "Illegal Immigration, Human Trafficking, and Organized Crime," WIDER Discussion Paper 72 (Geneva: World Institute for Development Economics, 2003), http://www.econstor.eu/bitstream/10419/52839/1/376632771.pdf. Accessed September 6, 2015.

16 Leisy Abrego, "Intervention and Displacement: How U.S. Involvement in Central America Pushes Children and Families to Migrate," *Stanford University Press Blog*, August 12, 2014, http://stanfordpress.typepad.com/blog/2014/08/migration-from-central-america.html.

17 Julia O'Connell Davidson, "Moving Children? Child Trafficking, Child Migration, and Child Rights," *Critical Social Policy* 31, no. 3 (2011): 454–477.

18 Nicola Ansell, *Children, Youth and Development* (Abington, Oxford: Routledge, 2005), 23.

19 Roy Huijsmanns, *Children, Childhood and Migration*, Working Papers Series No. 427 (The Hague, Netherlands: Institute of Social Studies, 2006).

20 Ansell, *Children, Youth and Development*; Lancy, *Anthropology of Childhood*. See also Marisa O. Ensor, "Understanding Migrant Children: Conceptualizations, Approaches, and Issues," in *Children and Migration: At the Crossroads of Resiliency and Vulnerability*, ed. Marisa O. Ensor and Elżbieta M. Goździak (London: Palgrave, 2010).

21 Oude Breuil and Brenda Carina, "'Precious Children in a Heartless World'? The Complexities of Child Trafficking in Marseille," *Children & Society* 22, no. 3 (May 1, 2008): 223–234. See Neil Howard, "Promoting 'Healthy Childhoods' and Keeping Children 'at Home': Beninese Anti-Trafficking Policy in Times of Neoliberalism," *International Migration* 54, no. 4 (2013): 87–102; and O'Connell Davidson, "Moving Children?"

22 Catherine Panter-Brick, "Street Children and Their Peers: Perspectives on Homelessness, Poverty and Health," In *Children in Anthropology. Perspectives for the 21st Century*, ed. Helen B. Swartzman (Westport, CT: Bergin and Garvey, 2001), 38.

23 Breuil, "'Precious Children in a Heartless World'?," 224.

24 Given the rates of single parenthood, divorce, remarriage, and resulting blended families, these ideals are no longer prevalent among Western families either and yet they prevail in the policy and legal frameworks.

25 For Latin America: Jessaca B. Leinaweaver, "On Moving Children: The Social Implications of Andean Child Circulation," *American Ethnologist* 34, no. 1 (2007): 163–180; M. Weismantel, "Making Kin: Kinship Theory and Zumbagua Adoptions," *American Ethnologist* 22, no. 4 (1995): 685–709. For Africa: M. Pilon, "Les determinants de la scolarisation des enfants de 6 á 14 ans au Togo en 1981: Apports and limites de données censitaires," *Cahiers de Sciences Humaines* 31, no. 3 (1995): 697–718; E. P. Renne, *Population and Progress in a Yoruba Town* (Ann Arbor: University of Michigan Press, 2003).

26 Leinaweaver, "On Moving Children."

27 Kerry Richter, "Union Patterns and Children's Living Arrangements in Latin America," *Demography* 25, no. 4 (1988): 553–566.

28 Carola Suárez-Orozco, Hee Jin Bang, and Ha Yeon Kim, "I Felt Like My Heart Was Staying Behind: Psychological Implications of Family Separations and Reunifications for Immigrant Youth," *Journal of Adolescent Research* 26, no. 2 (2011): 222–257.

29 Joanna Dreby, *Divided by Borders: Mexican Migrants and Their Children* (Berkeley: University of California Press, 2010).

30 Harry Ferguson, "Abused and Looked After as Children: Child Abuse and Institutional Care in Historical Perspective," *Journal of Social Policy* 36, no. 1 (2007): 123–139.

31 Nancy Scheper-Hughes and Daniel J. Hoffman, "Brazilian Apartheid: Street Kids and the Struggle for Urban Space," in *The Cultural Politics of Childhood*, ed. Nancy Scheper-Hughes and Carolyn Sargent (Berkeley: University of California Press, 1998).

32 Breuil, "Precious Children in a Heartless World?," 225.

33 Julia O'Connell Davidson, *Children in the Global Sex Trade* (Cambridge: Polity, 2005).

34 Caitríona Ní Laoire, Fina Carpena-Méndez, Naomi Tyrrell, and Allen White, "Introduction: Childhood and Migration—Mobilities, Homes and Belongings," *Childhood* 17, no. 2 (2010): 155–162.

35 O'Connell Davidson, *Children in the Global Sex Trade*, 463.

36 See David Oswell, *The Agency of Children: From Family to Global Human Rights* (New York: Cambridge University Press, 2012).

37 UNICEF, *Child Trafficking: More Precious Than Gold*, 2007.

38 O'Connell Davidson, *Children in the Global Sex Trade*, 464.

39 Jo Boyden and Joanna de Berry, *Children and Youth on the Front Line: Ethnography, Armed Conflict and Displacement* (Oxford: Berghahn Books, 2005).

40 Anthony Giddens, *The Giddens Reader* (Stanford: Stanford University Press, 1993).

41 See Anna Tsing, "The Global Situation," *Cultural Anthropology* 15, no. 3 (2000): 327–360; Janet MacGaffey, *Congo-Paris: Transnational Traders on the Margins of the Law* (Bloomington: Indiana University Press, 2000).

42 Julia Meredith Hess and Dianna Shandy, "Kids at the Crossroads: Global Childhood and the State," *Anthropological Quarterly* 81, no. 4 (2008): 765–776.

43 See also Greta Lynn Uehling, "The International Smuggling of Children: Coyotes, Snakeheads, and the Politics of Compassion," *Anthropological Quarterly* 81, no. 4 (2008): 833–871.

44 Olga Nieuwenhuys, "The Paradox of Child Labor and Anthropology," *Annual Review of Anthropology* 25 (1996): 237–251.

45 O'Connell Davidson, *Children in the Global Sex Trade*, 465.

46 Huijsmanns, *Children, Childhood and Migration*.

47 Ibid.

48 Myra Bluebond-Langner and Jill E. Korbin, "Challenges and Opportunities in the Anthropology of Childhoods: An Introduction to 'Children, Childhoods, and Childhood Studies,'" *American Anthropologist* 109, no. 2 (2007): 241–246.

49 See, for example, A. James and A. Prout, eds., *Constructing and Reconstructing Childhood* (London: Falmer, 1997); Christopher Jenks, *Childhood* (London: Routledge, 1990).

50 Nancy Scheper-Hughes and Carolyn Sargent, eds., *The Cultural Politics of Childhood* (Berkeley: University of California Press, 1998).

51 David M. Rosen, *Armies of the Young: Child Soldiers in War and Terrorism* (New Brunswick, NJ: Rutgers University Press, 2005).

52 Michael Wyness, *Childhood and Society*, 2nd ed. (Basingstoke: Palgrave Macmillan, 2011).

53 Jean-Robert Cadet, *Restavec: From Haitian Slave Child to Middle-Class American* (Austin: University of Texas Press, 1998).

54 UNICEF, *The State of the World's Children 2006: Excluded and Invisible* (New York: United Nations Children's Fund, 2005), http://www.unicef.org/sowc06/pdfs/sowc06_fullreport.pdf.

55 Kate Price, "Putting Children First: 'Innocence' in Childhood and the Risk for Child Commercial Sexual Exploitation in the U.S.," Wellesley Centers for Women, Research, and Action Report (Fall 2012).

Chapter 8   Healing the Wounded

1 Nick Mai, "'Tempering with the Sex of Angels': Migrant Male Minors and Young Adults Selling Sex in the EU," *Journal of Ethnic and Migration Studies* 37, no. 8 (2011): 1237–1252.

2 Loretta M. Kopelman, "The Best-Interests Standard as Threshold, Ideal, and Standard of Reasonableness," *Journal of Medicine and Philosophy* 22, no. 3 (1997): 271–289.

3 Peter C. English, "Not Miniature Men and Women: Abraham Jacobi's Vision of a New Medical Specialty a Century Ago," in *Children and Health Care: Moral and Social Issues*, ed. Loretta M. Kopelman and John C. Moskop (Dordrecht, Netherlands: Kluwer Academic Publishers, 1989), 247–274; Anne L. Wilson, "Development of the US Federal Role in Children's Health Care: A Critical Appraisal," in *Children and Health Care*, ed. Kopelman and Moskop; Loretta M. Kopelman, "The Best-Interests Standards as Threshold, Ideal, and Standard of Reasonableness," *Journal of Medicine and Philosophy* 22 (1997): 271–289.

4 Robert M. Veatch, *A Theory of Medical Ethics* (New York: Basic, 1981); Robert M. Veatch, "Abandoning Informed Consent," *Hastings Center Report* 25, no. 2 (1995): 5–12; William Ruddick, "Questions Parents Should Resist," in *Children and Health Care*, ed. Kopelman and Moskop, 221–230; Lucy S. McGough, "Children v. Child Custody," *Encyclopedia of Bioethics*, rev., ed. Warren T. Reich (New York: Simon and Schuster Macmillan, 1995), 371–378; Hilary Rodham, "Children under the Law," *Harvard Educational Review* 43, no. 4 (1973): 487–514.

5 Kopelman, "The Best-Interests Standard."

6 See Joan B. Kelly, "The Best Interests of the Child: A Concept in Search of Meaning," *Family Court Review* 35, no. 4 (1997): 377–387; Joseph Goldstein, Albert J. Solnit, Sonja Goldstein, and Anna Freud, *The Best Interests of the Child* (New York: Free Press, 1996).

7 Bluebond-Langner and Korbin, "Challenges and Opportunities in the Anthropology of Childhoods."

8 Jyoti Sanghera, "Globalization, Labor Migration, and Human Rights: Unpacking the Trafficking Discourse," in *Trafficking and Prostitution Reconsidered: New Perspectives on Migration, Sex Work, and Human Rights*, ed. Kamala Kempadoo, Jyoti Sanghera, and Bandana Pattanaik (Boulder, CO: Paradigm Publishers, 2005), 13.

9   Ibid., 6.

10 Kempadoo, *Trafficking and Prostitution Reconsidered*, xxv.

11 Steffen Jensen and Henrik Ronsbo, *Histories of Victimhood* (Philadelphia: University of Pennsylvania Press, 2014).

12 Alyson Cole, *The Cult of True Victimhood: From the War on Welfare to the War on Terror* (Stanford: Stanford University Press, 2006).

13 Diana Tietjens Meyers, "Two Victim Paradigms and the Problem of 'Impure' Victims," *Humanity: An International Journal of Human Rights, Humanitarianism, and Development* 2, no. 2 (2011): 255–275.

14 See, for example, Frantz Fanon, *The Wretched of the Earth*, trans. Richard Philcox (New York: Grove Press, 2005 [1961]); Che Guevara, *Radical Writings on Guerrilla Warfare, Politics and Revolution* (London: Filiquarian, 2006); Laleh Khalili, *Heroes and Martyrs of Palestine: The Politics of National Commemoration* (Cambridge: Cambridge University Press, 2007).

15 See, for example, Vanessa Pupavac, "Therapeutic Governance: Psycho-social Intervention and Trauma Risk Management," *Disasters* 25, no. 4 (2001): 358–372. For clinicians: Allan Young, *The Harmony of Illusions: Inventing Post-Traumatic Stress Disorder* (Princeton: Princeton University Press, 1995).

16 See Didier Fassin and Richard Rechtman, *The Empire of Trauma: An Inquiry into the Condition of Victimhood* (Princeton: Princeton University Press, 2009); Jensen and Ronsbo, *Histories of Victimhood*, 4 (quote).

17 James E. Bayley, "The Concept of Victimhood," in *To Be a Victim*, ed. Diane Sank and David I. Caplan (New York: Springer, 1991).

18 Ana Gonzalez-Barrera, "Record Number of Deportations in 2012," Pew Research Center, January 24, 2014, http://www.pewresearch.org/fact-tank/2014/01/24/record-number-of-deportations-in-2012/.

19 Bayley, "Concept of Victimhood," 62, cited in Jensen and Ronsbo, *Histories of Victimhood*, 5.

20 Daniela Reale, *Away from Home: Protecting and Supporting Children on the Move* (London: Save the Children UK, 2008); Victoria Hayes, "Human Trafficking for Sexual Exploitation at World Sporting Events," *Chicago-Kent Law Review* 83, no. 3 (2010): 1106–1146.

21 Patricia Hynes, "Global Points of 'Vulnerability': Understanding Processes of the Trafficking of Children and Young People into, within and out of the UK," *International Journal of Human Rights* 14, no. 6 (2010): 954.

22 See Alison Jobe, "Accessing Help and Services in the U.K.: Trafficking 'Victims/ Survivors' Experiences," in *European Slave Trade*, ed. P. McRedmond and G. Wylie (Basingstoke: Palgrave, 2009); Alison Jobe, "A New Sexual Story: Trafficking, Immigration and Asylum: The Converging of Discourses," in *Gender and Interpersonal Violence: Language, Action and Representation*, ed. Alexander Throsby (Basingstoke: Palgrave, 2008).

23 See also Michael A. Smith, "Cultural Sensitive Trauma-Informed Therapy for Youthful Victims of Human Sex Trafficking: Setting a Course to Healing," *Journal of Modern Education Review* 3, no. 7 (2013): 523–532.

24 The "diagnoses" were performed by case managers who referred the survivors to clinical social workers, psychologists, or psychiatrists.

25 As indicated earlier, USCCB lost a major federal contract to administer antitrafficking programs because of the perception that a Catholic institution would not provide a full range of reproductive health services.

26 Patrick Bracken, Joan E. Giller, and Derek Summerfield, "Rethinking Mental Health Work with Survivors of Wartime Violence and Refugees," *Journal of Refugee Studies* 10, no. 4 (1997): 431–442.

27 Derek Summerfield, "Childhood, War, Refugeedom and 'Trauma': Three Core Questions for Mental Health Professionals," *Transcultural Psychiatry* 37, no. 3 (2000): 417.

28 Arthur Kleinman, Veena Das, and Margaret Lock, *Social Suffering* (Berkeley: University of California Press, 1997).

29 Bluebond-Langner and Korbin, "Challenges and Opportunities in the Anthropology of Childhoods," 242.

30 Diane M. Hoffman, "Migrant Children in Haiti: Domestic Labor and the Politics of Representation," in *Children and Migration: At the Crossroads of Resiliency and Vulnerability*, ed. Marisa O. Ensor and Elżbieta M. Goździak (New York: Palgrave Macmillan, 2010), 48.

31 See President's Interagency Task Force to Monitor and Combat Trafficking in Persons, "Federal Strategic Action Plan on Services for Victims of Human Trafficking in the United States 2013–2017," http://www.ovc.gov/pubs/FederalHumanTraffickingStrategicPlan.pdf. Accessed September 6, 2015.

32 The quote is from Norma Hotaling, Autumn Burris, B. Julie Johnson, Yoshi M. Bird, and Kristen A. Melbye, "Been There Done That: SAGE, a Peer Leadership Model among Prostitution Survivors," in *Prostitution, Trafficking, and Traumatic Stress*, ed. M. Farley (New York: Haworth Maltreatment and Trauma Press, 2003).

Bibliography

Agustín, Laura. *Sex at the Margins: Migration, Labor Markets and the Rescue Industry.* London: Zed Books, 2007.

Albonetti, Celesta. "Changes in Federal Sentencing for Forced Labor Trafficking and Sex Trafficking: A Ten Year Assessment." *Crime, Law and Social Change* 61, no. 2 (2014): 179–204.

Allais, Carol. "The Profile Less Considered: The Trafficking of Men in South Africa." *South African Review of Sociology* 44, no. 1 (2013): 40–54.

Angel, Carole. "Immigration Relief for Human Trafficking Victims: Focusing the Lens on the Human Rights of Victims." *University of Maryland Law Journal of Race, Religion, Gender & Class* 7, no. 1 (2007): 23–36.

Aronowitz, Alexis, Gerda Theuermann, and Elena Tyurykanova. *Analyzing the Business Model of Trafficking in Human Beings to Better Prevent the Crime.* Vienna: Office of Security and Cooperation in Europe, 2010.

Banks, Duren, and Tracey Kyckelhahn. "Characteristics of Suspected Human Trafficking Incidents, 2008–2010." Washington, DC: Bureau of Justice Statistics, 2011. http://www.bjs.gov/content/pub/pdf/cshti0810.pdf.

Banyard, Victoria L., Linda M. Williams, and Jane A. Siegel. "Retraumatization among Adult Women Sexually Abused in Childhood: Exploratory Analyses in a Prospective Study." *Journal of Child Sexual Abuse* 11, no. 3 (2003): 19–48.

Barrick, Kelle, Pamela K. Latimorre, Wayne J. Pitts, and Sheldon X. Zhang. "When Farm Workers and Advocates See Trafficking but Law Enforcement Does Not: Challenges in Identifying Labor Trafficking in North Carolina." *Crime, Law and Social Change* 61, no. 2 (2014): 205–214.

Bastia, Tanja. "Child Trafficking or Teenage Migration? Bolivian Migrants in Argentina." *International Migration* 43 no. 4 (2005): 57–89.

Belser, Patrick. "Forced Labor and Human Trafficking, Estimating the Profits." Working Paper, 2005. http://digitalcommons.ilr.cornell.edu/cgi/viewcontent.cgi?article=1016&context=forcedlabor. Accessed April 6, 2014.

Bennet, John W. "Applied and Action Anthropology: Ideological and Conceptual Aspects." *Current Anthropology* 37, no. 1 (1996): S23–S53.

Bernstein, Elizabeth. "Militarized Humanitarianism Meets Carceral Feminism: The Politics of Sex, Rights, and Freedom in Contemporary Anti-Trafficking Campaigns." In "Feminists Theorize International Political Economy," edited by Kate Bedford and Shirin Rai, special issue of *Signs: Journal of Women in Culture and Society* 36, no. 1 (2012): 45–71.

Bertone, Andrea Marie. "International Political Economy and the Politics of Sex." *Gender Issues* 18, no. 1 (2000): 4.

Bourdillon, Michael. "Children and Work: A Review of Current Literature and Debates." *Development and Change* 37, no. 6 (2006): 1201–1226.

Brennan, Denise. "Competing Claims of Victimhood? Foreign and Domestic Victims of Trafficking in the United States." *Sexuality Research & Social Policy* 5, no. 4 (2008): 45–61.

———. *Life Interrupted: Trafficking into Forced Labor in the United States.* Durham: Duke University Press, 2014.

———. "Methodological Challenges in Research on Human Trafficking: Tales from the Field." *International Migration* 43, nos. 1–2 (2005): 35–54.

Bristow, Edward J. *Prostitution and Prejudice: The Jewish Fight against White Slavery 1870–1938.* Oxford: Clarendon Press, 1982.

Bruckert, Christine, and Collette Parent. *Trafficking in Human Beings and Organized Crime: A Literature Review.* Research and Evaluation Branch. Ottawa: Canadian Mounted Police, 2002.

Brunovskis, Anette, and Guri Tyldum. "Crossing Borders: An Empirical Study of Transnational Prostitution and Trafficking in Human Beings." Report 426. Oslo: Fafo, 2014.

Bump, Micah N. "Treat the Children Well: Shortcomings in the United States' Effort to Protect Child Trafficking Victims." *Notre Dame Journal of Law, Ethics, and Public Policy* 23 (2009): 73–107.

Bump, Micah N., and Julianne Duncan. "Conference on Identifying and Serving Child Victims of Trafficking: [Notes and Commentary]." *International Migration* 415 (2003): 201–218.

Burke, Alicia, Stefania Ducci, and Giuseppina Maddaluno. *Trafficking in Minors for Commercial Sexual Exploitation: Costa Rica.* Turin: United Nations Inetrregional Crime and Justice Reasearch Institute, 2005.

Caldwell, Bruce K. Idrani Pieris, Barkat-e-Khuda, John Caldwell, and Pat Caldwell. "Sexual Regimes and Sexual Networking: The Risk of an HIV/AIDS Epidemic in Bangladesh." *Social Science and Medicine* 48, no. 8 (1999): 1103–1116.

Chacon, Jennifer M. "Misery and Myopia: Understanding the Failures of U.S. Efforts to Stop Human Trafficking." *Fordham Law Review* 74, no. 6 (2006): 2977–3040.

Chapkis, Wendy. "Trafficking, Migration, and the Law: Protecting Innocents, Punishing Immigrants." *Gender and Society* 17 (2003): 923.

Clawson, Heather, Nicole Dutch, and Megan Cummings. *Law Enforcement Response to Human Trafficking and the Implications for Victims: Current Practices and Lessons Learned.* Washington, DC: ICF International, 2006.

Clawson, Heather, Nicole Dutch, Susan Lopez, and Suzanna Tialupa. *Prosecuting Human Trafficking Cases: Lessons Learned and Promising Practices.* Washington, DC: ICF International, 2008.

Clawson, Heather J., Nicole Dutch, Amy Salomon, and Lisa G. Grace. *Study of HHS Programs Serving Human Trafficking Victims.* Washington, DC: U.S. Department of Health and Human Services, 2009.

Coburn, Tom. "Blind Faith: How Congress Is Failing Trafficking Victims." Office of Tom Coburn, U.S. Senate, Washington, DC, 2011.

Coghlan, Deirdre, and Gillian Wylie. "Defining Trafficking/Denying Justice? Forced Labour in Ireland and the Consequences of Trafficking Discourse." *Journal of Ethnic & Migration Studies* 37, no. 9 (2011): 1513–1526.

Cohen, Stanley. *Folk Devils and Moral Panics*. London: MacGibbon and Knee, 1972.

Cook, Joanna, James Laidlwa, and Jonathan Mair. "What if There Is No Elephant? Towards a Conception of an Un-Sited Field." In *Multi-sited Ethnography: Theory, Praxis and Locality in Contemporary Research*, edited by Mark-Anthony Falzon. Farnham: Ashgate, 2009.

Coonan, Terry. "Human Trafficking: Victims' Voices in Florida." In *International Sex Trafficking of Women and Children: Understanding the Global Epidemic*, edited by Leonard Territo and George Kirkham. New York: Looseleaf Law Publications, 2010.

Corbin, Alain, and Alan Sheridan. *Women for Hire: Prostitution and Sexuality in France after 1850*. Cambridge, MA: Harvard University Press, 1990.

Craig, Gary, ed. *Child Slavery Now: A Contemporary Reader*. Bristol, UK: Policy Press, University of Bristol, 2010.

Cree, Vivienne E., Gary Clapton, and Mark Smith. "The Presentation of Child Trafficking in the UK: An Old and New Moral Panic?" *British Journal of Social Work Advances* (2012): 1–16.

Davies, Nick, "Prostitution and Trafficking—the Anatomy of a Moral Panic." *Guardian*, October 19, 2009.

Denisova, Tatyana A. "Trafficking in Women and Children for the Purposes of Sexual Exploitation: The Criminological Aspect." *Trends in Organized Crime* 6, no. 30 (2001): 30–36.

DeStefano, Anthony M. *The War on Human Trafficking: US Policy Assessed*. New Brunswick, NJ: Rutgers University Press, 2008.

Digital, I. I. P. "Resources, Better Coordination Needed To Fight Human Trafficking." IIP staff, April 25, 2007. http://iipdigital.usembassy.gov/st/english/article/2007/04/20070 425123409ajesromo.7475201.xml.

Ditmor, Melissa, and Juhu Thukral. "Accountability and the Use of Raids to Fight Trafficking." *Anti-Trafficking Review* 1 (2012): 134–148.

Dobson, Madeleine E. "Unpacking Children in Migration Research." *Children's Geographies* 7, no. 3 (2009): 355–360.

Doezema, Jo. "Loose Women or Lost Women? The Re-emergence of the Myth of White Slavery in Contemporary Discourses of Trafficking Women." *Gender Issues* (Winter 2000): 25–50.

———. *Sex Slaves and Discourse Matters: The Construction of Trafficking*. London: Zed Books, 2010.

Dottridge, Mike, and Ann Jordan. "Children, Adolescents, and Human Trafficking: Making Sense of a Complex Problem." Issue Paper 5, Center for Human Rights and Humanitarian Law. Washington, DC: Washington College of Law, American University, 2012.

Estes, Richard J., and Neil Alan Weiner. "The Commercial Sexual Exploitation of Children in the U.S., Canada and Mexico." Philadelphia: University of Pennsylvania, September 18, 2001.

Farmer, Paul. *Infections and Inequalities: The Modern Plagues*. Berkeley: University of California Press, 1999.

———. *Pathologies of Power: Health, Human Rights, and the New War on the Poor*. Berkeley: University of California Press, 2003.

Farr, Kathryn. *Sex Trafficking: The Global Market in Women and Children*. New York: Worth Publishers, 2005.

Farrell, Amy, Jack McDevitt, and Stephanie Fahy. *Understanding and Improving Law*

Enforcement Responses to Human Trafficking: Final Report. Washington, DC: U.S. Department of Justice, National Institute of Justice, 2008.

———. "Where Are All the Victims? Understanding the Determinants of Official Identification of Human Trafficking Incidents." *Criminology & Public Policy* 9, no. 2 (2010): 201–233.

Farrell, Amy, Coleen Owens, and Jack McDevitt. "New Laws but Few Cases: Understanding the Challenges to the Investigation and Prosecution of Human Trafficking Cases." *Crime, Law and Social Change* 61, no. 2 (2014): 139–168.

Finckenauer, James, and Min Liu. "State Law and Human Trafficking." Presented at "Marshaling Every Resource: State Level Responses to Human Trafficking" conference, Princeton University, December 2006.

Fitzgibbon, Kathleen. "Modern-Day Slavery? The Scope of Trafficking in Persons in Africa." *African Security Review* 12, no. 1 (2003): 81–89.

Fong, Rowena, and Jodi Berger Cardoso. "Child Human Trafficking Victims: Challenges for the Child Welfare System." *Evaluation and Program Planning* 33 (2010): 311–316.

Goldstein, Joseph, Albert J. Solnit, Sonja Goldstein, and Anna Freud. *The Least Detrimental Alternative: The Landmark Trilogy of Beyond the Best Interest of the Child, Before the Best Interest of the Child, and In the Best Interest of the Child*. New York: Free Press, 1996.

Goodey, Jo. "Human Trafficking: Sketchy Data and Policy Responses." *Criminology and Criminal Justice* 8 (2008): 421.

Gorham, Deborah. "The Maiden Tribute of Modern Babylon Re-Examined: Child Prostitution and the Idea of Childhood in Late-Victorian England." *Victorian Studies* 21 (1978): 353–379.

Government Accountability Office (GAO). *Human Trafficking: Better Data, Strategy and Reporting Needed to Enhance U.S. Anti-trafficking Efforts Abroad*. Washington, DC: GAO, 2006.

———. *Human Trafficking: Monitoring and Evaluation of International Projects Are Limited, but Experts Suggest Improvements*. Washington, DC: GAO, July 2007.

Goździak, Elżbieta M. "Challenges, Dilemmas and Opportunities in Studying Trafficked Children in the United States." In *Course Reader eBooks*. Belmont: Wadsworth Cengage Learning, 2012.

———. "On Challenges, Dilemmas, and Opportunities in Studying Trafficked Children." *Anthropology Quarterly* 81, no. 4 (2008): 903–923.

———. "Spiritual Emergency Room: The Role of Spirituality and Religion in the Resettlement of Kosovar Albanians." In "Religion and Forced Migration," edited by Elżbieta M. Goździak and Dianna J. Shandy, special issue of *Journal of Refugee Studies* 15, no. 2 (2002): 136–152.

Goździak, Elżbieta M., and Micah N. Bump. *Data and Research on Human Trafficking: Bibliography of Research-Based Literature*. Washington, DC: Institute for the Study of International Migration, 2008.

Goździak, Elżbieta M., and Elizabeth A. Collett. "Research on Human Trafficking in North America: A Review of Literature." *International Migration* 43, nos. 1–2 (2005): 99–128.

Goździak, Elżbieta M., and Margaret MacDonnell. "Closing the Gaps: The Need to Improve Identification and Services to Child Victims of Trafficking." *Human Organization* 66, no. 2 (2007): 171–184.

Gurgel, Ricardo Q., Jeanne da Fonseca, D. Neyra-Castaneda, Geoff Gill, and Luis Cuevas. "Capture-Recapture to Estimate the Number of Street Children in a City in Brazil." *Archives of Disease in Childhood* 89, no. 3 (2004): 222–224.

Guy, Donna J. *Sex and Danger in Buenos Aires: Prostitution, Family, and Nation in Argentina.* Lincoln: University of Nebraska Press, 1991.

Hall, Tom, and Heather Montgomery. "Home and Away: 'Childhood,' 'Youth,' and Young People." *Anthropology Today* 16, no. 3 (2000): 13–16.

Hashim, Iman. "Discourse(s) of Childhood." Paper presented to "Child Abuse and Exploitation: Social, Legal and Political Dilemmas Workshop," International Institute for the Sociology of Law, Onati, Spain: May 2003.

Haynes, Dina Francesca. "Used, Abused, Arrested, and Deported: Extending Immigration Benefits to Protect the Victims of Trafficking and to Secure Prosecution of Traffickers." *Human Rights Quarterly* 26 (2004): 221–272.

Heissler, Karin A. "Rethinking 'Trafficking' in Children's Migratory Processes: The Role of Social Networks in Child Labor Migration in Bangladesh." *Children's Geographies* 11, no. 1 (2013): 89–101.

Hepburn, Stephanie, and Rita J. Simon. "Hidden in Plain Sight: Human Trafficking in the United States." *Gender Issues* 27 (2010): 1–26.

———. *Human Trafficking around the World: Hidden in Plain Sight.* New York: Columbia University Press, 2013.

Hopkins, Peter E., and Malcolm Hill. "Pre-flight Experiences and Migration Stories: The Accounts of Unaccompanied Asylum-Seeking Children." *Children's Geographies* 6, no. 3 (2008): 257–268.

"Human Trafficking: A Brief Overview." *Social Development Notes: Conflict, Crime, and Violence No 122.* Washington, DC: World Bank, 2009.

Hynes, Patricia. "Global Points of 'Vulnerability': Understanding Processes of the Trafficking of Children and Young People into, within and out of the UK." *International Journal of Human Rights* 14, no. 6 (2010): 952–970.

International Labour Organization. *A Future without Child Labor: Global Report under the Follow-up to the ILO Declaration on Fundamental Principles and Rights at Work.* Geneva: ILO, 2002.

———. "Honduras: Child Labor Data Country Brief." Geneva: ILO, 2002.

———. "Unbearable to the Human Heart: Child Trafficking and Actions to Eliminate It." Geneva: ILO, 2002.

International Organization for Migration. "2011 Case Data on Human Trafficking: Global Figures and Trends." *IOM*, February 2012.

Izarola, Seri E., Erin Williamson, Catherine Chen, Ashley Garrett, and Heather Clawson. *Trafficking of U.S. Citizens and Legal Permanent Residents: The Forgotten Victims and Survivors.* Washington, DC: ICF International, 2008.

Jahic, Galma, and James O. Finckenauer. "Representations and Misrepresentations of Human Trafficking." *Trends in Organized Crime* 8, no. 3 (2005): 24–40.

James, Allison. "Giving Voice to Children's Voices: Practices and Problem, Pitfalls and Potentials." *American Anthropologist* 109, no. 2 (2007): 261–272.

Jobe, Alison. "Accessing Help and Services in the U.K.: Trafficking 'Victims/Survivors' Experiences." In *European Slave Trade*, edited by Penelope McRedmond and Gillian Wylie. Basingstroke: Palgrave, 2009.

———. "A New Sexual Story: Trafficking, Immigration and Asylum: The Converging of Discourses." In *Gender and Interpersonal Violence: Language, Action and Representation*, edited by Alexander Throsby. Basingstoke: Palgrave, 2008.

Jones, Samuel Vincent. "Human Trafficking Victim Identification: Should Consent Matter?" *Indiana Law Review* 45 (2012): 482–511.

Juhasz, Judith. "Migrant Trafficking and Human Smuggling in Hungary." In *Migrant*

Trafficking and Human Smuggling in Europe: A Review of Evidence with Case Studies from Hungary, Poland, and Ukraine, edited by Frank Laczko and David Thompson, 167–232. Geneva: International Organization for Migration, 2000.

Kappelhoff, Mark J. "Federal Prosecutions of Human Trafficking Cases: Striking a Blow against Modern Day Slavery." *University of St. Thomas Law Journal* 6, no. 1 (2008): 9.

Kapur, Ratna. "Migrant Women and the Legal Politics of Anti-Trafficking Interventions." In *Trafficking in Humans: Social, Cultural and Political Dimensions*, edited by Sally Cameron and Edward Newman. Tokyo: United Nations University Press, 2008.

Kara, Siddharth. *Sex Trafficking: Inside the Business of Modern Slavery*. New York: Columbia University Press, 2009.

Kaufman, Michelle R. and Mary Crawford. "Sex Trafficking in Nepal: A Review of Intervention and Prevention Programs." *Violence against Women* 17, no. 5 (2011): 651–665.

Kelly, Elizabeth, and Linda Regan. "Stopping Trafficking: Exploring the Extent of, and Responses to, Trafficking in Women for Sexual Exploitation in the UK." *Police Research Series* 125. London: Home Office, 2000.

Kyckelhahn, Tracey, Allen J. Beck, and Thomas H. Cohen. *Characteristics of Suspected Human Trafficking Incidents, 2007–08*. Washington, DC: Bureau of Justice Statistics, 2009. http://www.bjs.gov/content/pub/pdf/cshti08.pdf.

Laczko, Frank, and Elżbieta M. Goździak, eds. "Data and Research on Human Trafficking: A Global Survey." Special issue of *International Migration* 43, nos. 1–2 (2005).

Laczko, Frank, and Marco A. Granmegna. "Developing Better Indicators of Human Trafficking." *Brown Journal of World Affairs* 10, no. 1 (2003): 179–194.

Lancaster, Roger N. *Sex Panic and the Punitive State*. Berkeley: University of California Press, 2011.

Lange, Andrea. "Research Note: Challenges in Identifying Female Human Trafficking Victims Using a National 1–800 Call Center." *Trends in Organized Crime* 14 (2011): 47–55.

MacClancy, Jeremy. *Exotic No More: Anthropology on the Front Lines*. Chicago: University of Chicago Press, 2002.

Macy, Rebecca J., and Laurie M. Graham. "Identifying Domestic and International Sex-Trafficking Victims during Human Service Provision." *Trauma, Violence & Abuse* 13, no. 2 (2012): 59–76.

Macy, Rebecca J., and Natalie Johns. "Aftercare Services for International Sex Trafficking Survivors: Informing U.S. Service and Program Development in an Emerging Practice Area." *Trauma, Violence, & Abuse* 12, no. 2 (2011): 87–98.

Mahdavi, Pardis. *Gridlock: Labor, Migration, and Human Trafficking in Dubai*. Stanford: Stanford University Press, 2011.

Mai, Nick. "Tempering with the Sex of 'Angels': Migrant Male Minors and Young Adults Selling Sex in the EU." *Journal of Ethnic and Migration Studies* 37, no. 8 (2011): 1237–1252.

Malarek, Victor. *The Natashas: Inside the New Global Sex Trade*. New York: Arcade Publishing, 2004.

Markon, Jerry. "Human Trafficking Evokes Outrage, Little Evidence." *Washington Post*, September 23, 2007.

McDonald, William F. "Explaining the Underperformance of the Anti-Trafficking Campaign: Experience from the United States and Europe." *Crime, Law and Social Change* 61, no. 2 (2014): 125–138.

———. "Traffic Counts, Symbols and Agendas: A Critique of the Campaign against Trafficking of Human Beings." *International Review of Victimology* 11 (September 2004): 143–176.

Molland, Sverre. "'I am Helping Them': 'Traffickers,' 'Anti-Traffickers' and Economies of Bad Faith." *Australian Journal of Anthropology* 22 (2011): 236–254.

———. "Tandem Ethnography: On Researching 'Trafficking' and 'Anti-trafficking.'" *Ethnography* 14 (2013): 300–323.

Motivans, Mark, and Tracey Kyckelhahn. "Federal Prosecution of Human Trafficking, 2001–2005." Washington, DC: Bureau of Justice Statistics, 2006. http://www.bjs.gov/content/pub/pdf/fpht05.pdf.

O'Connell Davidson, Julia. *Children in the Global Sex Trade.* Cambridge: Polity, 2005.

———. "Moving Children? Child Trafficking, Child Migration and Child Rights." *Critical Social Policy* 31, no. 3 (2011): 454–477.

Oude Breuil. "'Precious Children in a Heartless World'? The Complexities of Child Trafficking in Marseilles." *Children and Society* 22, no. 3 (2008): 223–234.

Pennebaker, James W. *Opening Up: The Healing Power of Expressing Emotions.* New York: Guilford Press, 1997

Reale, Daniela. *Away from Home: Protecting and Supporting Children on the Move.* London: Save the Children UK, 2008.

Richter, Kerry. "Union Patterns and Children's Living Arrangements in Latin America." *Demography* 25, no. 4 (1988): 553–566.

Rigby, Paul. "Separated and Trafficked Children: The Challenges for Child Protection Professionals." *Child Abuse Review* 20, no. 5 (2011): 324–340.

Riioen, Kari H., Anne Hatloy, and Lise Bjerkan. *Travel to Uncertainty: A Study of Child Relocation in Burkina Faso, Ghana and Mali.* Oslo: Fafo, 2004.

Roby, Jini L. "Women and Children in the Global Sex Trade: Toward More Effective Policy." *International Social Work* 48 (2005): 136.

Roby, Jini L., Jennifer Turley, and JoAnna Garrick Cloward. "U.S. Responses to Human Trafficking: Is It Enough?" *Journal of Immigration and Refugee Studies* 694 (2008): 508–525.

Rosen, Ruth. *The Lost Sisterhood: Prostitution in America, 1900–1918.* Baltimore: Johns Hopkins University Press, 1982.

Salt, John. "Trafficking and Human Smuggling: A European Perspective." *International Migration* 38, no. 3 (2000): 31–56.

Scheper-Hughes, Nancy. "The Primacy of the Ethical: Propositions for a Militant Anthropology." *Current Anthropology* 36, no. 3 (1995): 409–440.

Shah, Svati. *Street Corner Secrets: Sex, Work, and Migration in the City of Mumbai.* Durham: Duke University Press, 2014.

Shannon, Sarah. "Prostitution and the Mafia: The Involvement of Organized Crime in the Global Economy." In *Illegal Migration and Commercial Sex: The New Slave Trade,* edited by Phil Williams. London: Frank Cass Publishers, 1999.

Shelley, Louise. *Human Trafficking: A Global Perspective.* New York: Cambridge University Press, 2010.

Shigekane, Rachel. "Rehabilitation and Community Integration of Trafficking Survivors in the United States." *Human Rights Quarterly* 29 (2007): 112–136.

Shively, Michael D., Dana Hunt, Sarah Kuck, and Jazmin Kellis. *Survey of Practitioners to Assess the Local Impact of Transnational Crime, Task Order Final Report.* Washington, DC: National Institute of Justice, U.S. Department of Justice, 2007.

Sigmon, Jane Nady. "Combating Modern-Day Slavery: Issues in Identifying and Assisting Victims of Human Trafficking Worldwide." *Victims & Offenders* 3, nos. 2–3 (2008): 245–257.

Smith, Kendal Nicole. "Human Trafficking and RICO: A New Prosecutorial Hammer in the War on Modern Day Slavery." *George Mason Law Review* 18, no. 3 (2011): 759–791.

Smith, Michael A. "Cultural Sensitive Trauma-Informed Therapy for Youthful Victims of Human Sex Trafficking: Setting a Course to Healing." *Journal of Modern Education Review* 3, no. 7 (2013): 523–532.

Soderlund, Gretchen. *Sex Trafficking, Scandal, and the Transformation of Journalism, 1885–1917.* Chicago: University of Chicago Press, 2013.

Soph, Cassia. "The Non-Prosecution of Human Trafficking Cases: An Illustration of the Challenges of Implementing Legal Reforms." *Crime, Law and Social Change* 61, no. 2 (2014): 169–178.

Spangenberg, Mia. "International Trafficking of Children in New York City for Sexual Purposes." New York, NY: ECPAT-USA, 2002.

Summerfield, Derek. "The Impact of War and Atrocity on Civilian Populations: Basic Principles for NGO Intervention and a Critique of Psychosocial Trauma Projects." *Relief and Rehabilitation Network* Paper 14. London: Overseas Development Institute, 1996.

———. "The Invention of Post-Traumatic Stress Disorder and the Social Usefulness of a Psychiatric Category." *British Medical Journal* 322 (2001): 95.

Swain, Surlee. "Sweet Childhood Lost: Idealized Images of Childhood in the British Child Rescue Literature." *Journal of the History of Childhood and Youth* 2, no. 2 (2009): 198–214.

Taibly, Rebecca. "Organized Crime and People Smuggling/Trafficking in Australia." *Australian Institute of Criminology No* 208 (2001): 1–6.

Trafficking in Persons: Global Patterns. Vienna: United Nations Office on Drugs and Crime, 2006. https://www.unodc.org/pdf/traffickinginpersons_report_2006-04.pdf. Accessed September 6, 2015.

Tyldum, Guri, and Anette Brunovskis. "Describing the Unobserved: Methodological Challenges in Empirical Studies on Human Trafficking." *International Migration* 43, nos. 1–2 (2005): 17–34.

Vance, Carol S. "States of Contradiction: Twelve Ways to Do Nothing about Trafficking While Pretending To." *Social Research* 78, no. 3 (2011): 933.

Vlieger, Antoinette. "Domestic Workers in Saudi Arabia and the Emirates: Trafficking Victims?" *International Migration* 50, no. 6 (2012): 180–194.

Walker, Edward A., Elana Newman, Mary Koss, and David Bernstein. "Does the Study of Victimization Revictimize the Victim?" *General Hospital Psychiatry* 19 (1997): 403–410.

Walkowitz, Judith. *Prostitution and Victorian Society: Women, Class and State.* Cambridge: Cambridge University Press, 1980.

Weitzer, Ronald. "Sex Trafficking and the Sex Industry: The Need for Evidence-Based Theory and Legislation." *Journal of Criminal Law and Criminology* 101, no. 4 (2007): 1337–1369.

———. "The Social Construction of Sex Trafficking: Ideology and Institutionalization of a Moral Crusade." *Politics Society* 34 (2007): 447.

Whitehead, Ann, and Iman M. Hashim. *Children and Migration: Background Paper for DFID Migration Team.* Brighton: University of Sussex, Development Research Center on Migration, Globalization and Poverty, 2005.

Whitehead, Ann, Iman M. Hashim, and Vegard Iversen. "Child Migration, Child Agency and Inter-generational Relations in Africa and South Asia." Working Paper T24. Brighton: University of Sussex, Development Research Centre on Migration, Globalisation and Poverty, December 2007.

Williams, Malcolm, and Brian Cheal. "Can We Measure Homelessness? A Critical

Evaluation of the Method of 'Capture-Recapture.'" *International Journal of Social Research Methodology* 5, no. 3 (2001): 239–254.

Wilson, Deborah G., William F. Walsh, and Sherilyn Kleuber. "Trafficking in Human Beings: Training and Services among US Law Enforcement Agencies." *Police Practice and Research* 7, no. 2 (2006): 149–160.

Zeitlin, Janine. "Groups Push State to Fight Human Trafficking." *Naples Daily News,* February 26, 2006. http://www.naplesnews.com/news/local-news/groups_push_state_fight_human_trafficking. Accessed August 25, 2014.

Zhang, Sheldon X. "Beyond the 'Natasha' Story—a Review and Critique of Current Research on Sex Trafficking." *Global Crime* 10, no. 3 (2009): 178–195.

Index

About the Author

ELŻBIETA M. GOŹDZIAK is a research professor at the Institute for the Study of International Migration (ISIM) at Georgetown University. She served as editor of *International Migration* for over a decade. She is a recipient of the George Soros Chair in Public Policy, several Fulbright grants, and a residential fellowship at the Rockefeller Center in Bellagio, Italy.

St. Louis Community College
at Meramec
LIBRARY

CPSIA information can be obtained
at www.ICGtesting.com
Printed in the USA
LVOW13s1918130117
520905LV00020B/331/P